This Much Is True –

14 Directors on Documentary Filmmaking

James Quinn

BLOOMSBURY
LONDON • NEW DELHI • NEW YORK • SYDNEY

For my daughter, Roxie.

Acknowledgements

I am grateful to Laura Hallam for her assistance with the initial research for the book; to Jane Kingsley-Smith for her generous and invaluable input during the editing process; and to my publisher Jenny Ridout, for her patience and support throughout. Above all, my thanks are due to the people who agreed to be interviewed, both for making time in their busy schedules, and for many entertaining hours of conversation.

James Quinn

Contents

Photographs

Foreword

Albert Maysles

Albert Maysles is a distinguished and hugely influential figure in documentary filmmaking. He is recognised, along with his brother and long-term collaborator David, as one of the pioneers of 'direct cinema', a method of filmmaking that relies on hand-held cameras and synchronous sound to capture unfolding human dramas, and that avoids narration and talking-head interviews, so that stories appear to tell themselves. He was made a Guggenheim Fellow in 1965, and is the recipient of many prestigious awards, including: a Career Achievement Award from the International Documentary Association in 1994; the John Grierson International Gold Medal Award in 1997; and the President's Award from the American Society of Cinematographers in 1998, the first time the award had ever been presented to a documentarian.

Maysles' extraordinary body of work, assembled over more than fifty years, includes: *Primary* (1960), following the Democratic primary election campaigns of John F. Kennedy and Hubert Humphrey; *What's Happening! The Beatles in the USA* (1964); *Salesman* (1968), a landmark portrait of door-to-door Bible salesmen, working in low-income neighbourhoods; *Gimme Shelter* (1970), following The Rolling Stones' 1969 US tour and culminating in the notorious Altamont free concert, at which the stabbing of a fan is caught on camera; and *Grey Gardens* (1976), the story of two reclusive socialites, a mother and daughter who are relatives of Jacqueline Kennedy Onassis, and who live together in a grand but decaying house. *Salesman*, *Gimme Shelter* and *Grey Gardens* were all released theatrically to enormous acclaim, and have since become cult classics.

Maysles has remained an active filmmaker into his eighth and ninth decades. In 2001, he received the Sundance Film Festival Cinematography Award for Documentaries for *LaLee's Kin: The Legacy of Cotton*, an account of one family's battle to escape poverty in the Mississippi Delta, which was also nominated for the Best Documentary Feature at the 74th Academy Awards. *The Love We Make*, following Paul McCartney as he prepares a

9/11 benefit concert at Madison Square Garden in October 2001, featuring Mick Jagger, David Bowie, The Who and Eric Clapton, amongst others, was released to great acclaim in 2011, on the tenth anniversary of the attacks on the World Trade Center.

Albert Maysles (left), together with his brother and co-director David, during the shooting of Salesman. *© Tony Anthony.*

As a documentarian I happily place my fate and faith in reality. It is my caretaker, the provider of subjects, themes, experiences – all endowed with the power of truth and the romance of discovery. And the closer I adhere to reality the more honest and authentic my tales. After all, the knowledge of the real world is exactly what we need to better understand and therefore possibly to love one another. It's my way of making the world a better place.

Introduction

James Quinn

James Quinn is an award-winning director of documentaries, earning critical acclaim for films such as: *Son of Mine* (2004), an observational film about a father's misguided attempts to save his miscreant son; *God Is Black* (2005), a pair of films about the rise of fundamentalist Christianity; *Nazi Pop Twins* (2007), an observational documentary about teenaged sisters learning to think for themselves, in defiance of their domineering mother; *Shannon Come Home* (2008), a film made with extraordinary access at the eye of an intense media storm, following the disappearance of a nine-year-old girl; and *My Daughter Grew Another Head and Other True Life Stories* (2010), a darkly comic observational film about ordinary people selling the extraordinary stories of their private lives to the tabloid press.

James is also a respected executive producer, developing and overseeing projects ranging from prestigious single films to a ground-breaking observational series about gypsy and traveller communities in Britain. For several years, he was Head of Factual at October Films, an internationally renowned independent production company, the winner of over forty awards for its documentary output. He left the company in 2010 to direct *Heroes of the 88th Floor*, a feature-length documentary, which was nominated for an Emmy in 2012.

Before beginning his career in television, James wrote a PhD in philosophy and taught at university level. He still occasionally lectures, and regularly writes for a variety of national publications.

He is currently working on a feature documentary for theatrical release.

James Quinn (left), on location in 2011. © James Quinn.

This book is a collection of in-depth conversations with some of the world's best documentary-makers.

It is *not* a filmmaking manual, though each chapter does feature practical insights and offers lessons learned over the course of an illustrious career. Nor is it an academic attempt to define what documentaries are; that has always seemed to me a pointless exercise, though each contribution is certainly full of thoughtful ideas about the challenges and opportunities that documentaries present. Nor, finally, is the book intended to plead the case for documentaries. It's often argued that documentaries need protection, but in fact they've never enjoyed greater popularity and prestige, particularly in cinemas. In my view, there's no need for cheerleading, though I'd like to think that, collectively, the fourteen interviews have a celebratory feel.

Rather, at a time when interest in documentaries has never been greater, and when filmmakers find themselves under unprecedented scrutiny for misrepresentation, manipulation and hidden agendas, the book is an attempt to honestly describe how documentaries are made, all the way from conception to completion.

The interviews that follow were conducted over the course of a year, and were fitted around the filmmaking commitments of the directors involved, as well as my own. I have left the interviews in Q&A form, so that the tone of each one is apparent – always passionate, often funny, occasionally frustrated, and sometimes even angry. Where press and publicity interviews can give the impression that a successful or memorable film was a mere march to glory, the interviews in this book follow Paul Watson's injunction to 'tell it as it really is'.

Each interview addresses an element of documentary-making that the director concerned has particular knowledge of, with detailed references to both his or her own work and other well-known films. Geoffrey Smith, Emmy award-winning director of *The English Surgeon*, opens the book by considering the pleasures and pitfalls entailed in the documentary-maker's urge to explore the world around us, while Paul Watson, elder statesman (and *enfant terrible*) of British documentary-making and director of *The Family*, *The Fishing Party* and *Malcolm and Barbara*, discusses what it means when you undertake to tell the truth. Henry Singer, director of the internationally acclaimed 9/11 film *The Falling Man*, discusses the role of journalism in documentary filmmaking, arguing that the filmmaker's drive to achieve a thorough understanding of his or her subject is a large part of what gives documentaries their claim to relevance and importance.

In the chapters that follow, Nick Broomfield, BAFTA- and RTS-winning director of *The Leader, His Driver and the Driver's Wife* and *Aileen: Life and Death of a Serial Killer*, and pioneer of a unique kind of immersive filmmaking, considers the challenges of following narratives as they unfold and thinking on your feet; and Molly Dineen, BAFTA-winning director of *The Ark*, *Geri* and *The Lie of the Land*, known for her revealing films about closed worlds and institutions, discusses the challenges of winning and maintaining access. Brian Hill, celebrated for the intimacy he achieves with his subjects, resulting in BAFTA, RTS and other awards for films such as *Feltham Sings* and *The Club*, describes how he prepares for and conducts interviews, a discipline that he suggests is at the core of documentary filmmaking. And Louise Osmond, director of the extra-ordinarily moving feature documentaries *Deep Water* and *Killer in a Small Town*, considers the crucial role of emotion in documentaries, and how a director can capture it, manage it, and put it on the screen.

Kim Longinotto, winner of many international awards for films including *Divorce Iranian Style* and *Sisters in Law*, most of which highlight the struggles of female victims of oppression, explains her own personal take on documentary filmmaking with an agenda; and James Marsh, Oscar- and BAFTA-winning director of visually daring films like *Man on Wire* and *Wisconsin Death Trip*, considers the aesthetics of documentary filmmaking. Fellow Oscar-winner Kevin Macdonald, director of *One Day in September* and *Touching the Void*, and Morgan Spurlock, director of the 'docbusters' *Super Size Me* and *The Greatest Story Ever Sold*, respectively discuss techniques for telling past-tense stories, and the challenges of making films that are funny, as well as full of purpose.

Julien Temple, internationally renowned director of *The Filth and the Fury*, *The Future Is Unwritten* and *Requiem for Detroit?*, as well as music videos for The Rolling Stones, Paul McCartney and David Bowie (among many others), reveals his take on both music in documentaries, and documentaries about music. Marc Isaacs, BAFTA-winning director of *The Lift*, *Calais* and *Men of the City*, discusses the importance of 'characters' in documentary filmmaking, and explains how he goes about finding and developing them. And finally, Andrew Jarecki, director of *Capturing the Friedmans* and winner of eighteen international documentary awards, talks about the subject of editing, perhaps the most alchemical part of the filmmaking process, when all other ideas and elements come together, and a finished film begins to emerge.

The foreword and afterword are provided by Albert Maysles, one of the world's most influential documentary filmmakers, and Leon Gast, Oscar-winning director of *When We Were Kings*. The former sets the tone of the book, explaining his faith in reality as an endless source of stories, all imbued with the power to transform and enrich the world we live in. The latter concludes the book with a simple but inspiring message: if you think you've found a story worth telling, just pick up a camera and shoot.

If there's a single larger point that emerges from these very varied contributions, it's that documentaries *are* special and separate to the usual demands and expectations of film and television. And what separates them is the attitude and approach of the people who make them – caring deeply for their characters, throwing themselves into their work, questing after the truth, aspiring to change the world.

In common with the other directors in this book, I've found people more and more sceptical about documentaries, and increasingly reluctant to take part in them. Whatever the reasons for that may be – and I don't think reality TV can be solely to blame – I hope that the passion, commitment, intelligence and sensitivity that's evident in the pages that follow might send out a simple message in response: you can trust us.

1

Exploring the world
Geoffrey Smith

Geoffrey Smith is the director of *The English Surgeon* (2007), a film which follows the brain surgeon Henry Marsh as he confronts profound ethical and professional dilemmas on his latest journey to the Ukraine, a country he has been visiting for over fifteen years to help improve the country's very basic standards of brain surgery. Marsh emerges as a man of great compassion and humanity, devoted to his own personal mission to help others. The film won an Emmy in 2010, and was awarded the prize for best international feature documentary at the Silverdocs Documentary Festival in 2008.

Smith is also the director of *Presumed Guilty* (2010), the story of Antonio Zúñiga, wrongfully sentenced to twenty years in jail in Mexico City. The film is also the story of two young lawyers who are struggling to set Zúñiga free, and to expose a justice system they see as corrupt and fatally compromised by an ancient conception of justice, whereby anyone detained is considered guilty until proven innocent. The film won an Emmy for outstanding investigative journalism in 2011.

Both films combine thoughtful and gripping narratives with a very strong sense of time and place – post-Soviet Kiev in wintertime and the vast suburban sprawl of Mexico City – and speak of a genuine passion for exploring the world around us.

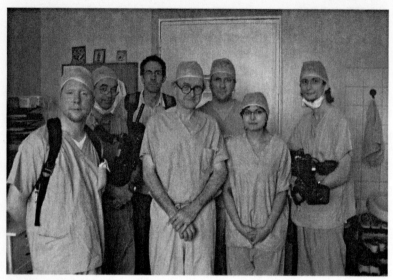

Geoffrey Smith (third from the right), during the filming of The English Surgeon. *Picture courtesy of Geoffrey Smith.*

Is it a duty of the documentary filmmaker to explore the world? Is it part of what a documentary is?

I find people, regardless of where they're from, deeply fascinating. I was a sort of bum throughout my twenties, even though I'd had a privileged education. I went travelling to the most bizarre places and I found myself enthralled and often very amused by people and their stories, and their different ways of being.

And I also found people very prepared to talk to me. It's maybe because I've got 'Sucker' tattooed on my forehead, and I'm one of those people that if I'm walking down the street the drunk will always somehow single me out as the easy touch. I don't know what it is but people feel happy talking to me; it doesn't take long for there to be a sense of trust. But maybe it's simply because I'm interested in them. You know, there's nowt stranger than folk, is there?

Exploration comes naturally if you're genuinely curious. And curiosity takes you into wonderful places. Perhaps slightly scary places sometimes. But I don't know if exploration is an abstract duty. For me, it's all about the audience. Everything I do is filtered back through the idea of the audience. I'm not interested in making indulgent pieces. I want to communicate, and show things that I've seen and found to other people.

The audience for a documentary is in a very privileged position. Audiences are privy to a world or a group of people, or even the thoughts inside one person's head, in a very intimate and voyeuristic way. The audience is sitting in the safety of the cinema, but documentaries take us into these extreme physical and psychological places. So, for me, exploring the world is part of the relationship between the storyteller and the audience. It's so much a part of humanity and human history. Storytelling, whatever form it takes, all comes back down to the campfire. It's that deep; it's that ancient; it's that perennial; it's that intoxicating, regardless of the culture. But now we've got a more powerful way to distil stories, with editing and with pictures on the large screen.

Do you think there are more interesting and intense stories to be told abroad, in the wider world?

It's a good question. As Orson Welles said, after eight hundred years of civil-isation, Switzerland has only produced chocolate and the cuckoo clock. So abroad isn't necessarily all that fascinating. You travel to places like Switzerland and you see very quickly that oysters don't make pearls without sand and grit to irritate them. Interesting stuff comes from having that grit – something to push against, some irritant, some sort of hardship or endurance test. The thing is that in our society – and I'm from Australia, which I find particularly anaesthetised and white-washed – there's just not enough to bang your head against. It's like living in a sort of fog, and I definitely want and need something to bang my head against. Whether it's, you know, a degree of poverty, overcrowding, pressure, people, competition, whatever it is. *Something.* So, yes, countries which are full of that are more interesting to make films in. It's only through conflict and drama that we can learn about the best and the worst of humanity. That's why people watch documentaries, because they can learn something. The third world, second world – they're full of conflict and drama.

Because people live more extreme lives?
Definitely, definitely, definitely.

It seems to me that another advantage of filming abroad is that things are done in a different way, which is inherently interesting, like Mexican law in

Presumed Guilty. *It's the same goal of justice, but the means of getting there is very different to the way it's done in Britain or the US.*

Yes, yes. I think that's a good point. The thing that we have to remember, though, is that not many viewers will be intimately familiar with the Mexican justice system, as I have become, because I spent six months living that film. So you have to give them a way in; you have to set up something that is accessible. You have to hold people's hands and take them on the journey. And that means giving them something essential they can identify with, something human. And then they'll come with you into the strange, new places you're taking them to. Keep your audience first and foremost in mind and you've got, I think, a much greater chance of communicating. To enjoy a story, an audience needs to know where we are and what's going on. You have to answer those questions. It's actually a big help in telling the story. And it's not dumbing down, it's just storytelling.

What were the advantages of the foreignness of foreign places, in terms of filmmaking?

Sometimes I'd say it's humour. I mean, when you analyse the basis of humour, it's often other people's difficulties or misfortunes or struggles and it's easy to find struggles and misfortunes in poorer countries. And we tend to laugh with or at situations that aren't normal, by our own standards. So, in *The English Surgeon*, when Igor happily goes to a DIY market in the street to buy drill bits for his operating theatre, he doesn't think anything strange about that. But it's a very funny scene for people outside of the Ukraine because you just wouldn't imagine a surgeon doing that and using a Bosch drill for brain surgery. But it's a needs-must society. There's a real ingenuity there, and that's something we take our hats off to. We like people who can achieve something on meagre resources, and a lot of individuals in developing countries have to do that.

There's a sort of drama to the rituals of everyday life as well, in a very foreign place. If, for example, you don't go to the supermarket but you shoot something and then skin it and then cook it ... that immediately is dramatic and visual and nice to film. That's true of the 'face-off' in Presumed Guilty. *It's a foreign way of doing something that's really compelling because of its foreignness.*

I think by the time you get to that point in the film you understand how much is loaded against this defendant, Antonio. I mean, he's visually already a convict, because he's behind bars and he has difficulty even hearing through those bars. But in this bizarre Alice-in-Wonderland system called Mexican justice, there is this allowance made for the defence to request the accuser to stand literally across the bars from them. We're talking, sort of, two or three feet away. That's the 'face-off'. And it's only at that point that the defendant can ask the questions, which is really important because, as you see in the film, the defence counsel is severely constrained about what he can and can't ask. So the trick in *Presumed Guilty* was that the lawyers – Roberto and Layda – trained Antonio to be his own cross-examiner. And then they said, 'You've got a chance to examine Ortega, who's the detective [who's framed Antonio] and the witness, Victor. That's our only chance, so we've got to make it work.' It's not just a case of having a shouting match and there being an emotional release. In fact, they use the face-off massively to their own advantage by training Antonio in a very short space of time to be a barrister. The scene is really powerful because of the way the face-off works. We're in the minds of the characters, and we're in the middle of some real-life drama, and we're hoping beyond hope that Antonio is going to hold it all together, ask his questions in the right way, keep the judge on side, and make a mockery of the policemen and the witness.

Is there more spectacle abroad as well, more visual rewards to reap?

I suppose that's true. But questions of ethics do come into that. You've got to avoid being pornographic. You know, can we find a six-year-old in Somalia carrying an AK-47? There's a kind of shallow, sensational, exploitative coverage that you see in news and docs sometimes that is ethically pretty dodgy. With the films I've made abroad, I've often had a strong personal connection with something: either the country or a group of people or a situation. And I feel there's some validity about that. But to turn up and cast an eye and make strong, if not damning, visual comments about a society is a bit too easy. People used to go to Northern Ireland and the kids in the Catholic areas would be shouting, 'Oh, you want to come down here and get it from this angle' – they were so used to having their world portrayed as a violent nightmare. It's an easy way out, and it's not very true. You have to look beyond the spectacle.

I'm sure you're right. But there's a real sense of spectacle about the Ukraine and that's part of the pleasure of The English Surgeon. *I'd never been to or seen that part of the world before, and it was something I enjoyed about that film.*

Sure. But you know, Marc Isaacs, for example, makes very telling films about people, often in London, and he doesn't feel the need to travel. And I respect that because he spends a lot of time with people and finds that inner world, the one that we can all relate to. The outside surface stuff may, of course, not be as colourful or dramatic as filming in some war-zone, but Marc's obviously made up for that by the psychological richness of things.

It's not that I think visual spectacle is an end in itself, more that it seems to me quite exciting, from a filmmaking point of view, to be somewhere that feels very new and strange – to have that as your canvas, I suppose.

Absolutely. I think from the point of view of going to watch films that are set in a far-flung place there's an element of tourism. There's a real power and magic in being taken somewhere else. I mean, people like being 'elsewhere'. It is a basic psychological thing – sometimes we like to escape. We all sometimes want to leave behind our dreary, everyday lives, and to be transported somewhere else, where things are different and people behave differently.

If those are some of the attractions and the advantages of filming abroad, what are the challenges?

I think one big challenge is determining the ethical basis on which you are there. I mean, 'What gives me the right to start making judgements about things?' And the answer to that question in the documentary world is all to do with the length of time that most documentary people spend with their subjects – the intimate knowledge they build up of another culture or a person or a family. There's usually been some huge bond of experience. So they're at the very opposite of the news and current affairs end of things. But sometimes the question remains: 'What an earth are we doing?'

I was on a jury last year and we watched three or four films, all quite well made. But everybody felt that there was a gap in some of them, a question mark over the moral basis of why they were made. So, okay, you've got access to this, this and this, but the missing piece in the puzzle was the moral validity of it all. And then we saw a film that was just so oozing with conviction – *Mugabe and the White African* – that all of us as jurors were just transfixed. The filmmakers had such a strong sense of purpose. They had put themselves and other people on the line, they'd smuggled footage out ... and you felt that. Somehow that moral cause, that moral validity, was imprinted on every frame, and people felt that it was somehow just 'right'. That's the key, really, isn't it? With a film made in a difficult place, you have to feel that the people in the film wanted, allowed or encouraged the filmmakers to be there. I can't stress this enough – when you are watching an observational documentary, you are watching the relationship between the director and the subject. That's what you're actually watching as an audience. And when it's good, when it's built on, dare I say, love, trust and respect, you feel all right to be in some pretty difficult places.

With *The English Surgeon*, for example, Henry's giving dire prognoses in English on people who don't speak English and have no idea how bad their condition is, but we still feel it's all right, because his relationship with me allows the audience in. But when you see something built on deceit or exploitation, audiences very quickly can turn against the film. I've seen that a number of times and I've felt that myself. I've felt some sort of outrage and repugnance about what's going on. There's a moral contract which is what documentary rests on largely. It's just human decency in a way. You are saying to the audience, 'What's happening in front of you is, in essence, the emotional truth of the situation,' but if the audience starts to feel they're being tricked and it wasn't that way, and there's some deceit or manipulation going on, audiences can get very angry. No amount of gloss or spin or great shots or sexy music can disguise a lack of honesty or a dishonourable purpose on the part of the director.

For the most part, what Hollywood wants out of fiction is authenticity. They want characters to be believable, doing believable, credible things. In documentaries, we start with that as a basis! We don't have to pay millions of pounds to generate it. We start with the assumption that what we're doing is real, and it's up to us to maintain that. If you've got a great story with great characters, plus the authenticity that comes from filming something that's real, in an honest way, then you've got a great film – one that equals most drama, if not surpasses it. That's the wonder of documentary and it's why documentary has become more and more important, and more and more popular. Certainly, in the audiences I've met over the last two or three years at film festivals, an enormous number of young people are seeking out the documentary because they're frankly sick of and annoyed with the fakeness and the fairy floss that's coming out of Hollywood mainstream cinema. They want to engage with the wider world. What's going on in Africa and Asia, you know? What's happening today in China? Or Russia? These vast countries that we only used to hear about with snippets of news. People have a huge appetite to soak up real stories with real characters that tell you how it really is.

So there are ethical challenges to filming in a different country or culture. What are the practical challenges?

Well, if one can get past the ethical basis on which one is there, the next thing that hits all of us is language, because not many of us can speak Haitian Creole, for example, or Mandarin. If you're going about it in the right way, there'll be a relationship, and your subjects will trust you and know that you aren't coming in for a day to film. We're there for the long term, we're there for three months, or six months or something like that; we become a part of people's lives. What you need is the trust and openness of the people that you're working with.

If that relationship and the trust are there, and you have a genuine reason for being in that place, you can overcome the more practical difficulties?

And, dare I say it, make a virtue of them. For example, in *The English Surgeon*, the main character is just that: he's English and has only a tiny smattering of Ukrainian. That could have been a real problem. But I made it part and parcel of the film. Probably one of the most powerful scenes in the film is entirely built around language barriers. Henry knows that a girl hasn't got long to live, but the girl concerned doesn't speak English and Henry doesn't speak Ukrainian. So that becomes fascinating to a viewer rather than being something to fudge or deny or hide.

Is that one of the tricks of filming abroad in general, do you think? To try to turn the difficulties and the strangeness to your advantage?

Yes. Well, look at Nick Broomfield's famous film about Eugène Terre'Blanche. The whole thing is about the difficulties of working in a far-flung, alien place and being an outsider. A conceit in a lot of modern television is that it's some-how seamless and effortless. There are shots up mountains and under water and from helicopters, but it's all made to look easy and natural. When it comes to documentary, the struggle that goes into making a film can be the most important thing, the most useful and revealing thing. Certainly, it's a way in which the audience can bond with the filmmaker and relate to the subject the film is about.

It's sometimes been my experience of filming abroad that, although there can be real practical difficulties – communication issues, logistical issues, struggling to get up to speed with different customs and ways of doing things, the danger of upsetting people without realising that you're doing it – in fact, filming abroad can be quite liberating for a filmmaker because there are fewer hoops to jump through. You know, in Africa, broadly speaking, you don't have PR departments; you don't have press officers. It's all a bit more natural. You can just get on with directing and not spend all your time producing problems away.

Yes, when it comes to questions of official openness, here people are incredibly sensitive and controlling about the access they'll give. Certainly, it would have been hard to film *The English Surgeon* in the UK. And many of Kim Longinotto's films, again dealing with law and the rest of it – there's just no way would they happen here. I think more people would like to film here, but the truth is access to public bodies just often isn't possible.

I made a film a while back that was about ordinary people selling their extra-ordinary stories to tabloid newspapers and magazines. It's been some time since I've made a film of that sort in Britain and I was shocked at how cynical members of the public have become about TV, and how suspicious they are now about the editing process. I wondered if filming with people in less 'sophisticated' cultures means that people are a bit more open and honest?

I couldn't agree more. It goes back to what I was talking about before. When contributors meet you, their experience of TV is largely as an audience member. And what they've picked up on from their viewing, perhaps because of watching reality television or the type of observational stuff that passes for documentaries nowadays, is the *wrong sort of relationship*, where everything is patently designed to be full of conflict and angst and pain and worry. People aren't stupid. They see that right away, and it leaves a bad taste in their mouths. When you and I come along and knock on their door and want them to participate in a film, they think they're just being stitched up because the moral contract is gone; it's evaporated. It's a poison, and I'm afraid there isn't any stopping it now it's in the system.

The viewers' sense that they're not being conned or misled is so paramount, but it's just ethereal; it's an intangible thing. It can't be enshrined in rules or legislated for; it just has to exist between people, and when it breaks down then it's a disaster. And what we're seeing now is the consequence of that. So, going to the Ukraine, where people do not have a tradition of exploitative television is a delight. And when you appear with a camera you're not an object of suspicion or mistrust. There's no sense in *The English Surgeon* of self-consciousness in front of the camera because people are not worried, and that's because they have no reason to be worried. It's so refreshing and liberating. I'm sure Kim Longinotto would say exactly the same thing about all her contributors. There just isn't that calculation going on, that fear of 'How am I coming across? What am I saying?' It just doesn't exist, and, as viewers, we just love that sense that we are an invisible observer. That's part of the reason why there's a huge, never-ending stream of really good international stories.

How do you go about filming and capturing a place which is foreign?

I think it has to be in the story, otherwise it's going to start feeling like wallpaper, as editors often call it. I mean, every city's got some landmarks and all the rest of it. But that's a postcard. Your story has to come, and the details of that geographical world have to come, through the people who inhabit that world. Otherwise, you know, you're simply making a travelogue, sending a postcard. And that can be pretty disastrous.

Other people's worlds are fascinating because they're theirs. Marian's tiny hut in *The English Surgeon*, out there in the village, is just so atmospheric. It's like a set, but absolutely perfect, and the church is priceless. It's all there. Just look at it! Your characters will take you into whatever part of the world it is that you're exploring. There was a character I filmed called Abujah in Haiti ... his world involves a sort of urban life in Port-au-Prince, but then there's a world of drumming and voodoo and healing out in the bush. So I went with him and became a part of that world and filmed it. You need a sound, intrinsic reason to be there. That's all I would ask: why are we here? If you've got a good personal reason built on a relationship, then you've got every right to be there. But to stray off the path and go, 'Oh, look at that, the Eiffel Tower!' or whatever ... I mean, come on. We're not going to buy that for very long.

Is it hard to find stories abroad? Is it a matter of time on the ground? Do you have to have an idea that you want to make a film in Africa and then go to Africa to find one?

Well, I suppose there are many different ways of doing it. But in my case, it might be a friend from another country. It might be that his or her parents are from somewhere interesting. It might be as flimsy as a good article, you know, which profiles what people are doing in an interesting situation. An article can only be a trigger though, because it's nothing more than a few hundred words. The problem with going out on spec to find a story is that it's a big leap of faith, and it's going to be your own money. So I'd say one would be better advised to try to have some deeper reason to go. The real key is to start from somebody that you have a personal connection with.

Is that how The English Surgeon *came about?*

Well, yes. The Ukraine is a country I had fallen in love with, and have been to many times since the mid-'90s. And I have always wanted to find a way to make a film there. It just didn't seem to happen. But then I met Henry Marsh in London, on the first film I did for the BBC, and I think it was on the first or second night, down at his house, drinking vodka, that he announced that he'd been going out to the Ukraine for many years to do his work. And it was like this instant connection that had to be consummated in a film. And the moment I got out there with him on a recce (I did two recce trips, two weekends with him), within half an hour of us being in that country, I knew! It was like I had the film in my head. I could completely see it and I knew exactly how strong it would be. And that's a great feeling to have: that sort of security and knowledge.

In 1987, I lived in Haiti. I was helping two Haitian filmmakers with their documentary about the first election in thirty-one years and, to cut a long story short, we stumbled across a massacre. Twenty-three voters were killed in small rooms just ten minutes before we arrived ... it was dreadful. And two of the same guys came back, and shot at some of us and I got shot through the leg and across the shoulder. I didn't want to leave the country but I was told I had to. I went back to London and my life was in pieces. It just wasn't a good time.

Eventually I realised I had to go back, and, in my sort of silly, white male way, I thought the reason to go would be to find the man who shot me, to confront the man who nearly took my life away. But one Haitian guy I knew very well – I know it sounds like a complete cliché, but he's a voodoo priest – he had a completely different agenda for me. Once he saw my plan wasn't working – which it was never going to in Haiti – he quietly and seductively introduced me to a different way of getting over this trauma, and that's what the film is.

So, again, the Haiti film is built on something very real, something very personal, and something that British people can relate to as a way into a very strange culture. It's the same with Laura Poitras' films. They're all built on strong personal relationships: *The Oath*, for example. She spent a lot of time recently with Bin Laden's driver, and, just through pure perseverance and putting in the hours and being around people, she's been able to capture a whole world in a film. There's no replacement for that time observing, understanding people, and wanting to say something significant.

If it is the case that there are advantages to taking an audience somewhere they've never been, do you think that filmmakers are having to go further and further abroad to give that sensation to the audience? The world is constantly shrinking.

Yes, but there are always new countries opening up. I mean, since '89 there's the whole raft of Eastern European countries. Suddenly, two or three years ago, there were films being made out of Kyrgyzstan and Tajikistan: *37 Uses for a Dead Sheep*, remember that? Films like that are a testament to the pioneering documentary spirit. I don't think there's any shortage of places to explore. The problem is more the way commissioning has been going. Over the last five to ten years, there's been a huge move away from international stories in TV. It's 'Give me something domestic' because (a) it's cheaper, (b) it's more controllable and reliable, and (c) they're saying that's what their audience wants. They reckon that subtitled programmes are a big turn-off. I wonder also if there's a resistance to international stories because you need very good people to tell those stories. It's much harder, which is part of what makes it much more expensive.

All that is depressing in many ways, but travelling to exotic places isn't the be-all and end-all. It's wrong to think that the interest in a film is in the surface details, in the geographic, the tangible. Good films are really just trying to tell heartfelt, revealing stories about the human condition. Why do we watch anything? It's because in the end it's about people. It doesn't matter if they're in a different place, speaking a different tongue, or if they're closer to home. A film has to try to lift itself above nationality. It has to have universals in place that make it appealing. There are great films made that are very culturally specific but the best films speak across borders because they're dealing with common, universal human experiences. It's all about being able to enter a world of emotion. The reason why we're going to keep watching is tension, suspense and caring about the people or the story. These are simple craft issues about storytelling. Get them right, and away we go; ninety minutes feels like fifteen.

Do you think it's easier to make a more philosophical type of film abroad?

I wouldn't say so. Fascinating people and circumstances and conditions honestly appear everywhere you go.

I agree. I don't mean that people and their lives are necessarily more profound abroad. I mean more that, in films made about life in Britain, you're not expected to be profound – you're asked to be more descriptive than reflective – whereas if you're making a film abroad you have permission to be more thoughtful and philosophical. It's very striking that The English Surgeon *is full of thinking and quandaries and dilemmas.*

I see what you mean. I think that the difference really comes from how they're funded rather than where they're set. Commissioning in terms of current domestic television is very much about keeping eyeballs glued to the screen, and that's not necessarily conducive to films that are poetic or reflective. International documentaries, on the other hand, attract much less money and get shown in very marginalised slots, so there's less pressure and more freedom to really say something. That's the advice to give anybody who is struggling with maybe the domestic agenda on British television, or the style of documentaries on mainstream TV, and maybe feels that it's not for them. Or they may have had experiences abroad, because a lot of people travel and they come across stories they really want to tell. My advice is to go and tell it. Find a way to make it happen. It's unbelievably easy now in terms of equipment. So the rest of it is really down to your own imagination and the strength of the relationship you have. That's the thing, really: behind every great film is an even greater relationship.

What is The English Surgeon *saying?*

It struck me early on that the film is best summed up as one man's struggle to do good things. And Henry Marsh, the surgeon at the centre of it all, is the type of self-effacing, enquiring, vulnerable person that allows a viewer into his doubts and difficulties. He doesn't want to sanitise those things. So we have a character who is genuinely struggling to do the right thing, but who allows us to enter his world. Ultimately, it's not a film about medicine. It's not a film about operating or a film about brain surgery. It's not a film about the differences between Ukrainian and British healthcare systems. It's a moral fable. It tries at all points to remove itself from the literal, from being overly concerned with details. It is always trying to float above that. So everything was couched in those terms and, most importantly, I would say that everything was seen through that prism. It's a really useful way to think about filmmaking. How do we introduce our central idea, our commanding idea to the audience? What devices do we use at the front of the film that encourage the audience to have that idea in mind when they view the rest of it?

That central idea, that the film is about a struggle to do good things, was enormously helpful to me and all the people I worked with on *The English Surgeon*, Henry particularly, because it reflects his own life. That's also why people respond to the film everywhere, from Melbourne to Moscow, from eighteen to eighty. Why does it work? Because it's not tied down to a specific time, place, culture or output. It is universal; it is our struggle to do good things. All of us make decisions about how we treat other people. With Henry Marsh, his canvas is bigger and more dramatic than ours, but the principle is exactly the same.

Do you feel attracted to dilemmas as a subject matter, as a way of exploring people and the way they live?

Yes, totally. I mean, I love dilemmas and I love the moral, ethical difficulties that life throws up. And medicine is very useful for engaging in those things, partly because there is a narrative already, which you don't have to construct. There is a problem, a process and a solution that's implicit in the medical model. All of us have flesh and blood. All of us know what it's like to be a patient. And because the audience can all identify with this general narrative, I don't have to waste valuable screen time building one. That gives me the freedom to bring in these really interesting, rather deep, complex dilemmas. It's a great way of working through or exploring lots of moral and ethical and emotional difficulties. And it's the same with justice as with medicine. They're both wonderful vehicles to get you to deep, interesting places fast.

What sort of person do you need to be to be good at making films that explore the world?

I remember coming back to England after those recce trips with Henry. I was very confident about this film and I wrote it up on two pages. I took it to a commissioner at the BBC who was a real champion and supporter of mine so I was expecting something very positive out of this. But it was like showing garlic to a vampire. I mean, she just looked down at this thing and it was like, 'Geoffrey, come on, get real here. The Ukraine? Ethics? Struggle? I mean, these aren't the things that people are interested in.' And this is the first thing I think directors have to have: you have to have a degree of conviction. You have to hold on to that belief about your film in the face of opposition. Okay, if twenty people turn you down and it's three years later and you still have never met anyone who believes in your story, well, maybe you need to readjust your position on it. But, having said that, you need to have an almost delusional degree of belief about it, because the path of least resistance is to say 'no'. It's easier to say no. And you have to simply endure a hundred 'nos' to get anywhere in this world with a film. Films are so often made simply on the strength of will that comes from a director's point of view. Listen to your peers. Listen to the people that you respect. But also you need a cast-iron will when it comes to the story you want to tell.

So that's the first thing. And the second is just listen; just spend more time listening than talking. You need to be a listener. Take Errol Morris. Look at a film like *Mr Death* – really funny, very clever, definitely one of his best films. Morris says virtually nothing because this man had drunk so much coffee that he had this torrent to unleash. Everyone's got a story. Really, they have. Everyone's got something special to say. But people can appear to be so grey until you find that spark in their life – the one thing that all of sudden they rivet you with, through their passion and conviction.

Remember that people have a hugely cathartic relationship with a camera. We can provide that outlet to a contributor who might be going through something difficult. I'm talking about films where there's a degree of observed drama in somebody's life. You and I turn up, and we get to know people. We're not family. We're not lovers. But we're fascinated and interested. And we also provide this box that acts like a confessional to some people. There is this genuine desire to tell a story, even though they know it's going to end up in a very public place. There's something about that process of unburdening or releasing or sharing the torment or drama or whatever it is ... I've always found that to be truly the most special, piercing and most emotional time. It all started for me in Haiti when I discovered the power of the camera. I could talk to the camera. It was a video diary. There was no crew. It was just me and a camera on a tripod. So I was pouring my heart out about my situation and realised towards the end that it was helping. And I thought, if it can do that for me, it can do that for other people. And that, in a certain sense, is the basis on which a lot of my films are made. I made a film on my own about Ralph Bulger, whose two-year-old son was killed. And I put all the budget into time, and I spent months with Ralph. It was three months before I even got the camera out. And then it was an incredibly cathartic and emotional film for him. But it was very, very hard for me to make that film. I didn't really have anyone to talk to. And he was going through a lot. You share a lot together; you can genuinely share a lot.

The other quality you need as a director is luck. But maybe you make that luck, by encouraging people to feel safe, letting them know that it's all right. People showing vulnerability is what bonds us with characters on screen. If someone's vulnerable and full of doubt but trying to do the right thing, we love them; we simply love them. Because that's who we are; we're all flawed and fucked up in our own funny ways. We love seeing other people struggle to move past that or get through that. So a good director has to be sympathetic. You have to identify with your characters, and with some of them, over time, you become a counsellor, a friend. Sometimes even a confessor.

Let's talk about the role music plays in exploring the world and opening up new places. Music can make somewhere feel safer, but it can also de-familiarise it.

I think that in the end, regardless of where we are in the world, the real journey – even if the film has a far-flung setting – is an interior one. It's what's going on inside people's lives. If you're attuned to that as the filmmaker, then that's what you will want your audience to see and walk away with. I see location as sort of window-dressing, whereas the psychological reality is something universal that we all find quite familiar, regardless of whether the people are from Mongolia or from Melbourne. And that's why films can work, because we share those universal things.

To me, music is the most direct emotional connection we can have with an art form. Music has that ability to completely cut through everything, and put you inside other people's lives. It allows you at the right moment to stop the exposition, to stop the words – which most documentaries, including mine, have too many of. It lets you put the viewer in a different place emotionally. And that's what we did repeatedly with the music in *The English Surgeon*.

You've got to keep asking, 'Where are we in the story?' when you're making a film, and music can help you answer that. So, when Henry meets Marian visually in the film, it's a long way before they meet in real life. The scene is Henry riding a bike from left to right, Marian walking from right to left. And I said to Nick Cave and Warren Ellis, who did the music on that film, 'What we're trying to put across here is that this is something special. Marian has reached out to a person he's never met who's trying to save his life. So how do we reflect that with music?' And, in the film, the thing that the audience is confronted with is this beautiful piece of music, which allows them to make an emotional connection between the two characters. You've got to use music to keep the audience inside the universe that you've created, and help them find their way through it. You can strengthen their connection with what's happening through music.

A lot of documentary-makers would use balalaikas in a film like The English Surgeon.

Yes, but that's like postcard GVs. That's the trap of being literal. This isn't about painting an anthropological, literal picture of life in the Ukraine, with silly-sounding instruments. It's a moral fable. It's the interior, psychological world that should be informing you and the musicians about what you need to be doing. You should give your musicians freedom, and use their music as rushes. In documentary, we can often cut our pictures around music. Try letting the musicians run riot! Let them create something that's wonderful and organic and strong from where they sit. And then play with it, and use it in other places that you wouldn't have first thought of. That's a fantastic process in the edit which they themselves, the musicians, also get off on because there's nothing more exciting than putting virgin picture and sound together.

There are loads of musicians out there, good musicians, that for no more than what people often spend on commercial music would love to be involved in shaping a soundscape. So go and talk to them. Go out there and find those people, because there's loads of great people that can give you something that's never been heard before, and it's liberating in the extreme to work like that.

What are the pleasures of filming abroad, from the filmmaking point of view? I've always loved making films abroad where quite often you've got three weeks and there's no going back afterwards, so it's quite pure and focused and immersive.

I think a lot can be said for the immersive experience. If you've judged it based on narrative, dramatic terms, you know that probably, or hopefully, certain things will happen across that period of time with these people you know. And then the beauty of that window abroad is that it's the beginning, middle and end of that shooting process. In *The English Surgeon*, it was twenty-one days. And if you can cover that with more than one camera – because in reality there'll be more than one narrative unfolding in one place – then you'll be able to make the film so much more energetic and dynamic, and you can cut from one narrative to the other, which is a completely liberating way for a documentary to work. Having a defined period of time can encourage you to make the most of it: to improvise and be creative.

Do you take personal pleasure from it in terms of being immersed in a culture, away from the distractions of home?

I always find shooting things incredible stressful. It's possibly the tension that comes from having seen things unfold in real life with the person you're filming, but without a camera because it's so much better for them and the relationship if you watch for as long as you can without filming. Then you're on the inside and they know that there's something genuine going on, and, when you get the camera out, you should be able to reap the rewards of intimacy and inclusion. Then the stress comes: 'Am I ever going to be able to film what I've seen?' But what you will get – and this is the great thing about the process of observational documentaries – is things that you could never have anticipated. I have this goose-pimple test. I just know, if I've got goose-pimples, that it's really going to work. You just know when something incredible is happening in the room. You might have shot three or four tapes that day, but then it all comes down to these five or ten minutes. And that ... man, it's worth living for! It's so exhilarating. I can endure all the pain and angst just for those few occasions on a trip where it really sings.

I love that feeling when you're away making a film that you're living it. You're not paying any bills. You don't have chores to do. There are no distractions. Just the film.

I couldn't agree more. I've always had an office or a place to stay either in the very place we're filming at or right next door. With *The English Surgeon*, we had an office actually in the hospital. It's all about being there, living, breathing, the cups of tea, the gossip, all that stuff. Because nothing ever goes to plan. People's lives are chaotic. And certainly when you're into medicine or anything official or bureaucratic, most of the plans that are written on paper go out of the window. You've got to be there to take advantage of all of that. You've got to jump in the river, in other words, and just get swimming. That's when you get the good stuff.

It's much more possible to do that when you're filming away.

Yes. It's a commitment to the film – one hundred and twenty per cent. Every fibre of your body is thinking, breathing, living the film.

People often say, 'Don't you get emotional with all that stuff happening in front of the camera?' Yes, but half of the director's brain at any point, regardless of what's happening in front of him, is preoccupied with questions like 'Have we got enough batteries left? Have we got enough tapes? Is the white balance right? Is it really in focus? Is it actually recording? What do I need next?' So half of your brain is protected from the intensity of the experience by the practical things you need to do when you're filming. We have a job to do. We've been given a role: 'Please document my story.' That's a huge privilege, but a massive responsibility. You don't want to miss that magic moment.

There've been moments in my life where I've been making films abroad, and then I've found it really difficult coming back to the ordinariness of the buses and the Tube and the bills and the dead pot plants. Because everything is hyper-vivid when you're filming a long way away, and intense and intoxicating.

It's addictive. It's totally immersive. It's like the falling-in-love addiction. It's intoxicating. It's a relationship, let's face it, and it's very intense when it begins. It's like a burning star. And there's a dark side to that. If you analyse it from a certain perspective, it is very like an addiction with all the attendant problems. Because 'normal' reality, if you want to disdainfully call it that, can't compete with the pressure cooker of a story and filming it. And then the thing stops, you confront reality again, which, all of a sudden, seems so dreary. The comedown is so impossible that directors are always looking for the next hit. And that's very hard on the people who are close to us. It's not healthy for personal relationships when those kinds of addictive highs and lows are happening. And we have to be honest, it's like a love affair. You fall in love with that story. And everything else – people, everything – has to give way to the story. If you're in the middle of filming and someone rings up and says, 'We've got to go now!' and it's your friend's birthday, chances are that it's going to be the film. It can be pretty bloody tough.

Films that venture out into the world have been very popular of late, in cinemas especially. I'm thinking of Werner Herzog and Encounters at the End of the World, *for example.*

Absolutely. Documentaries are on the crest of a wave. I honestly think that we do not need to fear competing with fiction when there are enormously powerful stories around us, that you just need to open your eyes to and engage with in the right way. To bring them to a screen requires discrimination and application, but the stories are there, and often they take place in quite a short period of time, and often they're filmable with more than one camera, so you can liberate yourself in the editing room. And then you can bring in other cinematic, dramatic devices, like the way it's shot and cut and scored and structured; to me, these are the best tools we have to bring our films to a much bigger audience. Tragically, the word 'documentary' carries with it a certain stigma for the general population: boring talking-heads, leftist, heavy, no fun, no production values ... you know, all that stuff. But there are definitely new ways now of telling vibrant, character-led stories about real life and people. And when audiences see those films, they love them.

Ultimately, documentaries can take people on a gripping, dramatic journey without travelling very far at all. The biggest journey we all make is between some sort of ignorance and some sort of realisation, whether it takes place in the suburbs of London or in the high plains of Chile – the location is academic. It's not really the point. Each time we watch something that's moving and true, we can learn something more about ourselves.

2 Telling the truth
Paul Watson

It is hard to do justice to Paul Watson's extraordinary forty-year career in documentaries in just a few lines.

He is perhaps best known as the director of *The Family* (1974), a pioneering and influential documentary series, which brought the realities of working-class family life to the screen in a way that was startling by the standards of the time. The series is often credited with inventing the 'fly-on-the-wall' genre. Some have also identified it as the progenitor of 'reality TV', a type of television which Watson himself wholeheartedly dislikes. In common with many of Watson's projects, *The Family* was very controversial when it aired, not least for the candid way it tackled taboo subjects such as sex and racism. Mary Whitehouse, president of the National Viewers' and Listeners' Association, led the calls for it to be banned.

Other films by Watson include *The Fishing Party* (1985), a landmark observational film, which both defines and skewers the 'Thatcherites', members of Britain's emergent ruling class in the 1980s; *A Wedding in the Family* (2000), the story of a single wedding, and the complex web of relationships that surround it; *Malcolm and Barbara: A Love Story* (1999) and *Malcolm and Barbara: Love's Farewell* (2007), a pair of heartbreaking films, which document the slow decline of a man with Alzheimer's disease; and *Rain in My Heart* (2006), an astonishingly raw film about alcoholism, which Watson filmed himself at the age of sixty-four.

Watson is extremely passionate and opinionated, and is disliked, loved and admired by people in the television industry in equal measure. After nine nominations without a win, he was the recipient of the BAFTA Special Award in 2008, presented for 'outstanding creative contribution to television'.

Paul Watson. © Guardian/Frank Baron.

Honesty is central to what documentaries are all about. Would you agree?

Yes, absolutely. My approach is warts and all – a terrible old phrase, but it's true. I make films as honestly as I can, because I don't want people worrying about them being fake in any way. I'm spending all those months of my life in other people's company – not my family's company, not my friends' company, not even my own company – and you've got to make sure that the end result is absolutely believable and true to make it all worthwhile. Things have happened around me in my own life, and all I can see is the rabbit going down the hole and I've got to get it; I've *got* to get it. I'm the fox. But, in the end, if you come up with something that delivers a fresh understanding of a situation, a situation that others have their own views about, then you've done something really worthwhile. But it absolutely has to be true. The minute you tell one lie, you tell two. And when you tell two, you start to write an essay in lies because each has to justify the other and explain it away. You get into a humungous bugger's muddle. You can't do it. Mustn't!

I'd say your films are, at times, brutally honest.

Do I object to your use of the word 'brutal'? People have used the word 'unflinching' about me. But that is exactly what I would expect if someone were to make a film about me. What does unflinching mean? Well, if it means that I haven't got sensitivity, if it means that I'm autistic in some way or blind to other people's problems or uncaring to those problems, or I'm so stupid and naïve that I can't see what might happen to these people as a result of their honesty or their exposure, then, no, I'm not unflinching. I think that I've questioned myself enough on those things to feel confident about that. People get upset if they're having a portrait painted and it's inaccurate. You know, it's for a wife or a lover, and she's got a squint in her eye, and the artist turns her head so you don't see it, or the artist straightens it or paints it out. If I'd learned to live with a squint in my eye, I'd be fucking offended if someone thought that it should be removed. The Chinese have squints and there are people who love that particular look. It's just wrong to say, 'Don't worry. I'll sort it out for you, love. You'll look perfect. You'll look like something out of *Vogue*.' That's not what I do. I think it's absolutely right to call a spade a spade.

You don't pull any punches.

No, I try never to pull my punches. In my earlier life I was a boxer; ducking and diving was my preoccupation, not pulling punches. When you do, you start being a play actor. You confuse the people around you and the audience and the people you're filming with if you don't play it absolutely straight and ask the difficult questions and call it as you see it. It's vitally important. I had to ask Vanda an extremely difficult question, towards the end of *Rain in My Heart*, about whether her father really did do all that she said he did. I found a tactful choice of words for it. I can't remember what they were now, but I do remember spending two nights worrying about it. It wasn't comfortable, but it had to be done. I could have just wimped out but I had a responsibility to check – was what she'd been saying the truth? And was it really the reason for her alcoholism? The question caused her real pain, but it had to be done. Filmmakers have a responsibility to their audience.

That's what I mean about brutal honesty. It's a very uncomfortable scene. When the going gets tough, you don't go AWOL. But you see lots of films on television that discreetly draw a veil.

No, no, when the going gets tough, I'm there to witness how it gets resolved. You know, there's really no point in making documentaries if you're not going to reveal some truth, and look the subject squarely in the eye, both physically and intellectually. As a documentary filmmaker, you have to want to record the world you live in, the changing world around you, including everything that's wonderful and terrible about it. It's a duty. Whether you approve or disapprove of your subject will come across in how you cut the film, but you are not there to be a crusader for a particular cause. You are there as an artist doing landscape pictures and portraits on film instead of on canvas. People aren't stupid. People can see a phony when it's in front of them. They can spot a dud a mile off. Duds can be very self-serving and the public doesn't want that. They get enough of that in *Big Brother*. They want to watch ordinary life. People are in their homes; they feel safe; they feel comfortable. They watch TV and they empathise with the people they see on screen; 'I would', 'I wouldn't'. They can scream and shout. They can have a conversation with the screen. They can think about their own lives and opinions and problems. That's what we're there to do as filmmakers, to feed that process. And it only works if what we put on screen seems honest. *Is* honest.

That approach can make your films quite unsettling at times, I think.

Yes, they are. I think *Wedding in the Family* is unsettling. I think *Fishing Party* is unsettling. *Fishing Party* was as unsettling as you could get in 1985. I think what makes them unsettling is 'there but for the grace of God go I'. I think we see ourselves in them, and that can be very unsettling. I think all my films ask you, after they've tried to explain the realities of a situation, to make a decision: where do you stand on this issue? Where do you stand in relation to these people? And that's very disquieting, because it means you have to come off the fence. Today, that isn't expected of people. Commissioning editors talk endlessly about 'jeopardy' and 'uplift' and buzzwords like that. But they don't talk much, these days, about films challenging the viewers or making them think.

I don't want people to be serfs to their jobs, serfs to society, serfs to the age. I want them to be questioning the status quo and questioning the people in charge and questioning themselves, and that can only happen if they get information. They can't all be on a hospital ward for people with liver failure. They can't all be in a chapel or a church when someone is getting married or in the lives of those people after they have got married. But I'm 'licensed' to go and get the information, and to put out stories they can watch and participate in, agree with or disagree with, and take a point of view on. Too often in this society we listen only to politicians, and we are told what to do the whole time. The law tells us what we have to do, and traffic wardens tell us what we have to do, and bloody cameras on streets watch us and monitor us. We need to have a defence, and that comes from understanding the world and thinking for oneself. Information!

If honest films are about telling it like it is and pursuing a subject no matter where it takes you or the questions it throws up, what does a dishonest film look like?

Oh, dishonest films are so easy to spot – absolutely easy! The action seems false. The characters look a bit dead behind the eyes, because they're just walking things through, or repeating 'lines' or actions according to the filmmaker's wish. You know, no one could have *acted* as Vanda reacted at times in *Rain in My Heart*. Her body was so resigned; the head was so resigned, the legs just not operating. If you fake a film, it's obvious – it's just glib. You turn people into actors and it loses all its power. They're not actors; they're real people. I never use lights because that turns them into actors. And I never re-do scenes; if you miss it, you miss it. Faking a film is disrespectful to the people you're filming. They're not actors. Take away the reality of a situation, and you turn them into *bad* actors. And that's just dishonest.

It can be hard to make a completely honest portrait, though, to capture an unfolding story in an entirely honest way?

You've got to be in the right place at the right time, and a lot of that is luck. And experience as well, I suppose. When the wife suddenly emptied her heart in *A Wedding in the Family*, I just happened to be there, and I just sensed it was going to happen. I'm not Svengali. It was always going to happen. I thought, 'Here's a boil waiting to be lanced. Here's a person waiting to be hugged. Here's a person who's got more to say. And in fact a person who can only say it to a "stranger".' I was a stranger, but also a mate who understood her point of view, as opposed to her husband who just didn't want to touch her and was looking out for his next mistress. I am an incredibly lucky filmmaker. Crap at life but a lucky filmmaker! I think I may have done a deal with the devil on those terms at some time in my life – not drunk, sober. And, who knows, it may have worked, but it comes at a price. My life in other ways is not that brilliant.

If your films are records or documents – of a wedding, for example, or how Alzheimer's disease plays out, or an alcoholic drinking himself or herself to death – what is it fundamentally that you're documenting?

Human frailty and how we might cope with it. If you can learn from Mrs Wilkins in *The Family*, or from Malcolm and Barbara, if they get you thinking, then that's a very useful process. They've *had* to do it, cope. You haven't had to do it. It's like they've done it for you. Maybe by watching them and learning from them, your family won't have to go through the same sort of hurt, or it might help you cope if the same thing ever happens to you.

That's the purpose of your films?

Yes! And for those who rule over us to see! Unfortunately, they spend so much time, like all the middle classes these days, dinner-partying each other, that they miss it. But, if the press catches your meaning, there can be a fuss, and that's when Parliament has to take notice. My films are about how our society works and whether we can better it, and not many documentaries nowadays share that purpose. Documentaries now are schmaltzy and bland and reassuring. They don't question or document anything that really matters. So, for example, if we go into a hospital, we don't find out how the NHS is coping or not with the demands placed on it. We get children who are very ill and mummies and daddies who worry. We all feel great when that child survives, or terrible if the child doesn't. And you think, 'I've displayed my own humanity by watching this.' But it's bollocks. Films need to be put in front of standing committees on health, or in front of politicians and decision-makers. Documentaries need to challenge what these people think they know. That's why people get cross with me, because I spoil how they've come to terms with a subject, and make them think again. Documentaries need to be *evidence*.

There's a line of narration in Rain in My Heart, *where you say, 'If some of us don't record it, none of us will understand it.' That's almost your motto?*

Yes, I look at situations and ask 'why?' Look, I've covered three wars and I've covered individual death. I've made films about families facing enormous difficulties. How people cope has to be seen and shared. I'm not a Christian, but I believe we are our brother's keeper. As filmmakers, we are there to use our privileged access to make records of 'things that happen', and, by doing so, inform the world. If we didn't have information freely available for people to examine and digest, we wouldn't be a civilised society.

You're trying to get people to understand each other?

In a simple word, yes! I am presenting neighbour to neighbour! I mean, you walk down the street in some parts of the world and all of the curtains are open. You walk down many of the streets in this country, and the curtains are drawn, and you want to stop and peer through the chinks. Do they have similar ways of living as me? You hear a row in the next garden, and you stop to listen: 'What are they arguing about? Is it like me? Is it like the arguments I have with my wife?' By presenting people's actions to the rest of the nation, I am saying, 'Know your neighbour.' We need to understand each other better. We need to tolerate each other better. And we can only tolerate if we understand each other better. What is it so many people seem to dislike about gypsies and black people? I want people to ask questions about *themselves* and their *own* attitudes, and documentaries that try to understand other people's lifestyles can prompt them to do that.

In A Wedding in the Family, *the groom's mum says that television shows things that shouldn't be shown.*

I put her comments into the film because it's the polar opposite of what I think, and what documentaries should be doing. Things *should* be shown, and discussed. Sometimes you might get something wrong, and you might offend against taste. You might offend against people's political sensibilities. But you've stimulated a debate. And that's the documentary's purpose: to gather the facts and put them into an order that explains, stimulates and pro-vokes. Documentary-makers should always be questioning the status quo, and showing how things really are. I'm not here to put the world right. I don't have the power, nor the intelligence you need. I'm a conduit for people who have a variety of views and experiences, which have the potential to add to the debate in our society and our communities. But films that do that seem not to be wanted any more because they are contentious. Maybe because the people who commission films fear for their jobs?

I suppose people might say that proper documentaries are hard to watch – depressing, even. But life is a fucking war, and it seems to me that it deserves some analysis. If the only job of television is to entertain, we all should give up and just make *Strictly Come Dancing*, or whatever. My job is to say, 'Okay, you have every right not to watch my film. But there are maybe things in this film that you should know, and that you might find useful.' It isn't there just to distract people and make the evenings go by faster. It's about telling it like it is. (Though of course a good documentary can be very funny and very entertaining, as well as very useful.)

What does your body of work add up to, would you say?
I have absolutely no idea.

Shall I make a suggestion?
You can suggest away, and I shall say 'Bollocks'.

A forty-year portrait of British society?
I would like to think so. I've really tried hard to document the times I've lived in. The problem when you're talking about a body of work is that films are locked away in vaults and cupboards. It is only seen when the good and the great decide it can be seen. It is not like when you come into my house, and there are paintings in every room. My films are distant memories of friendships, concerns and issues. Both they and I will be totally forgotten in a few years' time.

Because you take a very honest and unflinching approach to filmmaking, are you always looking out for characters who are robust enough to stand up to the way you work?
What I'm looking for is just somebody who believes what they're talking about, and who has their own way of explaining their situation – not self-publicists, just genuine people. They don't necessarily have to be tough or robust. You get a lot of people who agree to take part in a film precisely because they're quite vulnerable, and being in a film is better than sitting there on your own and worrying about whether he or she's going to leave you, or whether that lump that you've found is cancer. It's about 'a trouble shared', and all that. I just

assume an honest, *adult* relationship with my subjects. And it's true that that might involve asking some pretty direct questions. 'You don't seem very happy to me,' that sort of thing. That can seem a pretty innocuous form of words, but, when it's said at the right time and they trust you, both of your worlds change, sometimes forever.

Generally, I try to be as open and straight with contributors as I possibly can. And that starts right at the very beginning: 'It's not *your* film, Mrs Wilkins. It's *my* film of *your* story, of your life, of your times.' We might have sessions talking about what the *Daily Mail* and other newspapers might think of me, and whatever trouble I might have been in over my career, and Mrs Thatcher not being terribly happy with *The Fishing Party*, or whatever. We talk about the other films I've made: *Sylvania Waters*, or *Malcolm and Barbara*, or others of my films they might have seen or more probably heard about. We might talk about their relationships, my relationships, my failures in relationships, my obsession with what I do, who I vote for, the people I like, the things I don't like. They would know as much about me as I'm hoping to know about them. This is all much easier, of course, when you're not working under the kind of time pressure directors are under these days. In our conversations, I even try to be honest up to the very point of dissuading them from taking part in the film. I make it very easy for them to say no. I would hate it if they said no, but you've got to run that risk. They've got to know that it won't be glamorous or easy, and it certainly won't be financially rewarding.

If someone doesn't really want to be in a film, there's no point in trying to convince them and pressing ahead, because two-thirds of the way through the shoot they'll find out – oh, fuck! – they're in up to their noses and they're about to suffocate in shit because they didn't think hard enough about it at the beginning. That's when they want to pull out, and there's nothing worse than trying to film someone who doesn't want to be filmed. You walk in and they've got gaffer tape on their mouths, and they're sitting on their hands. Then you've got to go back to your bosses and say, 'I've spent your money, and nothing's come of it.' Better – much better – to be completely honest from the off.

Don't your characters worry about your approach? It requires quite a lot of them. They have to be willing to be as honest as you are ... There's a woman in A Wedding in the Family *who says, when you're asking her questions, 'This is exactly what the men are afraid of.'*

People worry about what might be disclosed, yes. There were a lot of those worries around when I did *The Dinner Party*, so I had another dinner party all lined up ready to go, in case my first choice fell through. I like talking to people, and they like talking to me. I have that sort of a face! You get into a conversation, and people realise that you don't want bullshit. You want it how it is. People worry, but they also know from me that they'll get their views across, and I'll be generous. I'm not out to get them. I ask that, if they say anything, that it's honest and meaningful. And they know that, if they *are* honest, I'll respect it and give them a fair hearing. You know, generally, when people are honest about what they think, even if it's not an especially flattering opinion, the audience will say, 'Fuck, they're actually a lot nicer and more human than I thought.'

You must need very strong relationships to make films the way you do. How do you go about building those relationships once a film is up and running? Is it partly a matter of trading intimacies?

Well, people want you to listen to their problems. They don't really want to discuss your problems, because most of them won't feel empowered enough to help you. They're too shy, and you're the posh person from the telly.

You just need to talk and listen, and show that you're human and you're sensitive to what they are saying, you've listened and you understand. You might let them know if you've been through the same thing yourself, but you're there to film *their* life. It's about them, not you. I've often told contributors things about myself. But it can't get too cosy, because then you're in for a bit of trouble. You mustn't lose the power to ask the difficult question in your quest to understand. If you become a friend, that gets much harder. Friends very often ignore the real questions, and let people get away with things. Friends take sides, which you can't do. You're there to ask the difficult questions. That's your job. And you need to retain the authority that television seems to give you. You need to know that if you make a request, even a seemingly unreasonable one, it will be considered and hopefully agreed to. I suppose the key to building good relationships is just being interested in what people show and tell you. If I'm not genuinely interested, then it's not going to work. I politely listen and leave and then send a note to say, 'Thank you, but we decided not to go ahead.'

The other thing is explaining very clearly what you want to do, and why you're making the film in the first place. I hate injustice and many of the people in my films have experienced or are experiencing injustice, in one form or another. I let them know where I stand on the issue, and I say, 'It would be very helpful if you were to explain or show your experiences on camera. I'd like you to let me hang around your life while these things you're going through or struggling with are happening.'

They pick up on your sense of purpose.

Yes, it's essential. The purpose is what binds you together. They're the experts, and you're there to listen and gather and record. In the old days, we would have middle-class people standing in front of subjects and saying, 'I am a Professor of Sociology. Behind me are poor people; let me explain them to you.' Fuck off out of the way and let the experts explain themselves!

There's a kind of solidity about you, which I think must help when you're building up relationships.

Solidity? I'm on a diet!

A physical thing, partly. A trustworthy physical presence.

Well, I don't wear expensive suits. I don't have much hair, and I don't try to hide it. I look people in the face. I touch people a lot, you know? Shake hands hello and goodbye. I'm quite feminine, I think, in some ways, which might make me more approachable. You've got to have a kindly presence. If you're asking to share a stranger's life, you've got to be quite warm and emotional. Why would they share their lives with someone who seems cold and unemotional?

It's not just being avuncular, though. It's also a kind of authenticity. Integrity, I suppose, is what I mean.

I'm like a bell jar; if you ping me, I'll ring true. My values are acquired over a long period of time, across a lot of varied experience. I don't judge people and I try not to agree with things when I really don't agree. I try to be honest. I never ask people to trust me. But I do expect it.

Maybe that's the secret.

I don't know what the secret is. I just like being with people. It's amazing what you can learn from them. I've made a fuck-up of my relationship with my father.

I've mostly made a fuck-up of my relationship with my mother; and my brother and I don't particularly get on. My daughter won't speak to me because she thinks it's my fault that my son died. He died of cancer, something over which I had no control. But I get on very well with strangers. I've worked most of my life with families other than my own. My wife thinks I'm odd.

Is there a line between telling it like it is and intrusiveness? Where is the line?

Well, the line is different for every filmmaker. Personally, I draw it very close to intrusion.

When do you say, 'Shall I stop?'

Well, it's very simple, I'm afraid. Some would say heartless. Others would say dedicated or committed, depending on their point of view. A few might even think my films necessary. My answer is you go on as far as you can.

I think you say to Barbara in Love's Farewell, *'Shall I stop?' Is it a defence against critics who might say you're going too far?*

Yes, it is in part. I mean, one is in two minds as to whether one ought to be filming at all. But my policy, my philosophy, is to film it as far as I possibly can. And if I'm heard saying to her, 'Do you want me to stop?' cynically I would say I get a brownie point for stopping and it makes the audience feel a little bit more comfortable with me continuing. It deflects some critic saying, 'Oh, he's remorselessly filming the poor old bitch when she's down.' There's all of that. But I care. Of course I care! I would have stopped if she had said, 'Yes, please. I can't take any more.' It's her decision.

There's a moment in Malcolm and Barbara, *where Barbara says, 'Oh, you just have to stop.' And you say, 'Okay, but can I just ask one more question?' And the question you ask is a killer question.*

It was. 'Do you want him to die? Do you want it to finish?' It was very important to get that across. She knew what the question was likely to be, and she told me later that she didn't want to face up to the answer. She was at her lowest ebb, and I felt that was the time to ask.

You ask yourself in the narration of Rain in My Heart, *'What right have I to film this?'*

I was very aware that the public would say, 'How fucking dare you film this very nice man and this very nice lady? He hasn't drunk for ten years but through no fault of his own he is not going to be given a liver transplant and is going to die and you are going to film it. You are filming her crying, the last kiss and her tears dropping on to his cheek etc. etc. How dare you? This is transgressing all our taboos. It's not on.' And here again I was filming, intruding on another death, and I'm sure people would be thinking, 'Well, that's just typical.' I think they're wrong, of course! I wanted to anticipate those objections and try to answer them in the narration of the film. Originally, I set out to make a film about the process of making a documentary and the morality of it all. But the material itself was so strong that it became a simplified film about what it appeared to be about, i.e. people drinking themselves to death.

The line between telling it like it is and intrusiveness – do you feel like you should always be pushing it?

Look, filmmakers are working in an industry in which they will never work again if they don't push. Boundaries are movable feasts. Different filmmakers have different boundaries: some closer to privacy, some further away from privacy. They have different values. That's what makes films so interesting: they're made by very different people. There is not a film I've made where I haven't felt something for the people I'm making the film about. It may seem corny to say, but I love everybody I have ever made a film about, even the men in *The Fishing Party*. I don't dislike them, only what they stand for: Tory arrogance. It's not a sexual love, of course. I say to students, 'For God's sake, never have an affair with anybody you're making a film about.' It's a stubborn love. Everybody has something you can love about them, despite whatever they do, despite whatever their situation might be, and despite what other people may think of them. It comes from learning so much about them.

There's a scene in Rain in My Heart *that illustrates that, I think. You're filming a guy gulping down red wine and throwing up in a bucket, then drinking and throwing up again. He's gasping and shaking. He's in a terrible state. It's hard to watch, but you don't turn away. You carry on recording in a way that really is quite harsh and exposing, but, at the same time, there's a real compassion and empathy to it. There's a real sense that you care about him.*

I do. I'd invested a year of my time in the subject. You can't do that if you don't care. It's like being a nurse or a nanny looking after people: you're firm and maybe tough sometimes, but warm about it as well. I'm not a jobbing film-maker. I'm a painter who happens to have a camera in his hand, rather than a paintbrush. I think it's an enormous privilege to film with people. There are times when I'm in a black mood and despairing, and I think I'm a complete wanker and a failure. And then you think of all those different people that have allowed you into their lives, and you think, 'Well, I can't be such a prick.' I hope and think most of my films celebrate the people they're about. And I don't think there's ever been a film where I've said, 'Oh, God, I can't wait for this one to end.'

Some people would say that a director who was truly compassionate would have turned the camera off when Mark started drinking pints of red wine and then throwing it straight back up.

I'm sure they would. Other directors would have turned the camera off; I know they would. I don't know a single filmmaker of your age that would have filmed it. I really don't. It's where society is at the moment – very concerned about intrusion and privacy. But the story is alcoholism, a pernicious illness that affects a vast number of people, destroys homes and family life. I have to ask myself: 'How heartless am I?' But I'm not heartless, absolutely not. I think it's cruel not to film the subject completely. Alcoholism is a filthy business. You might not like the film. It's not an entertaining evening around the telly. But I have to film it. 'Mark, don't do that. Mark? Oh, fuck, he's going to do it.' I have to show it! Switch off if you want! But, by allowing me to film him, this man is explaining something you may need to know one day.

It's obvious that you care, because you're begging the guy not to neck another pint of wine. But, at the same time, you're filming his degradation in a very square and unblinking way. I think, when people have a problem with your films, that's their problem ...

It's simple. If I don't film it, no one will. And you won't hear about the outcome, or learn about the lives of those who suffer. Government makes tax money out of alcohol. Companies and their shareholders make profit out of alcohol.

In whose interest is it to show the horrors of alcohol addiction? You *can be* both caring and unsparing in what you shoot and the way you shoot it. Not just can be, in fact, you *have* to be. You mustn't worry about people calling you a 'hard-hearted bastard'. I'm closer to those people than the people in the audience. I've made relationships with them, and we have unwritten, caring rules. And I think it would be outstandingly uncaring to simply turn your back on what is happening. You're there because of what is happening, and when it happens, there in front of you, it would be a sin to fall down on the job, to look away. My job is to do justice to their condition; to do justice to them agreeing to share their lives with you. If I chose to stop at any point, the portrait would be skewed. It would be incomplete and dishonest and the audience wouldn't have all the information they need to take a view.

Mark drinking and puking and drinking and puking – those are very powerful and revealing images. They're the unvarnished truth of what it's like to be an alcoholic. Are you always on the look-out for those sorts of images?

Yes, of course. Images that make people sit up and realise what alcoholism is! I didn't actually believe I was getting that stuff with Mark. I was on my knees, filming on a cheap, shag-pile carpet, which poor Mark had found somewhere, and slowly I got this warm feeling around my balls, and it was me kneeling in the vomit while I was filming, and it was coming up through my jeans. But when it started happening it was perfectly natural, and I was there to film it. I needed to get pictures which describe what's happening, without needing commentary all over it. I was privileged to witness Mark in that state. I could do that because he trusted me to be there and, perhaps, because as an alcoholic he couldn't wait for me to leave before he started drinking. Was I utilising that? Yes, I was. It was a horrible thing to witness, but the film-maker's sensitivities mustn't come into it. I might on another occasion have been filming the atrocities of war; what happens to my sensitivities then? Nothing! It's my job to get the information. You have to be sensitive to things, but not so sensitive that you can't face up to what is really there. I'm there to capture those bits of hell and say, 'These things are happening, dear public, in *your* society.'

What is the most raw thing you've filmed?

Well, Malcolm being washed in bed in the last months of his life ... he looked like something inside a concentration camp. It was shocking. But that is what happens when Alzheimer's takes hold. That's the shocking bit. And, if we are not doing something about it, that is shocking as well – more so than his body. He was like a living skeleton, without the ability to move, speak, recognise or function as a human being. Malcolm gave his body to the film. He agreed to be filmed, and, while I am sure he hasn't remembered that for many years, his wife agreed as well. Those images are not exploitative of Malcolm. What would be shocking is if having seen the film we chose to do nothing about finding a cure for the illness. As a filmmaker, my reward is to hear people and Parliament discussing the issue, rather than whether or not I'm a heartless human being. All the time I'm filming, I'm hoping the film will do some good!

You must be looking at things like that through the viewfinder of the monitor and thinking, 'This is awful,' but, at the same time, a bit of you is thinking that this is –

Good telly? Yes, I think so. In the sense that it serves the overall purpose. It's informative of the subject. And remember that directors are employed to make films, not to be social workers.

Do those unsettling images still have the power to shock you when you see them? Malcolm with his pyjamas round his knees in the loo and Barbara tending to him, and so on.

Oh, yes. I flinch when I film them, I really do. They haunt my head. They are exhausting. And of course you worry and wonder about the legitimacy of it all. I don't know whether I'm getting old and soft, but these days I'd rather write those parts in a play than make a documentary. The problem is with the broadcasters, and what TV has become. Television doesn't actually deserve people like Malcolm and Barbara, their candour, their secrets. TV trashes their honesty and their inner feelings. TV just wants exposure and sensation and ratings. Television is one of the great inventions of the twentieth century, and we've trashed it and turned it into something trivial. TV executives have all the power over a film these days. But when I'm making a film, I've *been there*. I've seen it. I've heard it. I've witnessed it. I'm going to make a film as truthfully and rigorously as I can. What I don't need is bureaucrats screwing with the film, playing political games and jostling for position in their careers. Executives worry that a documentary on an important social subject will produce a downer for the audience, and they'll switch off. They are fearful of bosses who are fearful of bosses. But my only interest is in explaining and revealing to you what it's like to be an alcoholic in the afternoon in a scruffy suburban flat. Fuck you and your worries about getting on in 'the business'.

You sacrifice a lot when you're making a film. Good filmmakers dedicate their lives to difficult objectives: to empathise, record and disseminate the truth of a situation, whatever truth means, so that other people might get something from it. It's bloody tiring, and, since I've been ill, I wonder whether I've got the stomach for it: whether television is still worth the effort. In TV terms, at seventy years old, I'm a dinosaur, and I hear a voice in my head saying, 'I don't think I want to be part of the TV circus any more.' I joined TV in the '60s wanting to change the world for the better, and that hasn't happened. But we are never, as a society, going to learn or solve problems if we're ignorant. So it's to the filmmakers we must turn, and there are plenty of good ones. Our job is to go out into the world, to meet people and get on with people and understand people, and then put it all together and say, 'This is the world we all share. What do you want to do about it?'

3 Getting to the bottom of things

Henry Singer

Henry Singer is best known as director of *The Falling Man* (2006), a feature-length documentary about a photograph of a man who fell or jumped from the World Trade Center on 9/11. Singer sets out to determine the man's identity, and to find out why the image was felt to be so shocking that it became subject to censorship. The film is typical of Singer's patient journalistic approach; as one newspaper commented, it is 'an extraordinary piece of journalism: thorough, dispassionate, thoughtful, incredibly moving, as interested in the philosophical journey as the pursuit of facts'. The film has been seen in over fifty countries, and was nominated for an International Emmy, a BAFTA and an RTS award.

Other examples of Singer's work include: *Waiting for Brian* (2005), about a mercurial street drinker in Bedford; *The Confession* (2005), a raw observational film about a compulsive gambler; *Last Orders* (2008), the story of a working men's club in Bradford, which faces closure amidst a profoundly changed social and racial context; and *The Blood of the Rose* (2009), a gripping investigation of the life and death of filmmaker-turned-conservationist Joan Root, who was found murdered at her home in Kenya in January 2006.

Henry Singer (left), during the filming of The Falling Man. *Picture courtesy of Henry Singer.*

Is journalism important in documentaries?

Well, it is to me. I was briefly a journalist. I nearly went to business school, which is a bit of a laugh among my friends – I'm financially not the most astute fellow. I went to business school and left after about an hour and wasn't sure what to do. I was twenty-six. I ended up realising that many of my peers, who struck me as doing interesting things, were actually either journalists or filmmakers, and I decided to explore that world. So I managed to get a job as a night-time cub reporter at a well-respected mid-sized newspaper in New Jersey. To apply for the job they just passed me a press release about some long-lost statue that had been found at a boys' Catholic school in New Jersey. And they said, 'Write a piece about this.' And somewhere in that press release, you know, Father Joseph, the headmaster at the school, was quoted as saying, 'It's a miracle.' And I thought, 'I'm going to show these people what a creative genius I am.' And I got a New Jersey phone book and I just started calling people up and asking them if they believed in miracles and if a miracle had ever happened to them. And I wrote what I thought was this kind of extraordinarily interesting piece about miracles. And the editor pulled me into an office and said, 'This is absolute shit! It is absolutely the worst thing I've ever read.' I had been to all the right schools and was a very confident and probably slightly arrogant guy who, you know, read the *New York Times* and thought, 'Anybody can do this.' And it had never occurred to me that journalism was actually a craft and it was a set of skills that you had to learn. And that moment was the beginning of an education.

I only worked at the newspaper for a little over a year, but I learned a lot. There is a distinction between American journalism and British journalism. I think American journalism is less driven by opinion: it's more of a profession based on a particular form of training where you attempt to detach yourself and be as objective as is possible. I guess that training, as an American journalist, left me with the idea that research is extraordinarily important. A film I made recently, for example, *The Blood of the Rose*, was the product of a huge amount of research and journalism. There was an article in *The Guardian* about an increase in murders of white people around Lake Naivasha in Kenya, the only fresh water lake in the country and the centre of the flower industry there. And the penultimate paragraph was on Joan Root and it mentioned her murder, the fact that she and her husband, Alan, were these renowned wildlife filmmakers, and the growth of the flower industry around the lake. It just struck me as a really interesting opportunity to look at the connection between what we do in countries like Britain and the United States and the effect it has on a tiny lake on the other side of the world and the people who live there. I mean, I had this vision: 'My God, I buy flowers on Valentine's Day and it's changed this lake, and those changes have prompted this brave woman to try to save the lake, and she's ended up being murdered for her efforts.' I started reading around the story even before I pitched it, and I found so many articles about how the flower industry had destroyed Lake Naivasha. And I got increasingly excited. I went to Kenya and did a recce for ten days. I met with Joan's ex-husband Alan Root and various friends of hers, and I met a couple of flower workers who described to me the evil doings of the flower industry, and I came back absolutely convinced that this was going to be an extraordinary film. And then I ran across – amazing I hadn't run across it until then – a piece in *Vanity Fair* which basically suggested that the flower farms had had Joan Root killed. So it all fell into place at that stage – brave woman takes on the flower industry for ruining a lake, and is murdered by them as a result.

I raised the finance. But the film changed the more research I did and the more journalism I put into it. The way I make films is I try to speak to anybody and everybody who's in any way remotely connected to the story, even if I don't think they'll be in the film. And over time it became absolutely clear in my mind (a) that the flower industry had not killed Joan Root, and (b) that to paint the flower industry as evil multinationals was just absolutely not fair; it was wrong. At least half of the flower industry is working to improve Lake Naivasha and save it. And, on top of that, the flower industry creates jobs, which, if you've ever been to a country like Kenya, is vital. I forget what the unemployment figures are but they're staggering and they're awful and they make your heart ache. So the simplistic thesis that I left London for Nairobi with just didn't stand up to proper journalism. And I think I ended up making a film that was far more nuanced and far more complex and far more 'true' than the one based on the idea I'd set out with.

The irony of it, and I guess in a sense the disappointment of it, is that I think the film would have been far more commercially successful if I had stuck to that initial agenda, the initial idea that I set out with. Because clearly at the moment films like, I don't know, *Food Inc* and *An Inconvenient Truth* and *The Cove* are highly successful commercially because there's a middle-class audience out there who in a sense already has these politics and wants them reconfirmed on the big screen. I have a real distrust of some of those agenda-driven films (though not necessarily those three).

They can be very simplistic.

Some can be incredibly simplistic. In my experience, every film I've ever made where I go in with an idea, when I actually make the film I find that my initial idea gets challenged and shaken up. I just think life is far more complex than those agenda-led films suggest it is. And it's much harder, I think, to make a film that is complex. It's less popular. It's less simple for people to take on board. We live in cultures where we like simplicity, and it's probably part of our natures as human beings that we like simplicity.

What is journalism in a documentary context? Is it a matter of trying to get to the truth, or is it trying to generate a new take?

Well, I don't think it's about generating a new take because I think that's kind of anti-journalistic. I think, for me, it's about an overall approach that tries to get at the truth. Now I know that I ultimately end up with a film that is driven by my sensibility, by the questions that I think are important, by the things that I find interesting, but the starting point is always trying to nail down the facts. Did the flower industry have Joan killed? Is there any evidence for this? Is it just hearsay? When I first started making films – when my journalism training was fresher – I used to read around the subject a lot before I actually spoke to people. Now I just speak to as many people involved in the story as possible. The way I go about researching may be different, but it's still basic journalism. In some senses, I would say it is just a matter of keeping your eyes and your ears open.

Is it getting to the bottom of things?

Well, it is for me. I am absolutely driven to get to the bottom of things. I don't know where it comes from. I think I'm an odd combination in that I adore and am fascinated by people. I mean, what drives me more than anything else is understanding who we are, and understanding who I am. At the same time, I'm a very analytical person – ideas absolutely interest me, and I think I've always been that way. And, you know, I did therapy for a few years during which I think I was trying to get to the bottom of who I am, trying to understand why I behave the way I do. And making a film isn't a whole lot different – it's about trying to get to the bottom of something. I just keep peeling back layer after layer after layer to really understand what the meaning of something is.

I think that's what ultimately really drives me: 'What is the meaning of the story?' I think a lot of films – certainly most films on contemporary British television – they're actually not interested in the meaning of things; they just tell stories. One could argue that trying to understand the meaning of things gets in the way of the story, but I would say that doesn't have to be true. I think it's harder to tell a really good story when you understand its complexity, when you're trying to suggest what it really means. But it's always possible. You just have to work that much harder in the cutting room. What did Joan Root's life and, in particular, her death mean? What can it tell us about post-colonialism in Kenya, in Africa?

Throughout the process of making a film, from the research to the shooting to the cutting, for me it's really about trying to get – as you say – to the bottom of something. Sometimes, it's not until you are in the cutting room that you realise what you were looking at, what you were trying to get to the bottom of, what the meaning of a story really is. In other words, it takes a while to figure out.

It seemed to me that there's an avatar for you in The Blood of the Rose. *There's someone who embodies that approach in the security consultant who is constantly digging away, trying to get to the bottom of what was going on.*

Yes, that's exactly what he is. In the six months that he overlapped with Joan Root before she died, that's exactly what John Sutton, the security consultant, was doing. He was absolutely trying to get to the bottom of what the hell was going on in Joan's life and, sadly, he didn't get to the bottom of it in time and she was murdered. The first time that I met him he spoke to me for eight hours, and I took notes for eight hours. It took so long partly because, for him, speaking was a sort of confessional. He felt absolutely overwhelmed by what had happened and in some way (falsely) responsible for what had happened.

One of the things I like about the film is how clear the question is at the beginning. I think, if you have a very clear sense of what the purpose is or what the goal is, then any amount of digging that takes you off in different directions or raises different questions is much easier to follow and much easier to enjoy.

Yes, I think that's true, but you mustn't confuse the clear question at the beginning of a finished film with the process of *making* the film. I am, by nature, an observational filmmaker. At the moment, I'm kind of flip-flopping between making observational films and more constructed, retrospective films like *The Falling Man* and *The Blood of the Rose*, and yet my process is always that of an observational filmmaker. So when I started researching *The Blood of the Rose*, and even when I was shooting the film, 'Who killed Joan Root?' or 'What killed Joan Root?' was just one of the many questions that I was exploring. I just had an instinct – and it was only an instinct when I started – that exploring her life, and particularly her death, might be rewarding.

Early in the research I hired a young flower-farm worker to find me somebody who was illegally cutting down trees and some illegal animal poachers, because I had an idea of this film being on a much larger canvas than it ended up being. You know, the 350,000 people who have moved there in the last twenty years are absolutely destroying the habitat in every way. And so I was juggling lots more than just the essential question 'Who or what killed Joan Root?' Even when I was shooting the film, you have a shape in your mind, but things shift, and you go off on tangents and explore different things. The film ends up with this essential question 'Who killed Joan Root?'

but that is really there as a narrative through which you can unpack all of the other ideas that have interested you in the making of the film. It's not as though I started off that film saying, 'Okay, I'm going to go out and figure out who killed Joan Root.' If I had done that, I think the film would have been rather different. I might even have shot the film myself. By looking more generally at her life, and particularly her death, I ended up exploring questions around colonialism, conservation, and racial relations, which is where the research, and the shooting, took me. Once in the cutting room, 'Who killed Joan Root?' took centre stage, and those larger ideas just became integrated into that one question and the overall story.

The Falling Man has a similarly clear question at the beginning, doesn't it? 'Who is this man?' It's that simple question that shapes the film. Was that the question from the start?

Yes, it was. But *The Falling Man* was a very different animal. It was an adaptation of an article by the American writer Tom Junod, unlike *The Blood of the Rose*, which was just me being intrigued by one paragraph in a newspaper and creating a whole film around it. You know, we all love telling stories and, as human beings, we love hearing stories. Most good films just tell really good stories with good characters, and have a beginning, a middle and an end. And certainly a detective story – trying to figure out who is the man in the photograph – just gave a fantastic narrative spine to the film. The question 'Who is the falling man?' was a great question to try to answer. It also gave you a through-line from which to hang a whole set of ideas that I think are implicit in the film, the most important being: 'How did America integrate 9/11 into its idea of itself?' But, watching the film, hopefully all you're caught up in is a great detective story.

It is interesting that, just like you've got the security consultant in The Blood of the Rose, The Falling Man *has two journalists on a quest.*

Yes. Tom Junod and Peter Cheney were totally on a quest to figure it out. There was also a character in that film named Richie Pecorella who's on his own mini-quest to try to discover what happened to his partner. He spent nights looking at every photo of people falling from the skies trying to find her. But there's a difference between the two films, and that is that Cheney is introduced reasonably early into the film, and then Junod picks up the quest soon thereafter, whereas, in *The Blood of the Rose*, John Sutton doesn't appear until – I don't know – maybe two-thirds of the way into the film. So *The Blood of the Rose* was a harder film to get right in the cutting room because the 'detective' wasn't there early on to give you a narrative thrust – the film had to generate that itself.

There's a simple question that you're trying to get to the bottom of, which is 'Who is the falling man?' But, in following that quest, the film gets to the bottom of all sorts of things, doesn't it?

Well, you know, I prefer watching and making observational films, because they are by nature – if you've got a good story and a good character or good characters – very, very complex stories. We are complex, and our interactions with each other and the world are complex. Retrospective films like *The Blood of the Rose* and *The Falling Man* can end up being less complex because their very content is made up of people 'telling' the audience things, rather than people just interacting and 'showing' the audience things. I think that a lot of people might have taken those two stories and made less complex and interesting and layered films than I did. But what drew me to both of those stories is that both clearly had within them lots of complexities and lots of layers, while still being fantastic stories.

What drew me to *The Falling Man* was that, first of all, it's an extraordinary photo and it's actually a beautiful photo, as perverse as that sounds. But I just knew instinctively that that photo would provoke lots of interesting ideas about that day. Obviously, it would provoke the very obvious question 'Who is that man?' But by looking at that you just knew it would throw up lots of ideas about censorship, you know, when you hear about how American newspapers dealt with the photo, quickly sweeping it and other images of the jumpers under the carpet. Also issues of our mortality – clearly, it's very difficult for any of us to look at that image, because it is of a man falling to his death and reminds us of our mortality. For some people, it provokes the uncomfortable idea of suicide, you know? Also the power of stills, and even how still photographs can lie, which is what you realise when you see the twelve outtakes of the falling man. And maybe most important, the idea that the falling man just didn't fit America's image of itself, because it's seen as un-heroic. As an aside, I find it extraordinarily heroic, but it's not heroic like the fire-fighters are heroic. So I just instinctively felt that that image was a wonderful prism to explore a variety of really interesting ideas that were tied up with the day.

It seems to me that, in documentary terms, good journalism is not just about getting to the bottom of things, it's about not being afraid of the ideas that go with that. The Falling Man, *for example, is very open to ideas.*

Yes, yes, I agree with that. I think the best films ... you know, you wake up the next morning and you're still thinking about them. I think, particularly in British television now, the wackier the story and the more freakish the characters the more likely these things are to get commissioned, but those are not the things that leave me thinking, and I actually don't think they leave most people thinking. But with *The Falling Man* there are ideas that stay with you because they are embedded in the story, and that, to me, is a thoughtful film.

I think a film should be thoughtful without you even noticing it's thoughtful. *The Falling Man* was a hard film to cut, and it took us a long time. I look at it now and there are places it feels a little rushed, but it's a thoughtful film in the way it's crafted, and the way it slowly unfolds. The detective story unfolds, and at the same time these ideas kind of unfold.

You know, I was absolutely overwhelmed by the response it had in this country, and it's sold to something like, I don't know, forty, fifty countries in the world. I can't tell you how many people come up to me and say, 'Oh, you made *The Falling Man?*' and they start telling me where they were on the day that happened. You know, I only made a film about a photograph. It's not as though I was the chief fire-fighter or something. I think people are responding to this idea of deciding whether you jump or whether you cling to the ledge. It gets at something very essentially human.

I nearly didn't make that film. Channel 4 called me up and said, 'Would you be interested in making this film?' My first reaction was no, because 9/11 was something that had just been so talked about; so many films had been made about it. I prefer making films about stories we don't know about, or don't notice, or avoid, as opposed to films about things like 9/11. But I'm certainly glad I made it because it seems to have become a bit of a classic.

But the jumpers in The Falling Man *give that film something in common with your other films: it's about something that's swept under the carpet.*

You're absolutely right. I did feel the jumpers had not been explored, that they had been swept under the carpet in the same way as street drinkers like Brian in *Waiting for Brian* and gambling addicts like James in *The Confession*, or even dying working men's clubs like the one in Bradford in *Last Orders*. Yes, absolutely. I think contemporary media, certainly documentary television in this country, is all about making films about things that we already know about, and I'm distressed by that; I like making films about things that we don't know about and that frankly we should know about. Those are the things that interest me.

I think that a trend in documentaries at the moment is just to document, to make records of things, so that they feel a bit like reportage.

Yes. Reportage is not interesting enough for me. I think reportage is really just news, whereas I think documentary-making is completely different, because what the filmmaker does is filter a subject through his or her sensibility. If there's one thing that I understand about myself, and there's a lot I don't, it is that I have a very, very clear sensibility. Even though an observational film and *The Blood of the Rose* and *The Falling Man* are very different kinds of films, I think anybody with any sensitivity would see that they've been filtered through the same sensibility.

What I think I try to do in all my work is to put people in the shoes of someone else. I try to make people feel a connection to the characters and the story. I think James in *The Confession* is a classic example. It would have been very easy to make a film that kept him at a distance. But I wanted to show that this overweight gambling addict is on the same continuum as we all are, and that he feels things – probably in a more extreme form – that we all feel.

I think another key to good journalism in docs is that they're thorough. I think you're very diligent and thorough. There's a sense that you're not looking for easy answers.

You know, I think being a filmmaker is a privilege and it's a wonderful way to go through life, but I also think it's a responsibility and I think you have to try to be incredibly thorough. I think it's a responsibility to be thorough because I actually think most people watch a film and they assume, 'This is true.' I mean, this is non-fiction and so you owe it to the story, you owe it to the people in the story, and you owe it to the audience to be as thorough as you can. The frustration I have now is that budgets have gotten so small that it makes it harder and harder to be thorough.

It can be hard in observational films, can't it, because you're following the story wherever it leads, and thoroughness in a way runs counter to that. Your time is taken up holding on to the coat-tails of the story. It's difficult to say, 'Now hang on a minute. Let's just be sure: is that the story?'

Yes, absolutely. But you have to be thorough in a different way to thoroughness in a film like *The Falling Man*, and that is you get to know a character well. You get to know their situation well. You have to make sure you're being true to their experience. There's these two women who do all my transcripts, who have always done my transcripts, and I've gotten to know them. And they said to me that they really like working on my films because they always feel that the final film really reflects the interviews that I do and the observational material that I gather. And they said, 'You can't believe how many times we get to know a set of transcripts inside out, and then we watch the final film, and we see how they've actually taken things out of context.' Changed, you know? Bent. And I found that terribly, terribly distressing to hear. I think, with an observational film, there's a responsibility in terms of making sure that what you're representing in your finished film is actually true to your experiences of observing that person – the whole time, even when you weren't rolling the camera.

I think that when you're dealing with provocative subjects, like racism in The Blood of the Rose *and suicide in* The Falling Man, *and addiction and so on, there is an additional pressure to be thorough, to be sure about what you're saying.*

Absolutely. No question. And, you know, if you look at my body of work, I'm drawn to subjects that are very dramatic and, I hope, significant. And if you choose subjects that are by nature incredibly dramatic and powerful, then, of course, you've got to get it right. With James in *The Confession*, on probably the fourth or fifth day of shooting he told me he was going to use my film as a suicide note. And, you know, you have to deal with that. You have to make sure that you're responsible, that you're thorough, that you get it right. You have a real duty of care, and you have to do the right thing, but without sacrificing what you perceive to be the truth of the story.

What were you trying to get to the bottom of in The Confession?

Well, *The Confession* is a film about a guy named James Burton who at the time was a compulsive gambler living in a homeless hostel for men in Bedford. I think what drove me in that film was really, really trying to understand James, trying to understand what made him tick. I was never interested in making a film that had him *describe* why he gambled. I wanted to try to understand why he gambled just by watching. He was a classic example of compulsion; he couldn't stop himself from doing things. And I wanted to understand that. I wasn't sure he'd be very good at describing why he did it. But I wanted to get to the bottom of him in other ways – mostly by being with him. And I think that film is a very, very slow unpeeling of a character where you are trying to fundamentally understand what makes him tick. Did I get to the bottom of James? I don't know. I mean, he's a complex person. Can you get to the bottom of anybody? I hope I got close. Certainly, James thinks I did.

It's an incredibly patient film, I think. Patience has a lot to do with getting to the bottom of things.

Yes, I think it does. I was drawn to James because of one essential question. He was going to get £7,000 from a pension fund, and he was a compulsive gambler who lived in a homeless hostel who kept his trousers up with safety pins. On top of that, his daughter was getting married. Yet he still said he would probably use that £7,000 to gamble rather than get himself straight or help pay for the wedding expenses. And I thought, 'That's a pretty interesting premise for a film.' I thought if I just spent time with him I would be able to kind of understand why.

I think I spent three or four months with James. I was with him four or five days a week. I often slept at the B&B around the corner. And I think that's what it takes to get to the bottom of things. You do have to be patient. You do have to be around. I'm always disappointed when I watch observational films where you hear about an important moment in somebody's life in a caption or in a voice-over. You know, I lose respect for that filmmaker. I think you need to put in the time and be there, and that the only way you are going to get to the bottom of anything is by actually seeing it. I really believe in showing things, rather than telling things. It's a bit of a cliché, but it's absolutely true.

There are some amazingly revealing moments in The Confession *that say it all really, like when he's hiding the money and then failing to find the money the next day. That looks like something that you could only film by being patient and sticking around.*

Absolutely, and I didn't even know what was happening as it was unfolding. I was just there, rolling. He actually started to count the money and put it in these little piles and I am just shooting and, mostly as one does, focusing on framing the shot. But in the back of my mind I'm just saying to myself, 'What the hell is he doing?' And then he started putting it in different parts of the room and I just didn't have a clue what was going on. And then the next morning he started trying to find the money, and he turns to me in frustration and he asks, 'Henry, where did I hide it all?' And I think that's when I started to understand him. The money game was to fill his head up. It's partly for the same reasons that people do drugs and drink alcohol – to focus on other things so he doesn't have to focus on the things that bring him such pain.

I mean, everybody that makes films works excruciatingly hard. You have to. I went to Kenya and I spent seven weeks there in the initial phase of research and I didn't take a day off trying to understand why Joan Root was murdered and the issues and all the ideas that that murder and that life brought up. That is the same impulse that had me wanting to spend time with James around the clock. You stop at nothing to try to understand. And as soon as I understand I can then make a film that I think reveals something to an audience about the kind of world we live in.

It's like you see James being stripped down. The lies that he tells himself are the kind of thing that stuck in my mind most. That he writes letters and cards to himself as though they're from the daughters he's estranged from. Did he understand that you were trying to get to the bottom of his character?

I said to him, 'Look, James, I'm interested in you because you're a compulsive gambler and I want to try to understand what's behind that behaviour.'

Because it feels, in watching the film, that he's going with you, that he's trying to help you understand.

Totally. That film has been described to me as sort of the rawest, most intimate film that many people have ever seen. And I could not have made that film in a sense unless he wanted to take that journey with me. In fact, it's almost like he wanted to take me on *his* journey. He basically said to me in an interview, 'Henry, this is my suicide letter ... I want people to know why I've done the things that I've done. And your film's going to explain that to them.' So he was an active collaborator in terms of trying to reveal to me why he did what he did. What I personally like about the film is I may have started off saying, 'I want to understand why this guy does what he does,' but I think the film ended up being a fifty-two-year-old guy looking back over the shambles of his life and trying to somehow make sense of it. To me, that elevates that film into something that isn't trying to unpick addiction, but is actually more interesting.

The film is very like therapy, really. James is coming to understand things about himself.

I think that film is hugely like therapy. When James announced to me he was going to kill himself, I became as much a therapist as a filmmaker. I was in and out of therapy for a few years, and so I certainly knew the process well. You know, if you're in therapy at all, it's not hard to think a bit like a therapist. There were many times where I'd be filming him and at a certain point I would put the camera down. Not because I felt, 'Oh, I don't want to go there with him,' but because I thought I had more than enough here about this particular moment or this particular idea. And then I would put the camera down and I would talk to him, partly as a therapist, partly as a friend. I do think, if you make observational films – certainly observational films about individuals – your subjects on some level are like people in therapy. You're watching them. And an observational film becomes a mirror for that person.

One of my agreements with James was that I would show him the film. I couldn't give him editorial control, but I would certainly let him comment on it, and if there was something that he felt strongly about I would discuss it with him, and, if he convinced me, I would change it. The first time I showed him the film I was obviously nervous because it is an incredibly raw film. And he wept throughout it. He had to leave the room a couple of times he was so beside himself. It was excruciating for him. It was a really, really hard thing for him to do. But I also think that that film on some level sort of saved his life. It was a real turning point for him.

Waiting for Brian is a similar sort of film; an observational film on a similar subject. But there's quite a lot of cat-and-mouse with Brian.

Yes. While James wanted so badly to explain why he was the way he was, Brian was very elusive. I met him when I was making the film on James. And I said to Brian, 'I'd like to make a film on you. Is that something that would be of interest?' Brian lived down the hall from James. And he had sort of seen what the filmmaking process was doing to James, and he was intrigued and interested. And after many, many conversations, he agreed. The truth of it is that Brian wanted to somehow escape his situation, but on some level didn't want it enough. Or he couldn't bring himself to look inside and share it in the way that James had. And the whole film became my very slowly trying to get to the bottom of Brian, but being rebuffed time and time again. And there were times I thought, 'Okay, Brian is finally going to open up and reveal to me why he is the way he is and why he left his family ten years ago, and never gave them even a phone number and disappeared off the face of the earth for them.' But I just couldn't get there in the end. I think that film is pretty revealing – not as revealing as James' film, but revealing nonetheless. I think it's almost as though they were on different steps of some kind of rehabilitation process. And Brian was just on a much earlier step and couldn't move beyond that.

Didn't you find it frustrating, making Waiting for Brian?

Hugely frustrating. You know, if you're driven like me to try to understand, and if you're driven like me to get to the bottom of things, to use your term, it's hugely frustrating not to be able to get there. I think I got into filmmaking partly as a public service. And this was public service writ personal; this was being in the position where I felt I could actually help two people. I really felt I could be there for Brian in the way that I was there for James. With James, I knew I was getting really strong material. And the process of getting strong material seemed to be helping this person. I wanted to do the same thing with Brian, but I just kept running up against a wall. And I found it hugely, not just disappointing, but distressing. Because I'd arrive from London to hang out with Brian for a few days and he'd be absolutely, completely drunk. And my morale would plummet. In the back of your mind all the time you can't help but be thinking about your film and the narrative, and is there a film that's slowly evolving? And, of course, I kept feeling like this film was just doubling back on itself, that he was just getting pissed over and over again. And I was hugely frustrated and demoralised.

In the context of your body of work, which is all about trying to figure things out, do you think it represents a failure?

No, I don't, in the sense that I think there are different ways of getting to the bottom of things. Brian died a few months ago. I actually gave the eulogy at his funeral. Via a text message at one point before his death, he told me what he felt was the great source of pain in his life and why he'd turned to drink.

The 'secret' that he keeps referring to in the film?

The secret, which I obviously can't share with you, nor can I share it with anybody. On some level, you could say that's a failure, that I didn't get that in the film. But I think there is a revealing story there nonetheless: a man who's a street drinker dries up for a time and then runs into another street drinker and falls back into drinking. And during that story I think you do get an insight into the man.

It's much less conclusive than The Confession.

It's less conclusive. But that doesn't worry me so much. I think we live in an age where we want conclusion; we want endings. We don't want ambiguity. We don't want questions. We don't want complexity. I'm not saying that it's an extraordinary film by any means, but it has all of the above, and I think it succeeds on many levels.

Personally, whereas The Confession *felt to me very satisfying in that we got to understand the guy, with* Waiting for Brian *I felt myself wanting you to push him harder and ask questions and make him tell you what the secret was.*

I think my great strength is my empathy, but there is a weakness with my approach, too, and that is that I'm really not someone that provokes people – that's just my nature. I'm a kind of un-confrontational person. The way I work with contributors is to build up a level of trust. I try to be honest about what I'm trying to achieve. I spend a lot of time describing what's important to me. I show them my work. And then I'm just there, trying to be an empathetic character in the room.

There's a moment in *The Confession* which is really a non-Henry Singer moment. It's the moment when James goes to gamble. He's gotten £700 in benefits and he goes to gamble in Southampton. And just as he's about to go in, I ask him if he ever thinks about his family at a time like this, and he gets angry and at one point he says, 'I'm going,' and I actually thought he meant that he was leaving the film, that he was quitting. I thought, 'Holy shit! I have just fucked this whole film!' Now, the question that I asked James was suggested to me by the executive producer and I think it's an incredibly good moment in the film. James says, 'Don't you understand, Henry? That's why we're here. That's what this is about.' It may be the most revealing moment in the film. And that's because I pushed a bit. But that's not my nature generally. I see the value of being more provocative and more confrontational. And yes, I think with *Waiting for Brian* another filmmaker might have taken that story further. A pushy, provocative, prickly interviewer at times might have gotten more out of him. But that approach might also have scared Brian off very quickly. In any case, it's not how I work, and I think I get the kinds of material I get with people because of the kind of character I am. It's interesting that you found yourself frustrated. Because I do think, with a really good film, the audience should lose itself and shouldn't think, 'Why didn't the guy ask him that?' or 'Why doesn't he push him that extra yard?' So maybe it's not as good a film as I like to think it is.

I think my frustration came from a slight suspicion that there wasn't any depth to Brian. I kept thinking, 'Well, maybe there is. Maybe there was something terrible and telling that happened.' But every time he would flirt with you over it, and then back off – 'Not today, maybe we'll talk tomorrow' – I kept thinking, 'Are you really interesting, though?' He says in the film, 'There's more to me than meets the eye.' I kept thinking, 'But is there?' That's why I felt, personally, that I really wanted you to kind of crack what that issue was, so I could work out whether he is just a weak character who's fucked his life up, or a tragic character because something bad has happened. But maybe it's good to end a film with that doubt still in your mind, I don't know.

I can tell you this: there was definitely a huge amount of depth to Brian. I think it's a weakness of the film if the audience has that reaction, I really do.

In terms of getting to understand Brian, he's playing this cat-and-mouse game. The thing that he won't talk about is the key to getting to the bottom of him. Did you talk to other people about it to try to work out what it was?

No, I didn't. I decided early on that both Brian's film and James' film were just going to be entirely them in their own words. What had excited me about the film on James – which had made me want to make a film on Brian – is that I became very interested in my relationship with James, and James' relationship with the camera. So, you know, in *The Confession*, the film is partly about the filmmaker's relationship with the subject, because at one point James admits that he'd lied to me just to get me interested in him. And, as we've already talked about, he said he was going to kill himself. With *Waiting for Brian*, I thought that was a really interesting thing to explore again. You know, another filmmaker might have talked to the social worker and the people around. But that just didn't interest me.

We create narratives of ourselves to try to understand ourselves. And I think that was what interested me. If you do a film about one person, what is the narrative that these people have to explain who they are?

Do you ever worry when you start a project that it may just be too confusing and too complicated to ever get to the bottom of?

You know, I'm not sure that you can ever truly get to the bottom of anything. One of the really hard things as a filmmaker is when you set yourself up to answer something, and you just can't. I mean, *The Falling Man*, in an ideal world, would have been able to say conclusively that Jonathan Briley was the falling man. But it can't quite say that, and I don't know if that's frustrating to viewers. When I made *The Blood of the Rose*, as I was making it, I thought, 'Wouldn't that be amazing if I could actually get somebody to confess to Joan Root's murder,' you know, like Errol Morris did so brilliantly in *The Thin Blue Line*.

I find it difficult to find subjects that I want to make films about, because it has to tick so many boxes. It has to have a really strong story with really strong characters, and it has to have depth. It has to instinctively provoke some questions so that I know it's going to be a really stimulating, interesting journey for me personally, and so that I feel I can make something that operates on several levels. That, to me, is the hard bit: whether I have the time to sufficiently understand enough of it to make a compelling film. One of the reasons I want to get out of television and just make big feature docs is that, if you can get the right story, you can raise enough money to have the time to ensure that you get it just right. But, generally, I don't worry. I guess I have enough confidence in my skills as a filmmaker to know that I can get pretty deep pretty quickly to be able to reveal some essential stuff and tell a great story.

My own feeling about it, when you're making something which is quite journalistic, is there's always a moment where you've set off into the forest, but you don't know how much further you've got to go and how much more dark and dense it's going to get before you emerge on the other side. You ask questions, but they generate more questions, and you end up with only questions. There's a point where you're halfway through a film and all you've got is a lot of questions, and maybe not many answers. That's quite scary.

It is scary, I think. With an observational film, that fear and that feeling of being completely lost partly comes with the territory. But I think a greater fear is 'Christ, is there a film here at all?' I guess with me there are things I do to ensure that that doesn't happen. One is that I'm really careful about the films that I take on. I only take on films that speak to me, where I feel that there's something there that I really want to explore. When I was in Kenya, I'd never been to sub-Saharan Africa before, and it really was foreign to me. And there was a period where I thought, 'God, I don't really know what this film's essentially about.' But the thing that always carries me through in those situations is that I know there's a film there. I knew there was a compelling character at the centre of it and I knew there was an incredible story. And you can always fall back on that. D'you know what I mean? You probe and probe and probe until you're not entirely sure what the film's about, or how you're going to tell it, but you just fall back on the fact that you've been there before and you've pulled it off before, and you're going to pull it off again.

What drew you to Last Orders? *What were you trying to get to the bottom of?*

With *Last Orders*, I was interested in exploring why the white working class in this country is drawn to voting for the British National Party, the BNP. But I think the film very quickly became much more interesting than that. It's really about the sense of alienation, despair and marginalisation that certain sections of the white working class feel in this country at the moment. I think that's what I was trying to understand. By looking at that alienation and marginalisation, it also became a way of deconstructing racism on some level. I think there's certainly some racism in some of those communities, but they get painted as being entirely racist because those are the terms with which they articulate their alienation.

I was brought up in that kind of area, and it's fascinating that a lack of eloquence is like a Yorkshire trait. People are proud to say, 'I speak as I find. I'm not complicated. I'm not a complicated person.' And, to some extent, the problem is that they're discussing these quite complicated feelings and a quite complicated situation in a very simplistic way, which can sometimes sound very racist.

I'm really proud of that film, and I'll tell you why: because it was as difficult an access film as I've ever taken on. You know, to go to Bradford and to a white working-class community, and to live there and get people to trust me while making a film that they feared could paint them in very simplistic ways. That was an incredibly difficult thing to do. My assistant producer and I lived there for four months and went to the club virtually every day. And, you know, there were plenty of people who said, 'You point that camera at me I will fucking shove it up your arse.' I mean, there were moments of real fear. From an access standpoint, it was a really, really challenging film. And I'm really proud that it tries to get to the nub of the alienation that that community feels. And it tries to use the potential demise of their working men's club as a metaphor for the fact that these people have lost their place in society.

It's quite rare to make films that openly talk about ideas, and that are a sort of mosaic of telling moments, but I don't think those are the ingredients for really strong storytelling. With *The Falling Man*, it's 'Who is this man?' With *The Blood of the Rose*, it's 'Who killed Joan Root?' I think, in those films, you see a story unfold. Or *Man on Wire* – I think it was really smart to turn that into a heist film, because it gives you that narrative clothesline, that compelling thing that carries you through and allows you to hang your ideas off it. Really good films have that. The problem with *Last Orders* is that it doesn't really have a story.

Last Orders seemed a bit unlike your other observational films in that you were drawing conclusions as you went along, much more explicitly.

Well, the brief which came directly from the BBC Head of Documentaries and the Controller of BBC2 was: 'We'd like Henry to explore this question.' So, you know, the film became more of an essay, I think, where I'm drawing conclusions. Looking back, I wish I'd done less of that. I think the best films show you things rather than tell you things, and that's particularly true of observational films.

It's just a different kind of journalism. I don't think there's anything wrong with it.

No, there isn't anything wrong with it. But it is less 'me'. I don't generally put myself in my films. I don't really like films in which filmmakers have a big voice, in which they talk to the audience. 'I couldn't help but think', and all that sort of thing. You know, I'm not that interested in what the filmmaker thinks. I'm actually really interested in what the subject thinks. And, in *Last Orders*, my journey becomes the story of the film, and I think that's less interesting.

What sort of person do you have to be to get to the bottom of a subject when you're making a documentary?

Well, you have to be a naturally curious person first of all. I think that's what drives most good filmmakers, that they're just curious about the world. I think, after that, it's just about following your nose. I mean, people always ask me to talk about how I interview people, and the way I interview people is I just listen to their answers and then the next question comes out of what they've said. I never have a list of questions. It's just a matter of really listening to people, and realising that in every answer there's always a follow-up question that takes you deeper. And, of course, there are certain basic things that you need to know in any story.

You need to be calm and patient, because the whole point of documentary-making is not simply to follow a story. Rather, the idea is to take time and to have a bit of distance, either from time elapsed or from the time in research and production, so that you can step back. You need a certain degree of detachment to really understand what something is essentially about, and to get the story right. And then you really have to keep your nerve, because it's never a calm process and you never have enough time. You never have enough time in pre-production, you never have enough days to shoot, and you never have enough time in the cutting room. If you come into a space where a film is being made, it rarely feels calm. There's always a lot of pressure. But I think you have to keep your nerve.

You need to be brave at times. When I arrived in Kenya, I was nervous because I had read this piece in *Vanity Fair* that suggested that the flower farmers might be behind Joan's death, and I was nervous because, if I am noseying around and it turns out that the flower farmers have murdered Joan, they might not appreciate that. And I was in the slums a lot. I was hanging out with fish poachers, and I was digging around in their world. I really didn't know where the story would take me, and you can find yourself asking some very inconvenient questions. An African friend of mine told me before I went over for the first time, 'Henry, you really have got to be careful. Kenya is the kind of country where you can very easily end up in a ditch.'

You need to be open-minded. You know, when I went to Kenya I really didn't know what I was going to find. You need an element of spontaneity. You want a film to be a continuing process of discovery. I think there's no question that the best films don't know where they're going to end up. *Capturing the Friedmans* – that film started off as a portrait of a clown, and at some point the clown said, 'You know, my family was involved in this scandal a few years ago and I've got in my possession all these tapes.' And suddenly that film became very different, and I think a really, really good film. It's a scarier place to be, but you try to make films that you don't know where they're going to end up. It's a much more productive and fulfilling form of filmmaking. You know, I distrust films that have agendas or even scripts, because I just think, if you're alert, so much happens around you that you should be picking up on in the moment, which actually is going to lead to an extraordinary piece of work. You don't want to be closed off. The surprising stuff is what makes the film.

And you need absolute tenacity. I mean, large portions of my life have just been taken over by my work and I don't have children yet. I think that's partly why. When I make a film, the rest of my life really falls away. If you're going to do this kind of work, you really have to just give yourself over to the work. You have to sleep on people's floors and so on, and you have to be hands-on and spend time with people and build up trust. I really think you should only do this if you can imagine doing nothing else with your life. It's so, so hard. And to pull it off, you have to give your life to it.

4 Thinking on your feet
Nick Broomfield

Nick Broomfield started his career in documentaries making observational films such as *Soldier Girls*, in the classic *vérité* style of Frederick Wiseman and D. A. Pennebaker. During the making of *Driving Me Crazy* in 1988, he responded to difficulties with the production by putting himself in the film, as 'the only way I could think of telling the story'. This led directly to the idiosyncratic style for which Broomfield is now known – a freewheeling, investigative approach, with Broomfield himself on screen, charming contributors, recording the sound, and picking his way through the story as it unfolds around him.

The best examples of this approach are: *The Leader, His Driver and the Driver's Wife* (1991), a film set in the last days of the apartheid regime in South Africa, in which Broomfield fences with the white supremacist Eugène Terre'Blanche, exposing him as a posturing buffoon; *Tracking Down Maggie* (1994), a game of cat-and-mouse in which Broomfield stalks former Prime Minister Margaret Thatcher in search of an interview; *Kurt & Courtney* (1998), in which Broomfield investigates the circumstances surrounding the death of Kurt Cobain, and allegations that Courtney Love may have been complicit in it; and *Aileen: Life and Death of a Serial Killer* (2003), in which Broomfield shares the final days of Aileen Wuornos, providing insights into her desperately unhappy upbringing and her parlous mental state, as she awaits execution on death row. His films have won recognition around the world, including a BAFTA, Prix Italia, a Peabody award and a Grierson.

Nick Broomfield (centre, with microphone), during the filming of The Leader, His Driver and the Driver's Wife. *Picture courtesy of Nick Broomfield.*

A lot of your films are very improvised and spontaneous.

Yes. I think probably what has always attracted me most to documentary is that it's so different from writing, which is more of a consolidation of impressions, whereas film can capture rawness in a way that no other form can. It can capture – well, I don't like the word 'capture' – it can mirror, it can record the rawness of a moment in a way that is much more telling. It can show not only how long it takes for someone to make a decision about something in real time, but also give you a sense of what it would be like to *be* that person, or to be with that person in the room, or to have that person as a friend.

So, probably what interests me about documentaries is almost the opposite of someone like James Marsh, who makes carefully constructed films out of formal interviews and carefully crafted dramatic re-creations, like *Man on Wire*. I suppose I would look to traditional drama to be beautifully lit and to be composed, whereas for me the wonder and the beauty of documentary is that it's wild and it's full of adrenaline and uncertainty, and it's not scripted, and no one really knows what's going to happen next. You're in the moment. You're trying to reflect reality, rather than re-enact it. And, for me, the great documentary filmmakers – not that James Marsh isn't a great documentary filmmaker – have the ability to go with the chaos and uncertainty, and to come back and give the audience a real flavour of what was going on in a situation, and what it felt like to actually be there. For me, that's what documentary has that no other form has.

It also seems to me that your films are often like adventures. They feel like an adventure in the sense that the outcome is very uncertain.

Yes. They're like a rollercoaster ride. They're much more like a relationship. They're like a diary into the future. But making those kinds of films is getting harder. You know, people expect – in these absurd pitch meetings with broadcasters – they expect you to know the beginning and the end of something that hasn't happened yet. I think the problem with raw filmmaking, the kind that I love and that I do, is that it's really unpredictable, and commissioning editors don't like someone coming in saying, 'Well, you know, I can tell you whatever you want to hear, but actually I don't know what's going to happen and I don't have access to half the people yet, and the reason I'm interested in them is because I don't have access to them. I'm interested because they've got lots to hide and the only people who really want to be filmed are the ones who don't have any secrets and I'm interested in people who have got secrets and finding a way through to those secrets.'

The cowboys have, to a certain extent I think, left television, which is a pity for documentary because, although you had a lot of terrible films, some of them were amazing because they have this rawness, like a kind of helter-skelter ride. They show you things that are a revelation to the filmmaker at the same time as they are to the audience. They're very much shooting from the hip. They are very much about the moment and how people will react in the moment.

Your films often have a quest structure, with you looking for answers in a way which is quite genuine; it's motivated by really wanting to know. Which gives them a real sense of urgency and tension.

Yes, I mean, for me, films are a lot to do with tension and holding an audience and making them curious so they watch till the end. Yes.

That search for answers is always going to be watchable and compelling, I think.

Well, in any film you have questions about people: who they really are or what their motivations are or why something happened – all those kinds of things.

I think inevitably as a filmmaker there are things about people you don't understand or things that puzzle you. And if you're working in the particular style that I eventually ended up working in, instead of just asking yourself the question, which is a lonely and tiresome and boring thing, you can share it with the audience. You can share a lot of the humour and a lot of the thoughts that normally you only have with yourself. You can share your frustrations. You can share your perceptions. You can share seemingly irrelevant bits of stuff that nonetheless form an impression or add a little colour or shade.

What I'm interested in doing is having an idea about something that fascinates me and then just finding a way through it. And so you build this kind of montage of impressions and thoughts, which is fun to do. I love a lot of those *cinema vérité* films, you know the Pennebaker ones, like *Don't Look Back*, and Frederick Wiseman's films, like *High School* and *Hospital*. I think they've very entertaining and they're also just a moment in time. They're very pure and observational. And I suppose my style is a bit of a refinement of that. I think all too much of the stuff you see on television is full of bland information that you don't really necessarily need to know. Or it would be much more fascinating to learn it in a different way. A seemingly oblique bit of information or an impression would actually give you much more of a sense of cracking something open and getting to the heart of something.

It's like the difference between an insight and a fact.

Exactly. Insights are interesting and facts aren't.

So you've got this improvised, spontaneous style, where you're feeling your way, looking for answers and forming impressions. Do you feel in at the deep end?

Yes, completely, because you really don't know that there's an end. I mean, occasionally for me it's been a great luxury if I've known that I'm even going to get an interview with my main subject – with Heidi Fleiss or even Aileen Wuornos or Margaret Thatcher, although of course I didn't really get it with Thatcher. In all of those films, it was all about 'Are you ever going to find this person?' I think the problem, for example with the Thatcher shoot, was it just didn't go on long enough. The other ones all went on for about twelve weeks or so but the Thatcher one was much, much shorter. And so, I suppose, one of the aspects of making a film that is very unstructured and deliberately so is that a lot of the research is done as you go. The film *is* the research. Because you're not setting things up ahead of time with people, and because you want to catch the spontaneity of their reactions as you move along, it actually takes much longer. So it's a rather expensive way of making films. And, I suppose, more and more television has less money and it wants to be secure in what it does.

Do you deliberately under-research things going into a film?

No, you don't under-research them. You read everything that you can, and you find out as much as you can about that particular person, although I do think it's probably quite a good idea to be relatively open and fresh when you start, so you don't have lots of preconceptions that you're simply going out to fulfil. I think that you want to meet people with an open mind when you first meet them, and form impressions as you move through the film.

Your approach is to go and find a film. Are you always sure when you've found it?

Yes, I think you know. You just kind of know emotionally. You know you've got a good subject and you know it's going to be fine. I think it's instinct. I think you just know you've got a good, rich subject. And, if one thing doesn't work out, something else will, and you'll be able to tell a good story.

That style of filmmaking, going where the story wants you to go, can sometimes lead you into difficult situations.

Well, I think sometimes you're forced into doing things that you don't necessarily want to do. You know, like getting up at the ACLU (American Civil Liberties Union) dinner, at the end of *Kurt & Courtney*, and asking lots of questions in a very public way. I found that really hard to do but the film sort of called for that to happen. I think you make a kind of deal with the audience that you're going to follow whatever comes up. You can't suddenly play it safe and say, 'Well, actually, I'm not interested in going there any more; I'm not going to do it.'

You've been in some quite dangerous situations, like in Biggie & Tupac when you're clearly in an area where wandering around with film equipment is a risk, and the police stop you because they think it's a slightly mad thing to be doing.

Well, yes, but that's obviously all part of the texture of those situations. I suppose the films are kind of anthropological in their portraits of that world, so you make them as accurately as you can, really.

Have you ever felt in over your head?

I think at the beginning of the films often they're very frustrating. I remember the Heidi film was, and the Biggie film and the Kurt and Courtney film to a certain extent. The first few weeks were very difficult because there weren't any interviews set up and it was very hard to get anyone who wanted to talk and to find a way in and to just get going, because there was so much suspicion in one way or another. And, you know, maybe it takes three weeks to really start to get anywhere. And that time is spent on the phone or just trying to get a lead. So maybe a lot of it is journalism. A lot of it is trying to get information or trying to get a character to talk to you who probably has been talked to by lots of other journalists and is rather doubtful that there's any point in talking to you as well. I mean, I remember with Biggie's mum, Voletta, we only got to speak to her after we had convinced her that we weren't doing just another sensational piece on her son, but that we were genuinely trying to unearth new stuff and we were doing a proper investigation. And then, once you've got that one person, lots of other doors open. But probably if we'd tackled the film in a traditional way – which is to do lots of research, then make your pitch to the commissioning editors, and then go out and do the film – I don't think it would have happened, because I don't think Biggie's mum would have taken our calls. She would have just thought it's another MTV thing or whatever. I think there is something about the reality of there being a film crew *in situ*, of the fact that you're already filming. You're not playing it safe. You've already kind of made your commitment to it. I think it makes a lot of people come forward and talk to you and take you seriously who wouldn't if you were just doing a sort of speculative proposal. It's a precarious way of working.

You get great moments that way, though. Like in the Heidi Fleiss film, when you encounter another film crew.

Yes, that was interesting. I mean, funnily enough, that's one of the reasons I had such a hard time on that film. Normally, filmmakers and journalists are incredibly helpful to each other. I always am if there's another film crew doing a similar story. I generally give them as much help as I can, partly because it's just so difficult. But on this occasion there was a British film crew doing a film about the vice squad in LA or something. They went around telling everybody that they shouldn't have anything to do with me and that I was going to stitch them up and blah, blah, blah. It probably put another month on to my schedule, just meeting people and convincing them otherwise.

But, generally, yes, working in that particular style, I think you do come up with things that are unexpected, that surprise you. I've always felt that filmmaking isn't really about going out to confirm your research. I remember when I started, you'd go off and you'd meet lots of people before you started filming and chat to them. And you'd come across great things, and then you'd try to re-create them in the interviews, on camera. But it's never the same the second time, partly because the person subconsciously knows they've already told you it and there isn't the same kind of electricity that there was the first time. Because it's sort of old hat, and you're both not really on your toes, feeling each other out. I do think there is a specialness in you, them and the camera meeting altogether for the first time. And I think film picks that up. But, you know, the more I talk about it I can see that it is a very eccentric way of making a film, really.

There's another great moment in Kurt & Courtney *where you're in a building that Kurt Cobain used to fight with his wife in. The receptionist sets the alarm off and calls security ...*

That was a mad moment. God, it's all such a nightmare! Most of those films were very, very hard work. And they were very precarious and the financing was very precarious. They were tough going. I think it's a tough way of making a film. But you absolutely do get those magic moments. I have a feeling maybe it's a young person's way of making a film. I think you need to have lots of energy and lots of bounce and lots of cheek and lots of adrenaline, you know? Because it is a very exhausting way of making a film, because nothing is certain at all. You haven't got anything very definite to hang on to.

It strikes me also that you need to be quite smart because you need to think on your feet. That's part of what puts your heart in your mouth when you're watching your films – you're thinking, 'Fuck, he's in a jam here ...'

Well, there is an element of that, yes. I was very, very lucky that I did them at a particular time when people were much more interested in taking risks. Working in that way means that the structure and shape of the film evolve as you go, in a building-block kind of way. And that's the fun of making them, actually: thinking as you go. You have your first encounter or interview which then propels a whole lot of questions and you go on to the next thing. And so you're constructing it in a logical series of building blocks that become more and more specific, and in a sense more and more tense, I suppose, towards the end of the film.

They feel like quite linear films.

Yes, very linear. And they're quite easy to cut in the editing room. Because, you know, a lot of that thinking has been done during the shoot. I suppose what I'm doing is structuring the film all the time, as I go, knowing pretty much what I need out of every scene, and how many points I really want to cover in a scene. At the beginning of the film, I'll cover lots of different subjects and throw it pretty open. I never view the material back. But you remember one or two things someone said that are things that you're curious about, and you want to follow up on. And then you go on, refining it down, getting more and more focused. Sometimes you write down a list of things that you think you need. Sometimes it's shots; sometimes it's points of the story that you feel you want to cover. And I would normally make sure that I get that list, that it's done one way or another. It might take several days, maybe even weeks, but those things just need to be covered. And it's actually a way of stopping you going mad, because you're slowly making it achievable. You're not taking on the whole big thing; you're just taking little specific points. And, little bit by little bit, you're getting there. You're getting some good, solid scenes. You're building something that you know is relatively solid.

Aileen: Life and Death of a Serial Killer is interesting in terms of a style which requires you to respond to what's going on, and to think on your feet. That approach makes for funny films and funny moments, but in that particular film it felt like so much is going on, and it's so serious, that it was becoming too much.

I think it was. Yes, I think emotionally it was a very draining film. And I think it was much more emotionally involving than the other ones, really. I mean, the other ones ... there was a lot of wit and humour to them, and wit and humour are great in that they allow you to skip around and do the shuffle and you don't really have to take it seriously, whereas that was a rather serious film. That was about the end of someone's life.

It felt to me that, where your films usually have that quest structure or you're pursuing answers, in Life and Death *you were sort of caught up in it.*

Yes, I was very much a participant, and I think I cared a lot about her. I cared a lot more about that film than I did the others. I was pretty detached with the others, really.

Did Life and Death *change the way you think about making films?*

I think it probably did. I think it did change me in some ways.

I wonder if it marked a transition between one way of making films for you and another?

Well, I sort of decided that I wanted to try to make different films for a while. I mean, I was doing a film a year for quite a few years and I think that that style was enormous fun when I first thought it up. It amused me; I was amused doing it. And then I stopped being quite so amused. I think I definitely stopped being amused with *Aileen. Biggie & Tupac* was a factor too. It was kind of a pain in the arse because it just went on and on and on. And it was difficult. And, you know, *Kurt & Courtney* was difficult too. You took something as far as you could possibly take it, which was generally just a little bit short of a lawsuit or several lawsuits, which again were fairly exhausting.

I think after *Aileen* I was quite frustrated politically, as well. I thought people didn't really care very much about people like her and, you know, nothing's really going to change very much. I wanted to make things that were probably more overtly political and in a different style.

The legal element must have been on your mind a lot of the time, making these films. You must have had to be very careful with such a responsive style of filmmaking.

Well, you had to know how far you could take it, so that you would manage to get the film out, so that there wasn't a cause for legal action. Fortunately, I'd had some legal training so I had a pretty good sense of all that. It's a matter of knowing how far you can go and how far things are accurate. You know, a lot of it is that you have enough evidence or you have enough reason to take a position. In a way, the films were all about that – accumulating enough reason to take up a definite position.

Do your films spend a lot of time being legalled?

Yes, they do. I legal them a lot. Then I have my lawyer, who's very good at libel, and then obviously the channel will go through it painstakingly. And there are sometimes changes you have to make.

There are lots of moments in your films where you think, 'How did you get to include that?' People talking to other people on phones, someone selling taped phone calls to you and so on. It's amazing that you got away with it.

Well, the more stuff like that you get the better. We live in a world obsessed with celebrity – I mean, to a really infuriating extent. And, of course, one wants to take it on, head-on really, and find a way of having some fun at its expense. And a good time will be had by all. I don't see how you can do that officially. I mean, why would they want you to be there? It has to be done in this guerrilla style.

You're always on your toes when you're filming. Have you ever felt that you've made the wrong choice?

Yes. Sometimes in the editing room it's really interesting ... you look at an interview and you just see, at a certain point, you made the wrong choice, and the whole thing just falls to bits because you've taken the wrong road. It was just not the right direction to go in. What I would tend to do with interviews is I would work quite hard in assimilating as much information as I could. Maybe I would think of some questions I wanted to ask, and I'd try to work them in conversationally. But sometimes you pick up on a point and you keep hammering it home, and it's just the wrong point. There are other points that are more interesting. Or you actually close someone down. You misjudge the occasion. I did feel like I was slightly cheating sometimes in the editing room, when you have to sort of cover up fatal flaws and mistakes you've made – you know, complete misjudgements. And there were, of course, lots of those.

You do leave quite a lot of stuff in, though, which makes your films feel very honest and transparent. For example, when you do that last interview with Aileen and you're trying to ask questions almost for balance; you're trying to put the other point of view. And she gets very angry with you and walks away. And then you say, in this really heartbreaking way, 'I'm sorry, because I fucked that up. I didn't mean to –'

Piss you off.

Yes. 'I didn't mean for it to end like this.' And that is a very transparent, honest thing to include, because you could have just come out of it earlier if you wanted to.

Yes. I also felt that this is the last chance to find out what really happened, like, 'Actually, did you do some of these things? Or what really went on...?' And I thought maybe, as she was clearly going to be executed, she'd want to talk about it. She'd want to engage because it was the last time she could. But, obviously, that was not the case.

Brave to leave it in, though. Because it's messy and a bit confusing.

Well, it was confusing. It is very jarring, I think, because she's built up in the film as somebody one likes enormously, so it was quite contradictory to upset her.

Sometimes there are really serious judgement calls when you're thinking on your feet. It's a high-wire act. I'm thinking particularly of the decision with recording Aileen. You know, when she says, 'Actually ...', in a moment of clarity, 'Actually, when I killed people, it was in self-defence. I've just had enough of all this. I want to die ...'

Yes, I'm often asked about that because, I guess, people think it's a really significant thing. I felt that it was incredibly revealing about the fact that she so wanted to die that she was prepared to say that she'd killed in cold blood, when she actually believed she'd killed in self-defence. I mean, it's pretty significant. So, I didn't really have any hesitation. I mean, people have said 'You know, you kind of made out you weren't recording ...' But I felt that it was incredibly revealing of her, and one of the most revealing things about that particular time. It made perfect sense that she said it when she thought she wasn't going to be recorded.

When you're asking questions, are the questions you're asking a reflection of your own curiosity, or are you motivated by what you think people want to know or what they should know?

Well, I don't think you can really separate them, because you have a sort of inherent relationship with the audience, and every time you turn the camera on, it's kind of like, 'What am I telling the audience? What are they learning from this scene? What are they seeing? What questions might they have? What do they need to know?' You're constantly thinking, 'I've said this, this, this, this, you know, what does that add up to, and where do I need to get to? What is this scene about in terms of the story?' And, obviously, the more defined the story becomes, the more you ask that question because it's a kind of ongoing adventure, and you can only probably have two main points or ideas in a particular scene. I'm not somebody who has long, long interviews, and I never come back to interviews because I think the film is like a moving road show; if you keep coming back to an interview, you're not really moving forwards geographically.

I think your films being so full of questions and answers and information you've discovered makes them feel quite complex.

I learned a lot when I did the Heidi Fleiss film because there were three people – Madam Alex, Heidi Fleiss and Ivan Nagy – who were all incredible liars. And they were supported by a cast of not quite such good liars, but people who just lied professionally all their lives, whether it was the head of the LAPD or Heidi's girls. And the three main people had a very different take, their own personal take, on a particular set of circumstances they all shared. So it became like a kind of *Rashomon* story of three people's versions of pretty much the same facts and of each other, but quite different takes on the facts, depending on their point of view and how they wanted themselves to look. So the film became a task of splitting hairs between the characters and taking the audience down that road. It was a story which had a lot of detail in it. And it was a matter of seeing how much detail the audience could actually take. What I learned from that is actually the more detail the better because there's more for them to hang on to and they get more involved. And the more specific the detail, the more interesting it all gets. So, actually, you can go into great detail, great hair-splitting detail, about a particular fact. And the more you can involve an audience in that particular fact, the more fascinated they are, especially if it's a significant fact.

Kurt & Courtney is a good example of that, it seems to me, in that what everybody's arguing about is maybe four facts: what exactly happened and in exactly what order.

Yes. You want an audience to get caught up in those questions, so they want to know the answer. That, in a sense, is what you are leaning on in these films, which otherwise are just out of control.

How did your style of filmmaking – very lightweight and responsive and researching as you go along – how did that come about as a style?

At the film school that I went to – the National Film School under Colin Young – the model was the two-person crew because he was into really anthropological films. So it was very much you and your partner. My partner was Joan Churchill. I then had to make the crews a bit bigger because I'd have a researcher on board, who would just be making phone calls and finding out stuff and sometimes they would load as well, because we were shooting on film. I think that small crews aren't as intimidating. You know, Kim Longinotto works with the same sort of size. I guess Molly Dineen would do as well.

In terms of the on-screen stuff, having a presence in the films, that was something I sort of just did. It was an experiment, really. It was an experiment which I did with *Driving Me Crazy*, all the way back in 1988. That was the first film I ever appeared in, and the only reason I did it was that the situation was out of control, and being on screen was the only way I could think of to tell the story.

I think when you try a new idea out and it works, it's great fun, isn't it? You know, it's a wonderful thing. It's always wonderful to try new ideas out. Being on screen gives the audience something more specific to identify with, which is you, and your adventures, so that you become the audience. And you're the thing that batters down the doors and has the confrontations and asks the questions. And in a way, you're the motor of it, aren't you?

It's a great way of structuring films that don't have structure as well.

Yes, because you can bring in lots of seemingly irrelevant strands. I mean, it's obviously quite easy to do rather badly as well. Unfortunately, it's now everyone's favourite style on television. I think it's become a little downgraded. I mean a little bland, I guess.

I think it works especially well when it's used on people who have things that they don't want to talk about.

Yes, it's wonderful for revealing all the things that people don't want to reveal. In fact, the harder they try not to reveal things, the better a film you have. The more stipulations they make about what you can't do, you're secretly thinking, 'Yes, yes!' Because you know it's hilarious and it's wonderful and it's so revealing about them.

In being on camera like that, because there's this need for you to think on your feet, have you ever felt exposed?

Well, sometimes you don't want to do it; you don't feel like doing it – which is why you want to have a great crew around you that you feel at ease with, so that it's fun. It's all great when it's fun, really. I think when you feel you've really got to do certain things, then you're like a performer, which I've never really felt. Then I'm not interested in doing it. I never really saw myself as a performer. I saw myself as somebody who was the filmmaker but who happened sometimes to be in front of the camera because it helped, because it gave me a structure, because I was the thread that was holding it together. Not because I had some kind of overwhelming need to be in front of the camera.

And is that you in front of the camera, or is there a Nick Broomfield 'persona'?

Well, I suppose in a way you become a persona. But it's basically who you are. Sometimes you buffoon it up a bit, I guess, but it's pretty much just who you are. I mean, it's not like you're being Borat and then you're being Bruno.

Making films in this spontaneous, thinking-on-your-feet way, do you need to be a lucky filmmaker?

A lucky one? No, because it's really, really hard work. It's obsessively hard work. You just have to go on and on. Most of it is just persistence.

5 Access
Molly Dineen

Molly Dineen is a BAFTA-winning documentary director, known for her intimate and revealing portraits of British institutions threatened by change, all of which appear to be founded upon remarkable access. She shoots her own films in classic *vérité* style, patiently waiting for her subjects to reveal their secret thoughts and frustrations.

Her best-known work includes: *Heart of the Angel* (1989), a portrait of life at a run-down London tube station; *The Ark* (1993), following the keepers and managers at London Zoo at a time of great upheaval; *In the Company of Men* (1995), the story of Welsh Guardsmen on a tour of duty in Northern Ireland; *Geri* (1999), following Geri Halliwell in the weeks after her departure from the Spice Girls; *The Lords' Tale* (2002), about those affected by the UK's 1999 House of Lords Act, in which many hereditary peers lost their historic constitutional power; and *The Lie of the Land* (2007), an examination of the effects of the 2005 ban on hunting with dogs in the English countryside.

Molly Dineen, during the filming of The Lie of the Land. © *Channel 4.*

A critic once wrote that you have a talent for access …

I don't know what that means.

What do you think he meant?

Oh, God knows. I mean, I don't know. What is a talent for access? I think sometimes the way I film gives the impression of better access than I actually have, because of the apparent informality. My access in the House of Lords for *The Lords' Tale*, for example, was appalling. It was to corridors and offices, none of the meeting areas, really. I mean, I could film a vast meeting with hundreds of people in the Moses Room but I didn't have proper access to the workings of the place, and certainly not to the recreational areas, which was where most of the deals were made – the bars and restaurants. I remember sitting in a corridor with Earl Ferrers outside Lord Strathclyde's office. That was the only place I could film him, so it was hardly good access – a completely public corridor! But because he's leaning back and speaking quite quietly and because the shot is informal, I think it makes you feel that you're at the heart of an establishment, which I really wasn't. I had very good access to certain individuals, but since I'd made a decision to stay in the Palace of Westminster and not film anyone at home, I'd really shot myself in the foot. It became quite hard to make it the sort of film that I like to make, where you put people in a situation that is informal, so that they respond as people and not as what they stand for. So, Earl Ferrers may be a Conservative peer, but I'm trying to talk to him about being accepted or rejected and what that makes you feel like. So it's trying to relate on a human level, and therefore I don't really want him sitting behind a desk doing a formal interview. So the corridor worked.

On *The Ark*, I had good access to London Zoo in the end, but that was the peeling of the layers of an onion. I tried for ages to get in and failed. Then, when they finally let me in, bizarrely, it was the day that the curator Jo Gipps was making ninety-two people redundant. So I had access to nobody, not a single keeper or animal house, but he happened to be an individual who was completely one hundred per cent prepared to be open. So I just attached myself to him and followed him round, and some doors opened, some doors shut. He was saying, 'Hello, we need to have a meeting to talk about redundancy. And do you mind I've got Molly with me?' I mean, how bizarre! What an absolutely textbook way of not getting access to people! I didn't know it at the time but it was the beginning of a very long involvement. In fact, it was just the first step of a very long, slow process. And every step of the way there'd be problems, even when you were really in with the keepers. Suddenly, an animal gets sick, and it's being treated by a vet, but a vet you haven't got access to, and the vet says, 'No. Sorry, no.' It's not easy to walk into a situation and explain what it is that you're trying to do, and why you'd love to talk to the people concerned. There's always the question of what's in it for them. Why should they bother? And a lot of the answer to that is to do with basic human emotions: do you like each other or not? Do you trust each other?

What kind of personality do you need to be good at documentaries, to be good at access?

I don't go with this 'good at access' thing. I don't think there is a technique. I don't think access is something that you have the personality for or a technique for. I really don't. I mean, there are certain things that are obvious. You need to be persistent. And you need to do research and know the area you're going into, because, if you go in not knowing anything, they're not going to respect you or trust you. If I'm going to see somebody, I make sure that I know enough about their world beforehand so that we've got some kind of currency. For example, when I was thinking about making the series that eventually became *In the Company of Men*, I went to the Ministry of Defence with a fair bit of information already under my belt, because I was living with Anthony Beevor as a lodger. He was writing books about the Army, and I picked up quite a lot from him. You need to know what to talk to them about and who it's worth getting access to. In *The Lords' Tale*, I understood so little about the machinations of the Parliamentary system, the bouncing backwards and forwards of Bills. If you don't know that, you're completely lost in their world. And, actually, I floundered there so much for so long. By the time I'd shot it, I really understood how it worked and where I should've been, which is not where I was for most of the film.

The research is really one massive, massive effort and push, completely full-on, constant. Not just the main subject but all around it – institutions around it, people around it. You bother to go across the country to meet somebody who might have known your central character ... It just makes your picture richer. That also means you're not researching the person you want to film or that organisation too much, because they just get exhausted. If it's a big organisation, like London Underground, you can immerse yourself. I could mess about in stations night and day and never meet the same person twice. But there came a point where I knew a lot about London Underground. I didn't know where I was going to make the film or exactly what it was about, but I was building up a very strong feeling of the psyche of the organisation at that time that I could bring to bear on the station I eventually settled on.

Integrity's very important when you're negotiating access?
What do you mean?

People want to have a sense that their story is in safe hands, don't they, when you're negotiating access? They want to trust you. So they want to know that you have integrity, that you're someone who has a moral compass and that you wouldn't do just anything to get the access you want. It's being honest about what you're there to do?
Yes, that's surely the ideal, but there is absolutely not a set of rules. I mean, there just isn't. Every film's been different. I can't generalise because it's different with each film, each situation, each relationship, each stage of my career.

How did you get access to London Zoo?

I'd written letters, and phoned them up – just tried to persuade them. But it was already a very big media story which then means that you're just another person who wants to come and gloat over their demise. And so my line to them was: 'Everybody knows what's going on from the outside, but would it not be worth showing what's happening on the inside?' If an institution's going through change, you've always got a chance that they will realise it's worth telling the story because they're changing. I think, in lots of my films, whether it's redundancies in the Zoo or redundancies in the House of Lords, or the amalgamation of the regiments within the British Army, there's been a backdrop of change that has given me a springboard – a way in. But the management at the Zoo really wasn't having any of it. They let me in, finally, but not to film them at all. Once I'd started with Jo Gipps, and we'd gone round the houses with him delivering his news of redundancies, then obviously I had to go back round and try to meet all the keepers and apologise and explain why I was on his coat-tails and that I was sympathetic to their situation. And then, while I was filming the keepers, I continued to try to work with the management and explain to them that, if this film was only with the keepers and nobody was ever aware of the decisions the management was making or why, then they would come across very badly. That began to shift it a little.

But filming decision-making and power and people in charge of organisations is very, very difficult, because they've got every reason to say no. They don't want to be filmed decision-making because people are worried about being filmed in discussion. I had so little of the management at the Zoo, but actually there was one wonderful chap, Andrew Forbes, who was the Operations Manager who was making the redundancies, and he had a way about him that was fantastic to offset against the keepers ... Not that I wanted to set him up. It would've been cleverer and nicer if he'd given me more access, and then he would've come across as a proper person. But, unfortunately, he made the decision to just give the occasional interview, so his interviews became a sort of springboard. He talks proudly about his daughter's entrepreneurial approach to earning pocket money which, when you then compare to the koala keeper who's about to go and be assessed for redundancy ... it lends the film this wonderful balance.

Something that must have been quite a hard thing to pull off in that series is that you're friends with everybody, but there are factions at war with each other.

Yes, yes. It was difficult. I would be in the office of David Jones, the Director General, and he'd sit in the window opposite the service gate where all the keepers would come in and out, the very keepers who'd been confiding in me about what they felt about David Jones. Yet, there I am, sitting being chummy with him. I used to try to position myself just in front of the wall rather than in front of the window, which was always a problem for sound because I was a bit too far away. I was trying to be inconspicuous. Why should the keepers trust that I wasn't sharing their secrets? It was a very public battle, and it was quite a nasty one. It got to the Zoological Society, and then there was a rebel group that rose up and that was another problem: would *they* trust you? Because there you are, filming discussions in all the different groups and factions. When I showed David Jones the film, in the end, I think he quite enjoyed it. He said, 'Good God!' because there were these scenes of us sitting around with the people who were plotting his demise. It is very tricky, morally, not to be going behind people's backs. You're trying to show an institution or a situation for its complexities and the fact that from each different point of view people believe they're right or they have a particular job to do for a particular reason. But it puts you in a very precarious position and you do feel sometimes very duplicitous, or you're longing to say, 'No, that's not what he said at all. Let me tell you what he thinks,' which you really shouldn't do because then you screw things up. So I think you really need to work alongside somebody else. I don't like the idea of working on your own because there's nobody to share it with, nobody to chat to and just discuss. I mean, you can get into incredibly complex situations.

How did you pull that off, being friends with all sides?

It's character, isn't it? It's just how you are. People say, 'How do you get people to talk to you?' And you say, 'Well, by being bloody interested in them.' It's not a mystery. People go out all the time; they talk to each other. I think people want to be listened to full stop, don't you think? I mean, that's what friendships are about, at the school gates or wherever. Usually underlying it is that people want companionship, to be heard, to be with people who find them interesting. And if, on top of that, you're getting attention, and someone is really listening to you and finding what you do interesting, when, in fact, you've been ignored all your life – you know, like Derek the ticket seller in *Heart of the Angel* – then that's attractive. And I suppose it's about people having a reason for talking. Geri says it was because she was lonely and she just wanted a mate, which I sort of believe, because she was in a very in-between phase. She was very alone. At the Zoo, if you think you might be made redundant and you feel indignant about it, then you want to talk to somebody. People were ready to talk, which made it so much easier than just going in cold and saying, 'Tell me about your life as a keeper.' People had things they wanted to get off their chests, because the whole place was being stirred up.

I think people always have a reason. I think Crispin Black in *In the Company of Men* was bored, and he's also a very good, natural actor, a bit of a show-off. And, if you're going to sit in a police station day after day, night after night, with just your men for company, then frankly why not have a bit of entertainment? But then, boy, did he go off it! When he got back to barracks, you felt suddenly that he didn't need it any more. He didn't need this person to offload on. I think that's part of what you're looking for, generally speaking – it's not just the story, but the stages of life people are at or their moods, or their situation. There are times people just want to talk, and there are times they really don't. And, if they don't, you'd be best not to bother, because what you're going to get is like blood from a stone.

But it's not just timing; with your characters, there seems to be real trust as well. In The Ark, for example, all those competing factions must have had to really trust you to be so honest?

It's your personality that makes people want to trust you, and open up to you. But I think it's partly how you film people, as well: how you stand with your camera; how you compose your face when you look at them; whether you are being a 'camera operator' or a person with a camera; how *au fait* you are with your equipment – whether you can make that so second nature that all your energy is actually going into them. How you talk to them, what you ask them, your awareness of their situation, their mood, what might be about to happen to them. You've just got to feel free enough to have all your antennae out. And the longer you're in a place, obviously, the easier that is because you really are embedded in it. That's why wildlife photographers sit and watch animals and wait and watch their moods and try to move into their cycle. I always try to make my shoots very low on people and overheads, because to me a lot of it is about time – the time you spend with people. The time you're prepared to give them.

You trained as a camera person?

I trained with a crew and did a proper apprenticeship, so I was very on top of the equipment for a while – for as long as people were using the film cameras I trained on. Ever since it's been digital cameras and tape, I have to say, I get really thrown by all the switches, so quite often terrible things happen and I can't solve it, and it completely takes away everything. Then it collapses, which is when you realise why it's so important that that's second nature. There was a marvellous moment with Geri Halliwell in *Geri*. She was doing some press thing and it was all formal and slightly superficial. But then she needed to go to the loo, and she went running, and I loved her for it, running from door to door, ringing people's doorbells, saying: 'Can I use your toilet?' How wonderful would that have been! Just because it was everything about what she's actually like. She's very upfront with people, and she was at the height of her fame then. And I pushed something on the camera and everything was bleached out white and I couldn't get it back. And I was on the phone to Sony and, I mean, I really didn't know my way around the equipment. And not only did I lose the scene but I sort of lost the day. I felt so overwhelmed by the technological side of it all. I couldn't be mobile and run around because I just didn't understand the equipment well enough. But now I have got it more sorted.

When I was making *The Ark*, I loved Mick Carman, the ape-keeper with the moustache. He was very funny and chatty. The trick was, because he was a very funny man and also really knew his stuff, to keep the conversation and relationship going when you picked up the camera. You can be having a great conversation, you pick up the camera and it's all gone. That whole vibe has gone. You know, it's access to people's moods and access to their thoughts; that is what you're working at getting. The initial access to the institution or the person – everyone would play the same game about that. You're trying to get their permission to film, make them feel confident about it. But then it's what you do with the access that matters.

In The Ark, there's an argument the series makes about public institutions and funding and commercialism. Was that something that you went into it with – the idea that the Zoo had the potential to be a metaphor for changes that were happening more generally?

Yes, that's why I went into it. I think during Thatcher's time a lot of institutions were heaved out of their post-war structure and made into more commercial organisations that had to sell themselves, and basically adopt a completely different psyche. And there was a kind of natural comedy to the fact that an American leisure company had come over and tried to make London Zoo sell itself to the punters, to make it much more modern and commercial. A friend of mine, who was a news reporter, he'd gone to do a report there, and he said, 'It is just fantastic what's happening.' And that's when I started trying to get in. But, by the time I did, that had failed as a project. I got in and they were suddenly having to make lots of keepers redundant. But the principle of the American leisure company remained, which was that they wanted people who could say 'Hi' to the public, rather than people that knew anything about rhinos and giraffes.

Did the managers at the Zoo, the people who were in a position to grant access, have much sense of where you were coming from?

Well, at the beginning, everything was up in the air, and nobody knew what was going to happen. Nobody knew they were going to get rid of thousands of animals and then the management. That all developed as I was there. All they knew was they had to cut a lot of costs. And I would have been saying to the management that people will criticise you from the outside for redundancies, but surely they have to understand that you've got to run a commercial organisation and it's very difficult in this day and age when people don't want to see animals behind bars. So you have a problem and it's an interesting problem. The fact that they didn't let me film them for a long time means that they probably didn't listen to that and just thought, 'No way.' But it could also have been that they were insecure about what it was they were doing.

It's important to like the people you're filming in an access-based documentary. Whether you like your characters is a big deal.

Huge. I do not film people I don't like. And I prefer not to film groups of people who stand for things I don't like. So, for example, if I were massively anti-hunting, I wouldn't have gone and tried to film a hunt. Not even if the idea was to go about it really honestly and say, 'Look, I hate hunting but I'm going to try to get my head round it.' If I'd really hated hunting, I just wouldn't have even considered making a film about it.

Why is that?

Because you're giving so much of yourself to try to get the same out of your characters. You have to put a lot into the conversation, the being there, the hanging around. And you can't put that in and try so hard to represent them or their point of view if you really don't give a shit about them or you don't like them. Or you think that it's not worth it. And that's very, very personal. I'm not being grand and saying, 'Why would you do the fashion industry, for example? It doesn't mean anything.' I'm just saying, for me, I have to care hugely about the issue and really like the people. A lot of people don't think like that. A lot of people want to film people they don't like or don't approve of, in order to expose them for what they are. I find I can't do that because it's not that sort of filmmaking I do. It's much more complicit. It's that sort of quite deep access to the psyche, if you like … What I'm trying to get to is a level of humanity, so that, whatever situation they're in, you want people to like them. Because then, if people like them as people, they might just think more about their situation and why they are as they are.

It's very immersive, the approach that you're talking about. It's a very committed and round-the-clock way of working.

It is. And do you know something? I can't do it now because I can't do it and also look after my children. It kills me. I sort of did it in *The Lie of the Land* but it just made me realise what an intense swamp I'd always got myself into in the past when I was making a film, working in a totally obsessive way. And I found that I just couldn't do it any more. I couldn't stay down there on the farms and do what I would normally do. And that really affects the film, because the rushes don't join up. You film for a while, and then you don't film for three days, and then you film again and then you stop again, which means there's all these fucking gaps, so you can't make a seamless, organic product. You end up with a very different animal, and I don't want to be in that situation again. Filmmaking really does become your world ... I think I've always given it too much, a slightly pointless amount. I mean, 'Come on, Molly, get a life!' But then, it's also your pleasure, your social life. I've always had quite a social time with people I've filmed – and not cynically. It's very difficult because, of course, it's useful, but I've always chosen to merge the two and lived life in these funny chapters, so you have a few years where your whole life is about the Army, and then another few years where your whole life is about London Zoo. You inhabit those worlds. I really loved the Zoo. And I really loved the Army.

Do you think it's true that maintaining access is almost as much about what you don't film as what you do?

Actually, that is quite key. I really didn't love Geri's world. I loved Geri, but not the whole business of PR and the selling of yourself and the utter crap of it all. Because it's so cynical, when you see how those PR companies operate, and how much of the news and the newspapers is planted and created. And, in fact, even in her life there would be 'created' stories, which I could have made much of in the documentary. But I'm not going to do that, am I? Because I'm making a film that's *with* her, and I'm interested in the human condition.

Sometimes I've thought I'm journalistically very irresponsible for the things I've omitted. You know, when I was filming the Zoo, there were rumours that land was being sold off, and shady deals were being done behind closed doors. The whole place was so rife with intrigue and drama, and I found out about the land being sold through the rebel group who came up to me and said, 'Do you realise...?' But, if I'd started sniffing round that, I would have probably lost the texture of the story. I hate to sound pretentious but, you know, the texture of how people are responding to success and failure, things that are much more universal, that concern all of us. If I go off and start working on an exposé, then they're all going to start feeling very unsettled and they're probably going to stop me shooting. Long films require very long relationships with institutions and people, and therefore you've really got to behave yourself, because, if you don't, you're fucked. In the Army it mattered a lot who you were seen with, particularly *vis à vis* the sergeants' mess, and what questions you asked and what you wanted to film. In any situation where you have access to an institution, people watch how you behave and what you're interested in and who you're friends with, and they decide on the basis of that whether to trust you or not. But that went double for the Army; they're arch disciplinarians with their men, but, my God, they're protective of them! And I think, if they'd felt I was filming something that would in any way shaft any of the Guardsmen, they would've been on me like a ton of bricks. It would have been game over.

So by not pursuing the journalistic story with the Zoo, for example, you were making an investment in the larger project?

Yes. Not just because of how you would be perceived, but also because you can only spread yourself so thin.

Was it hard to maintain access to Geri Halliwell? She's very up and down.

Yes. She was moody. She was a bit all over the place and a bit unclear as to where she was going. I was very hostile to the whole PR thing. I would love to have made a much more intimate portrait of her and her family, but she was too public for that. And, boy, did they not want that! But, because it wasn't a shoot where I'd invested a huge amount at the beginning, I never felt enormous fear that it was all going to collapse. Not like I felt on the Army film, where I'd really worked to get the thing going. Or *The Ark*, or *The Lords' Tale*, where at any moment something could go horribly wrong and you're out. With her, I had never really decided to make a film. I was just shooting footage. Then, I think there came a point when Geri thought, 'Actually, this is going to be quite useful.' But, yes, there were lots of times when she just wouldn't be up for it. And sometimes I pushed and sometimes I didn't.

There's a very interesting moment where she's complaining about her family not being on the edge of their seats when she's doing a TV appearance, and you point out that they're busy people, with their own lives, and she looks furious about it. It made me wonder if the whole process of making that film was like walking on eggshells?

No, not normally. I wasn't scared that Geri was going to say, 'Right, well, piss off then!' It was quite an odd moment. Wasn't it wonderful when her brother says, 'We got into trouble for it'?

You seem in that film like genuine friends.

Yes, I'm very fond of her, and we do still see each other. There are some moments, like the moment you've just cited, where, in fact, I'm holding the reins, because I'm suggesting that maybe her behaviour is inappropriate or out of order. But there are other moments when she is absolutely holding the reins, because she's basically showing off and singing, and I am going along with it filming it and there it is in the film, and of course she's doing it for the camera and performing. So I think the film goes on quite a strange meander through whether it's me in control or her. The moments I really like are where I think the access between us is on quite a deep level, like after Johnny Vaughan on telly has slagged her off after she sang to Prince Charles. And you see how she really is, just how desolate it makes her feel. One moment she's a fabulous-looking star, and then she gets run down on telly, and you see what that means to her. And she's looking very dishevelled. Do you remember that scene? And she's saying, 'I just think it's really unfair. They pick you up and they drop you.' I'm very proud of that as a moment. I'm genuinely interested and she's genuinely sharing. Whereas there are other moments that are very good access, like with the father and the letter behind the picture, where I'm very aware that I'm not being honest, because if I was really being honest, like a friend, I'd have said, 'Geri, put it away. That's embarrassing.' But I'm not. I'm thinking, 'My God! This is great TV!'

You know, we've all got our different things that we think are or aren't okay to show, which you capitalise on when you make films. You have to be bloody careful. You're in danger of seducing the person into thinking, 'Oh, it's fine. Everyone will think I'm great.' You do have to be careful. What I don't want to do ever is film people in a way that strips them of their dignity. I think that there's a very fine line you walk and you can overstep the mark if you do have very good access. I had to be very careful with Geri. When you follow her up to the bedroom and she takes off her shirt while she's chatting away, obviously part of you thinks, 'Oh, are we crossing over something here and the viewers shouldn't come with me? Or is this, in fact, great because it's showing just how relaxed she is with the camera, which doesn't mean anything other than you really feel as a viewer you're seeing a real person?' It is a huge responsibility, but then it's so lovely to get into a position where you and your camera and the subject are all at ease with each other, and there's no jockeying. These days there are whole PR departments who are paid to stop you doing what it is that you do. I say this arrogantly but I think quite a lot of people in PR have no idea what is good material. I had this problem with the Tony Blair film I made [a profile of the New Labour politician produced as a party election broadcast in 1997], where what they wanted me to film Blair doing was ridiculous. You just have a fundamental hunch to let people see he's a nice bloke. PR people and PR departments are the bane of my life now, and they often aren't very sophisticated in their perception of what it is that touches or moves people.

The debate that you have on the train about editorial control at the beginning of Geri *is very interesting. She expects to be in charge and for the film to leave out anything she doesn't approve of, and you tell her that's not possible.*

It had to go in, because I think the relationship had to be made clear to people. But I think, largely, conversations of that sort don't belong in films, because it's just part of making a documentary: the access struggle. I don't like to put it in because I think that's part and parcel of your job. One assumes you've got access, so you leave that behind and you go into that world. It's the world I want to bring to people, and the characters in it. But it's different when it informs the whole way you're filming, or if it's going to obstruct people watching it because there'll just be a huge question mark: 'Why did she let Molly do this?' I had to film the story of the making of the film.

How did it work out with Geri, the question of editorial control?

Fifty/fifty. It didn't bother me because it's the relationship I generally have with people in an unspoken, un-legal way. I think morally you need to let people have a say about the way a film is taking shape when they're giving so much of themselves. But I never usually formalise that into a contract or agreement, as such. *Geri* was just the first time it had ever been made official.

Do you always show people films before TX?

Yes, I do. Absolutely. Because if you're not trying to stitch someone up or mock them, but what you want is the most interesting thing out of them, then you do better to show it to them. Because then they can say, 'Well, actually, what I meant there was this ...' The hairiest screening I had was with London Underground, about *The Angel*, although *The Lords' Tale* was pretty ghastly, and

The Ark, because of showing David Jones the rebel group plotting his demise. It was so fantastic how big he was about it. Often they're very wonderful bonding moments, those screenings. But often they're a bloody nightmare.

There's a lot of responsibility that comes with access. It's easy to betray people.

Yes. Overstepping the mark with people, flattering them into giving away too much and then putting that material into your film in a way that makes them feel exposed. And then when you have a screening, you know, people can agree to it because they're all caught up with the moment of the screening. So I think it's quite important that you do screenings in quite a boring one-to-one way at a Steenbeck or on the computer, not a screening where you pack it with people who all approve. I think that's really important.

Having a camera and making a film does give you a lot of power.

Yes, it gives you enormous power, of course. Although I've never felt able to use that power, because I've always felt very beholden to the people I'm filming. If you like, I feel much more on their side than an audience's side – like I have to protect them. Filmmaking does give you power, but it also makes you massively vulnerable because you're often committing hundreds of thousands of pounds, and months and months and months, sometimes years, of your time to a situation which is all about 'are these people actually going to give it up? Is the situation going to deliver? Am I going to be allowed to carry on through?' That's what happened with *In the Company of Men*. I had my character, then I lost the location so I had to shift location and character. And then I was left with an unfinished film, so I had to shoot another one with the same character but back at base. It's not a series. It's not even a trilogy. I don't know what it is. It's three films about the same situation from different perspectives.

Is documentary access getting harder, do you think?

I do feel I'm part of a totally tainted, debased profession now. And I'm ashamed to have a camera and I'm ashamed to be part of the media. For the last three or four films, I mean back as far as *In the Company of Men*, most of my time is trying to explain 'I'm not like other people and I don't do that.' They've all got examples of telly they've seen which is about taking the piss out of people, setting them against each other, cutting them to contradict each other, and so on, which is why they don't want to be in a documentary themselves. I think the relationship between real people and television has fundamentally changed over the last fifteen years or so. And I think it's the amount of reality TV around that's done it. It's the way people see themselves being on television. And if you have fewer examples within documentaries of people having their lives taken seriously, then people are naturally scared about what it is that you're asking them to be part of, because it's light entertainment, which makes people feel vulnerable. They feel very unsafe now about documentary. There's pressure often from broadcasters to do with how spicy, how edgy, how full of conflict and sexuality they want television to be, which means that you're not free to be interested in something and actually look closely and honestly at it. And for me, for the relationships I want, it gets harder and harder and harder. I definitely used to feel I was the one with the power, and I really don't now. I feel quite uneasy that I've got to persuade people of the fact that it's going to be all right and that I'm going to be all right. These days, I don't feel powerful at all. I'm the person crouching at the door wondering whether Lord Strathclyde might be good enough to give me an interview. It's quite humiliating, a lot of making documentaries: the position you have to put yourself in, the grovelling, the waiting, the being shafted. I can't tell you how badly the Government Chief Whip treated me in *The Lords' Tale*. He was an extremely nice man, but he was foul to me.

You have to swallow the anger and frustration down, don't you?

Oh my God! Absolutely. The rage! The knocks you have to take! ... It's very difficult to justify your rage, but rage is what you feel. You're wasting hours and hours. You make an effort to be somewhere, and they don't turn up.

The power question is a funny thing, because the power exists in as much as you've got the camera and in theory the authority and you're going to make public their private thoughts. And in the edit you could do all sorts of stuff. But actually the bottom line is that the power is with your contributors, because they have this total ability to withdraw, or do it in a half-hearted way, or just not really let you in.

So access has become harder to rely on? More precarious?

I think you have to keep re-selling to people what it is that you're doing. In the

Army, there were, let's say, a thousand men in the barracks at Ballykelly, and the fact that I knew only seven of them meant that everywhere else I went I had to do the whole sell again. People would turn up at the officers' mess, drink too much, and it would be 'you buggers in the media'. And that would happen every single evening. And that was so exhausting, constantly having to explain what you were doing, but with equal passion and commitment, because if you just did it half-heartedly they'd think, 'Oh, what bollocks!' I mean, that business of keeping the relationship good, the door open, reinforcing the access is so important to do all the time. I'd never think, 'You're in, and you're in, and that's that.' It's never something that's actually sorted. God, it makes me tired just thinking of it! *The Ark* was the only one where I was in and it got deeper and deeper. But that was something peculiar to do with the nature of its very closed, village feel, and, of course, there weren't as many people as with *In the Company of Men*.

Was access to Geri a much easier proposition in that sense? More focused and manageable?

I'd just done the Blair thing. And I thought, 'It would be very interesting to make a film about somebody famous but in the way I make portraits.'

I had a friend who was involved with the Spice Girls, and knew they wanted a film making. I knew nothing about the Spice Girls. It wasn't my sort of music or age group. And I went and saw them perform in Manchester, and it was fascinating. And that's how I met Geri. I think both the Spice Girls and I knew that I was not going to be the person to make that film, and that they were not going to be people whom I wanted to make a film about. Then it was later when Geri had left the Spice Girls ... I think she phoned me up. I had had a new baby, and I thought, 'God, that's interesting.' And I was really flattered because she was all over the telly, 'Where is Ginger Spice?' And I really liked her. But, having mainly made films about male institutions, it just wasn't my cup of tea. And I didn't enter into it, I'm afraid to say, with the sort of aggression that you need to enter into a documentary with. I should have gone to see a lot of people around her. Maybe not family, because that would be a non-starter, but a lot of the people she went to see for advice. But that meant quite a lot more time on the road, and time on the phone, and really hammering it, and I wasn't going to give it that. I just wasn't. I had a new baby and I think I also thought, 'This is very unchartered territory; I don't know where I'm going with this woman.' But I got more and more interested as it went along. And, in fact, I think it ended up a really good film because she is very open.

You're in it much more than your other films. Is that because you were maintaining access even as you were filming?

No, it was because there was no other human dynamic. I was not filming her talking to Richard Branson. I was not filming her talking to Bob Geldof. I was not filming her being instructed by Matthew Freud. I was not filming her sobbing with Natalie, her sister. Because all those would have been further access man-oeuvres and I didn't have it. I hadn't pushed it; I hadn't even tried. So it was just about me and her. It was much more a personal journey, because getting good access to other famous people, especially when they're giving advice to Geri, would have meant a huge amount of negotiation. You have to pay your respects to them, and phone them, and go and see them, and explain what you are doing, and then say, 'So, if I come with her, is that all right?' And then she'd have to be okay about me doing that, and she might not have wanted me to, because she would have felt too vulnerable. Remember that Geri was apparently going into retreat at the time. So it's not as if I'm making a film about her as a Spice Girl, which would have been a very, very different thing. She had no idea where she was going and what she was doing. She was just terrified of losing her fame. And all that helped to make the film quite intimate, with just me and her, talking.

Have you seen Being Mick?

I think Mick Jagger is a god. But *Being Mick* is like an article from *Tatler* magazine, isn't it? About the homes, the babes, the children, the lovely lifestyle. It's just devoid of content. I know from talking to Kevin Macdonald that he got some incredibly interesting material, which wouldn't have done Mick Jagger any harm at all. He told me about some great scenes that weren't in there because he just couldn't get away with it, because Mick Jagger was running the show and had absolute veto over the film. I would have been so frustrated. Imagine! You make a fabulous film that never gets shown. Nobody can see it! It would have killed me with frustration. On the other hand, I suppose people like Mick Jagger have every right to manage things that are made about them. Their public persona is their business. I was very interested in doing a film about somebody famous after the Blair one, but I wouldn't now. No, thank you. It's impossible to do your job properly, because the tension is too great between how they want to be perceived and how you would like to show them, and because they need it as PR. And you've got to respect that.

Is it right that you once had talks about making a film about The Rolling Stones?

Yes, but it was a case of failed access. Their manager, Prince Rupert, wanted me to do it. Keith Richards would have been fine with it. He said, 'Move in with us. Do it like the Maysles brothers did it with *Gimme Shelter.*' He was incredibly interesting. But Mick Jagger was very, very honest about the limitations he wanted to impose: 'It will not go out if I don't like it, and I'm only going to like it if it's full of me basically being quite bland.' I said, 'I want an open-door policy.' What arrogance! I was really, really clear to the point of self-destruction. I regret it, because maybe if I'd started, and maybe if we'd got on, or I'd found a way of having not much Mick in it but a lot of everyone else ... maybe then it would have been fine. But it's a really big deal, making a film and committing that time. You can't put yourself in situations if you know you are going to be fucked about. You'd be silly to. In the end, Jane Treays went on tour with The Stones, and it's never been seen. It went into a cupboard because they didn't want to release it. That's the nightmare.

Do you usually send copies of your films to the subject when you're pursuing a piece of access?

Yes, absolutely. People should make their decisions based on what you've done, I think. You look at a filmmaker's work and you know if they're going to shaft you. So you should certainly send your work off, particularly if you are proud of it. I was very proud of, for example, *The Ark.* I felt that if the Lords had seen that, or the people who made decisions there, it might have been different. Easier. Mick Jagger did bother to watch them. He watched two or three of them, and he was very nice about them.

Did Geri watch your films?

Yes, because I'd sent them to the Spice Girls. I remember Posh Spice fast-forwarded through them and asked me at the end why people in a restaurant were eating mice, because she hadn't realised it was a zoo, and she was watching the tropical-bird keeper chopping mice up to feed to an eagle!

What do you think about paying for access? I think, these days, contributors are much less content with the honour of being chosen to be filmed. They're much more aware that people make money out of documentaries, and expect to get their share.

Well, on principle, I would keep money out of it. Just, I think, because it would make me feel awkward about why they're doing it. I don't know, it would just feel strange. It would be like bribery. But I've often paid people afterwards as a thank you because there's a sort of moral issue. If you're making money and you're filming people who have got no money, it sort of stinks if you don't say, 'Look, as a thank you, can I give you X,' or in the Army, you know, we put hundreds of pounds behind the bar. When I made *The Lie of the Land*, for both the hunts I filmed I made them DVDs of them hunting out of footage we didn't use in the actual film, because I'd shot so much. And they sell them to their members and make a bit of money from it. So I always try to do something that says 'Thank you'. But, no, I'd never pay. Not because I'm holier than thou, but just because I think it would really contaminate the relationship.

Do you think that access is always better when it's long term? You can make a film with a week of access quite often – you just get in, film it and then get out. But, if you could turn that week of access into a month, would it be a better film?

Not necessarily. *Heart of the Angel*, I remember very particularly, was two weeks upstairs and two weeks downstairs. I mean, it was two weeks of nights and two weeks of days. That was the shoot. It wasn't epic. There was a lady who was supposed to stand with us and she lasted about a day and then she got so bored because Sarah, the sound recordist, and I just sat there at the top of the lift shaft. So she disappeared and then we got going. I've often put two weeks on it as a limit, particularly if you're in a confined situation. I think people just get bored of you after two weeks. You go through a courtship with your contributors, which lasts about two weeks, and then something snaps and it's just too much, too exhausting for both sides. Even though you maybe carry on and on and on filming, you notice you use that early footage because there's such an energy to it. I think there's a tension in the early stages of making a film born of them actually not knowing you that well and you not knowing them that well. It's sort of birth-of-a-friendship-type tension. But I think it's important that it's there. If you know them too well, possibly there are too many insider references, or it's too intimate, and it excludes an audience. Somehow it's got to be just at the right stage that it engages them and that it's fresh enough. There just is a way you talk to people whom you don't really know, but maybe you want to.

The sorts of films that you've made, like The Ark *and* The Lords' Tale, *over a long period of time – those deep, long-term access films are becoming quite rare now. Is that just a matter of budgets?*

Yes, but I don't think it's *just* about budgets. You can play about with how much you're given, and be creative. If you spend your money carefully and thoughtfully, you can get away with giving a film a lot more time.

You're always constrained by your budget to some extent, of course, and budgets these days are getting smaller and smaller. But it's really about the attitude of the filmmaker. It's a question of whether you're going to commit in quite a vocational way to a subject and a way of working. Because, frankly, the amount of time that went into *The Ark* had nothing to do with the budget. *The Ark* was not a massive budget for four hours of telly. It was just that I spent the budget on time, and it made a huge difference that they saw me so committed to it all for such a long spell. That's a very persuasive thing. Drip, drip, drip, like a tap.

You stretched the production out?

Yes! Because you're so obsessed, and that's all that was going on in my life. For years and years, I was one hundred per cent in whatever film I was working on, living it every moment of the day, pouring everything into it.

Ultimately, filmmaking isn't that complicated, you know. It's about time and attitude, a commitment to understanding people and how they feel, and a will to make sense of their experience and the things that are going on around them. It's easy to say, I know, but, if you get those things right, everything else will follow.

6 Interviews

Brian Hill

Brian Hill is one of Britain's most respected documentary filmmakers, known in particular for his interest in documentary innovation, and for his great skill as an interviewer.

His films include observational films such as *The Club* (1994), about an uprising at a suburban golf club; testimony-based films such as *The Not Dead* (2007), which tells the stories of soldiers from three different generations, all of whom suffer from PTSD, and *The Bigamist Bride* (2009), about a five-times married (but never divorced) young woman named Emily Horne; blends of drama and documentary, such as *Consent* (2007), and *The True Voice of... Murder, Rape* and *Prostitution* (2006), in which actors deliver monologues based on documentary interviews; feature documentaries like *Nobody Someday* (2001), the story of Robbie Williams' European tour in the year 2000; and *Climate of Change* (2010), about the efforts of ordinary people around the world to make a difference in the fight against global warming; and documentary musicals (a genre that Hill can claim to have invented), such as *Drinking for England* (1998), *Songbirds* (2005) and the BAFTA-winning *Feltham Sings* (2003).

Brian Hill, during the making of Climate of Change. *Picture courtesy of Brian Hill.*

What is the key to a good interview? Is there one?

I used to work with a guy called Nick O'Dwyer. We'd talk about the films we were making, and we had very different opinions about how to interview people. He was very journalistic, and he would prepare all his questions beforehand. He would go into the interview knowing what he wanted to get out of it, and he would proceed accordingly. But, for me, that is completely the wrong way to approach an interview for a documentary. I don't think you should go in with an idea of what you want the person to say, because, if you're trying to get them to say it, you're really narrowing down what you're going to get. And you're closing off all sorts of other stuff that might come out if you approach it differently. So my approach is to be very conversational, to keep it very open-ended. I don't have any written questions; I have nothing written down. I mean, I prepare, but I prepare by just thinking about it. And usually, if it's a big interview for a film, if it's a really significant character, then I won't have spent too much time with them beforehand. The researchers will have seen them and talked to them, and I'll go and meet them for maybe just half an hour before we get going. I don't like to get to know them too well, because when I first do a big interview with them I want that to be a genuine voyage of discovery for me. I don't want to go into an interview knowing everything about them. I want to go in knowing that they're a good character and they're useful for the film. I want for me to be genuinely finding stuff out about them.

The other thing that I think is really important is to give enough time to it. People think you can knock off an interview in twenty minutes or half an hour and you can't, I don't think. If it's a really important thing and if that person is a big character in your film, I would spend at least a day on an interview with somebody. I made a film recently called *The Not Dead*. It had three characters: three soldiers from different conflicts. And I spent an entire day with them. Not talking all day – we were stopping and starting. We'd stop after a while if they wanted to go to the bathroom, if they wanted to get a drink, if they wanted to just get up and walk around for a bit. But I think it's important to give them all that time, with as few unnecessary interruptions and external pressures and distractions as possible.

And one other thing: I think that the big lie of the last ten years of documentary-making is that, because digital technology means smaller cameras, it means you can be more intimate with your subjects. I just think that's nonsense. I don't think it means intimacy at all. It just means it's cheaper and you can spend longer with people, and you get some really badly shot films. But it's not cameras that create intimacy, it's how you set things up. So if I'm doing something like *The Not Dead*, or a recent film that I made called *The Bigamist Bride*, I make a big deal of the interview. We create a studio. It's all lit; we have a chair there for the subject; there's crew and cables and mics; and it's all done in quite a formal way. Very controlled. And then I bring them into the studio and say, 'Look, this is where you're going to sit.' And I think what it's saying to them is: 'They're taking my story seriously.' It's not just some twenty-two-year-old with a camera pointing at me and wobbling all over the place; they're taking it seriously and they care about it. It has legitimacy and gravitas. And then once they're in the chair, people relax very quickly. Even with lights on and cables everywhere and a camera crew and stuff, I think it's quite easy for people to relax in that situation, and for an interview to become intimate.

I'll give you an example. I made a film called *Drinking for England*, about people's relationship with alcohol. It wasn't censorious. It was really a celebration of what people are like, what the British are like with alcohol. But I wanted one person who had reached a point where they'd decided they had to give up drinking because it was ruining their life. It was so difficult to find that person. And Katie Bailiff, who works with me, one Sunday afternoon she rang me and she said, 'I'm up in North Lancashire, and I've found this woman and she's going into rehab tomorrow so she could be ideal for us. She's just decided.' And I said, 'Well, what's she like as a character?' And Katie said, 'I don't know. She's pissed; it's really difficult to tell.' So I went, 'Okay ... err ...' It was a BBC *Modern Times* budget which meant a limited number of filming days. I hadn't met her and I said, 'Well, what do you think? Will she be any good?' And she said, 'I don't know. It's really hard.' And I said, 'Look, it's your call.' She said, 'Okay, call the crew. Come up here 10 o'clock tomorrow morning.' So I rang the crew, but I'm thinking, 'Fuck, is it going to be any good?' She was drunk when we turned up, this woman Jane; she'd gone on the sherry as soon as she woke up that day. She was going to rehab that afternoon and I thought, 'This is going to be a disaster,' because she can barely string two words together. So I said to her, 'Okay, look, we'll set up. Do you mind? We're going to turn your living room into a bit of a studio. We're going to light it.' And she went, 'Yeah, yeah, that's fine, whatever. Do what you want.' So we got everything set up, and we were shooting on film in those days so there was a bit more of a hoo-hah about it, and I said, 'Turn over,' and I asked her the first question. And she just immediately locked on to me and started talking brilliantly about her drinking, about why she was going into rehab. It was a gamble. But that whole thing about setting it up in a formal way and giving her a bit of space and a bit of respect – she kind of responded to that, and really opened up. I think she must have felt, 'This is going to be a really big deal. They're taking it seriously. There are all these guys here and cameras and the clapper-board; it's like the movies.'

Sometimes you want to be on the spot where something important happened, of course, to give an extra frisson to an interview. Or you might want to be in a teenager's bedroom, for example, because that's where their stuff is and they feel safe and comfortable there. Or someone might be most comfortable in the pub. You need to think about where you're going to get the most out of your character. But you really can achieve a lot in a studio set-up. It's become my favourite way to do interviews over the last few years.

Is it the pressure that makes the difference with studio-based interviews?
I think it's partly the pressure. I also think sometimes people are very flattered that somebody's taking an interest in them, that somebody thinks that their story is important enough and their life is important enough to be carefully

recorded on film and shown to an audience. And I think that can be immensely flattering to people, particularly people who are just regular, ordinary people: not celebrities. There's nothing they think is particularly special about themselves. I think people respond to the attention.

Do you feel like you do better interviews when you're under pressure yourself?

Not really. I think if you're any kind of decent filmmaker you're always under pressure, and that's usually self-generated pressure. We could all make a living by taking the easier route and making that kind of middle-of-the-road, mediocre stuff that television has a huge demand for. But if you've set yourself high targets, you're always under a lot of pressure. I always feel under pressure making films.

Do you have an interviewing persona that you click in to?

Yeah, that's a good question, actually. When I interview people, generally speaking, I'm quite inarticulate and quite bumbly and I repeat myself and go round in circles and off the point, which I think is all really unthreatening and more like a real conversation. I think it's partly a deliberate thing but partly also – because I don't prepare interviews in the sense that I have written questions – it's just me trying to think on my feet about what to do next, and sometimes remembering something the interviewee might have said five minutes ago and thinking, 'Oh, that's quite interesting. I should have pursued that,' and then skipping back. I think it just feels more natural to people, and they like it.

Do you vary that persona much, according to who you're talking to? You need quite a strong character always to be the same with people.

Yes, I think I might have variations. For example, if I were interviewing a politician, I would be less kind of bumbly and more incisive. I might have a list of questions, not written down, but in my head, that I wanted to go through. There would be certain points I'd want to nail them on. But, generally speaking, I think I am pretty much the same, whether it is a porn star or an old lady on a council estate. I think I pretty much have the same attitude and the same persona.

I'm asking this as a Yorkshireman: do you think it helps, being a Northerner?

I've always thought that I was able to go more places and be more accepted because I come from a Northern, working-class background. I feel comfortable with working-class people in a way that some middle-class directors or researchers might not. I also feel perfectly comfortable with toffs and landed gentry. I also think it is much easier to make films in the North. It is easier to find institutions that are willing to let you in and that are going to be open and straightforward there than it is in London. I don't know why that is. I don't really subscribe to the view that everybody in the North is really friendly and helpful and Southerners are posh and standoffish. They aren't really. I think that's obviously nonsense. But I suppose all I can say is that being Northern hasn't held me back, you know? It seems to work.

But in terms of that kind of easy intimacy you're aiming for with an interview, the Yorkshire accent is top and Lancashire is second top for friendliness and trustworthiness in those surveys that call centres do of what accents people prefer to listen to. That's why there are so many Northern call centres.

I made a film called *Slaughterhouse*, which was an interesting experience because I was born a mile away from the particular slaughterhouse we filmed in. I thought, 'This is going to be fine, you know? I will walk in and they'll welcome me with open arms as a long-lost brother. I will just be able to slot straight into some kind of rhythm with these guys who work in the slaughter-house.' But it didn't work. They just thought I was some Southern poof. Most people can spot that I have a Northern accent. But in the North it is not very Northern and they all thought I sounded like some Londoner. Even though I said, 'Ay, lads, I was born a mile from here.' They were just like, 'So fucking what?' And it didn't really help at all in the one place where I thought it would help. It was, if anything, a disadvantage.

What makes a good interviewee?

I think, turning that question on its head, what makes a bad interviewee is someone who's desperate to be in a film. I don't think that people who desperately want to be in films should be, really. Because of things like *Big Brother* and *Wife Swap*, there are lots of people who will put themselves forward to be in a film, thinking that it's a platform for them to perform on. You can very often see people in films who are really putting it on. I try to steer clear of people like that. You want to make films with people who are genuine and honest: not too guarded, and maybe not too self-aware, not defensive, just open and honest. The best characters I've found are people where you say, 'We're making this film about X, Y and Z, and we're looking for characters,' and the good people just go, 'Well, I'm not that bothered, but yeah if you want. I'll tell you about my life.' And they don't really care that much.

We're doing a history series about London at the moment. We're trying to find characters to tell the story of London. And, just this morning, we were sitting with the team going through some of the characters that they've filmed, and sometimes, within a minute of just looking at somebody's tape, I can tell if it's a good character. I've been trying to explain to the researchers what makes a good character. It's partly that they've got a story to tell and they can tell it engagingly – because, let's face it, most people can't. Even the nicest people in the world often can't tell their own story and keep it from being boring ... So you want people who are engaging, which often means that they've got a dramatic way of telling the story; they know how to be a raconteur. And they've got to have something to say as well. It's no good having great presentation skills if you don't have anything to say. So those two things are really important. Even then, even if someone is a natural storyteller with interesting things to say, they also need to have a level of sincerity.

And sometimes it is important how people look. I don't mean they necessarily have to be beautiful, but a characterful face, you know, an expressive face can really help with an interview. Faces are vitally important, because it is a visual medium, which a lot of documentary-makers seem to forget a lot of the time. Like Emily in *The Bigamist Bride* – her face was a big part of that film. When I did the first interview with her, she asked for a make-up artist and we shot it in a studio, and there is that extraordinary close-up of her which just dominates the screen and those eyes looking at you. I really like that. I think she is so arresting to listen to and it's partly the way she looks and the way she holds that look. In fact, people generally had good faces in *The Bigamist Bride*. Going back as far as Noleen in *Sylvania Waters*, she had a very arresting look, a face that was very expressive. It was making that series where I first realised that the look on a person's face can tell you so much about what they might be thinking, or give you a clue as to their character, particularly when they are interacting with other people. I remember on the first day of filming *Sylvania*

Waters I noticed a look that passed between two of the characters which told me a huge amount about the relationship between them.

I was really struck by Cliff in The Not Dead, *as well. He really took me by surprise. There was something about the look on his face as he was talking that had me in tears.*

Cliff is so dignified and he has got this amazing face and piercing blue eyes. We had some Chinese visitors come over. They wanted to see some stuff and none of them spoke English. We showed them some of Cliff from *The Not Dead* and they were really moved, even though they couldn't understand what he was saying – just his face and the fact that tears were trickling down his cheeks. I think it is good to be able to light characters and photograph them in a way that does their faces justice.

A good face is almost like a shorthand, in the sense that you don't have to explain that much about a character if their face is right, because you look at them and you can read quite a lot about them.

I think you can. You can garner so much information, whether or not you are conscious of it at the time from the face, from the way that they do their hair, from the jewellery that they are wearing, the clothes they are wearing, the way they sit, the way they stand. You can tell so much, particularly in a country like Britain where we are obsessed with class, although we don't really talk about it that much. But it is a constant factor in people's lives.

It helps when characters are likeable as well, doesn't it?

It does help when people are likeable, even if they're people who you've got big problems with in many ways. I've filmed with burglars and criminals and junkies and people like that, who are not really what you'd call salt of the earth, but you can usually find something in them to like. And I think it's important that you do. I made this film called *Saturday Night* and it had a character in it called Ian who was a really violent young man. He'd just come out of prison for attempted murder and he had a massive drug habit. In most people's eyes, this guy was just a scumbag, but I did find quite a lot in him to like. I thought he was really intelligent, for one thing, and I thought he was very perceptive about himself and about his place in society. And he was interesting. He wasn't just some kind of junkie no-hoper; he had things to say. Similarly, going back to *Sylvania Waters* again, a lot of people were very critical of Noleen; they regarded her as vulgar and brash and far too fond of the bottle. I'd have people asking me, 'How could you bear to film with her for twelve months?' But actually there were a lot of things I really admired about her. She was tough, she was fiercely protective of her family, and she had a definite sense of humour.

I've always thought that you should ideally only make documentaries about people that you like, to some degree or other. It's very difficult when they are thoroughly unpleasant. I recently made a film with a character I really didn't like, and I found the whole process of making the film hard-going as a result. That was Emily, this woman who'd got married several times without ever getting divorced. I don't really care about the morality of breaking the law, but the fact is she'd really hurt and damaged people along the way. It wasn't just the act of getting married; she'd deceived people and she'd hurt them.

If you can't find anything to like about your characters, you at least have to want to understand them. There's a guy in *Slaughterhouse*, which was filmed in Oldham, who was very unpleasant, always kicking the animals and bullying people and making racist comments. I hated the racism of those characters, of course, but I was also *interested* in it. Men like that have grown up in one way and then suddenly there are areas of the town they've lived in all of their lives that have become no-go areas, and the whole culture has changed. I'm not saying that their perspective is right, but it is worth trying to understand, and I came away with some sympathy for their position. They feel lost and beleaguered and let down and betrayed, and they're not necessarily bad people. There are reasons why they are as they are.

Is there a kind of person you most like interviewing?

I used to think that I got more out of women, probably just because women tend to be a bit more open and honest. I've certainly always enjoyed making films with and about women. These days, I wouldn't make any gender distinctions. I've sometimes enjoyed the tussle of trying to dig something out of someone who might be a bit of a closed shop. But, overall, I think I just like talking to ordinary people about their lives and experiences.

Chemistry is important in interviews, I think. You can be a very skilful interviewer, but, if someone doesn't take to you or is just wired up in a way that you're not going to be able to communicate with them, it's going to be a struggle. There are just some people who are going to be resistant to you personally, whoever you are. Is that true, do you think?

Yes, I think it is. Probably most good documentary-makers that you'll meet have a certain amount of personal charm. People like Paul Watson. He's kind of bullish and a bit aggressive, but he's got charm with people. Nick Broomfield, he's got charm, you know, a certain amount of charisma. Kim Longinotto is charming and friendly, and I would imagine that the people in her films feel comfortable talking to her. I think that's an important quality. You know, nobody's going to talk to you if you're cold and distant and what they regard as snobbish or frigid. Nobody's going to want to talk to you then.

Apart from charm, I think that most people respond to filmmakers who they think are being honest and straight with them, and who are genuinely interested in them. I recently got involved in one of those beauty pageants that happen when there is a big news story and lots of people are chasing it to make the documentary. In this case, it was the story of Mark Kennedy, the police officer who spent seven years undercover, posing as an environmental activist and passing on information to the police. Lots of directors and production companies were trying to sign Mark up for a film. I was one of the last people to get to meet him. I went along with Katie Bailiff and there was no question that we would be anything other than straight with him and honest about what we wanted from the filming process, and what would be required of him, and what the possible consequences might be. The first thing I said to him was: 'I know you've met lots of directors and producers and I'm sure that a lot of them have talked about the films they've made and what they can do for you, but I'd like to start off by asking what *you* want from the process.' Nobody else had asked him that. Nobody had thought that he might have some kind of vested interest in the process. It was pretty much that one question that made him decide to make the film with us.

But sometimes the stuff that people might object to about you are things you can't do anything about.

Yes; even with charm and integrity, sometimes it just doesn't work. People just don't like you. It's very hard for me to accept that somebody might not like me! And I'm guessing, you know, as I get older, I'll find that with younger people, that they don't want to talk to a granddad. I can still get away with it now but I might not be able to in a few years' time.

It's interesting the assumptions that people make about you as an interviewer. I had a character once who was a Nazi, and she took to me, partly, I think, because of my shaved head. Sometimes the assumptions people make are helpful and sometimes they aren't.

Yes, I mean that's what we all do: we all pick up on visual signals about people. Social psychologists tell you if you smile at people then that's going to help. I don't know about that. But, yes, your characters are going to form judgements about you as much as you're doing it to them. I think Mark Kennedy, the undercover cop, for example, just felt comfortable with us. I have to say that having Katie (also a Northerner) in meetings like that is always a huge help. She's very perceptive about people and she has the great gift that people feel very comfortable around her.

There's a lot of tension in the interviews with Emily in The Bigamist Bride. *It feels like a storm brewing.*

Yeah, I felt I had to get after her a bit. The first interview with her that I did on the first day of filming ... it was all set up, it was lit in the studio, and it was her chance to tell her story. Now whether she knows she's lying all the time or whether it's part of her illness that she lives in this fantasy world, I'm not sure. I think she probably knows that she's lying and she likes to present herself in the best light, which I suppose is a fairly human thing to do. But then, as I researched the story more and talked to some of the men that she'd affected and some of the people who'd been in her life, I came across all these things that contradicted everything she'd said. At the end, on the last day of filming – I had to leave it until the last day – I cornered her. And it wasn't done in the studio all set up and lit; it was hand-held in the living room. She knew what was coming because she's not stupid. I said, 'Emily, we've got to talk.' And then she went, 'Okay, go on.' And I had to really say, 'You told me this, but this is the truth. You told me you've had at least twelve abortions or miscarriages; that's just not true, is it?' I just confronted her with all these lies because I felt if I don't do that then the film has no value. It was uncomfortable and difficult. She didn't like it and she got upset, and probably a lot of people watching it thought, 'He's a bit of a twat for doing that.' But it just felt necessary. In retrospect, though, I'm not sure I should have made that film. I don't necessarily think it was in her best interests or mine.

Your questions are very simple and direct with Emily. Are simple questions always best, do you think?

Yes. I think, if you want people to talk to you, then you have to have a conversation, which is usually a simple affair. It's no good asking them really complicated questions that they have to think hard about, and then they think 'Christ, I'd better say something clever.' I just have a conversation with people: 'So, tell me about Emily when you first met her. What was she like?' You know: 'Emily, did you really love him?' And so on.

Is there always, with every interview, a killer question?

I don't know that there is, actually. I think there can be with some. I think there is a killer mood that you establish and an atmosphere which enables people to open up. But killer questions are probably more relevant to things like news and current affairs where you lead people down a path and then you spring that question on them and it is the question you have always had in mind. I don't really work like that because I prefer to respond to what people tell me rather than going in with 'I must ask these questions'. It was a bit different with Emily in *The Bigamist Bride*. I knew that, in the final act, we had to confront her and you had to hear my questions because we didn't want to let her off the hook, after she had lied to me for so long – 'Have you worked as a prostitute?' and so on. It felt quite uncomfortable, doing that.

Did it feel a bit cruel?

Yes, it did feel a bit cruel. It was very hard with Emily. I was conscious of the fact that she is clearly not in the best of health mentally, but I didn't want to fall into the same trap that everybody else has done, which is to treat her with kid gloves, because I don't necessarily believe that she is, as she told me, bipolar. I don't necessarily believe half the things that she says she is. We did have her psych-tested and we always had access to a psychologist, a counsellor who we could call at any time because she was vulnerable. It did feel uncomfortable, badgering her like that at the end, and a bit cruel. Maybe it was cruel, but I thought, 'Well, she has been incredibly cruel in her life and probably will be again.' I thought she was robust enough to take it, and she was fine afterwards. Well, she still spoke to me, at least.

The Bigamist Bride was a film that was made up of interview, really: it was centred on an extended interview with the central character. It's quite unusual for a film to take that form these days.

It is. Testimony used to be the bedrock of documentaries, but testimony-based films have all but disappeared now. Broadcasters think they're too serious, but I like to experiment with different ways of making films that might swim against the tide. Recently, I've made a few films which are largely interview-based, largely 'talking heads' – people just talking about their lives. The big mantra for a long time with broadcasters has been: 'You've got to do first-person narrative.' But that's really hard to pull off in documentary. There just aren't that many stories where you get a great narrative unfolding. You know, something like *Capturing the Friedmans* was unusual in that the producers had a great narrative unfolding in front of them. But most documentaries aren't like that. And even if you do have a great story unfolding, that you can tell observationally, you need time to do that, and directors are very rarely given that time these days. You've got to really invest in good actuality. You've got to really spend time on the ground. I had a whole year to make *Sylvania Waters*, for example. What happens in the absence of time is that people try to construct unfolding narratives that don't really exist and the film's very unsatisfying because of that, whereas I think doing a film that is mainly interview, with some reconstruction or archive, can be really satisfying and complete. I wouldn't say that one way is better than another, or that these are the only ways to make documentary films. You have to choose the style that you feel comfortable with as a filmmaker, and that suits the tale you're trying to tell.

I'm currently halfway through making the film with Mark Kennedy, the undercover cop. It's largely a past-tense story, about what he did for the seven years he was living a double life. One of the things I'm trying is quite new for me. I interviewed him for hours and hours and ended up with around 160,000 words of transcript. Then I edited this down to thirty-odd pages and turned it into a script and asked him to perform it in a studio. I suppose it's similar to the kind of thing I've done with the documentary musicals – *Feltham Sings* and *Songbirds,* and so on, where I got people to sing about their lives. But in this case I'm asking him to perform his own life story from a script culled from his own testimony. I'm still right in the process, and I don't know whether it is going to work.

My favourite character from your films is the old guy in The Club, *the guy who's a terrible golfer.*

Preston Lockwood, yes. He became a kind of narrator in that film. The film was about a suburban golf club, and, for me, it was almost an anthropology film. It was a tribe of people that I didn't really know much about: you know, the British, suburban middle classes who read the *Daily Telegraph* and voted Tory and had a very peculiar view of what is British and what is acceptable and worthwhile. I didn't really know people like that and I hadn't really made films about people like that, so it was a really interesting exercise. But I was really struggling with that film, and I went back to Channel 4, to the Commissioning Editor, Peter Moore, a couple of times and said, 'I can't make this film. There's nothing happening. There are no great characters; some of them are slightly amusing, but there's nothing really going on. I should stop and not waste any more of your money.' And Peter said, 'Carry on with it. Just see – something will happen.' And that's a great piece of advice, actually, to filmmakers or people starting out. Something good did happen, which was that I found Preston Lockwood, this character who was just amazing and different and very watchable. What I liked about him was that he was like a licensed fool, in a kind of Shakespearean sense. He could say the things that other people couldn't say or would get in trouble for saying, but nobody minded with him because he was so genial about it. So he could be very critical of the club's policy towards women, and the power of the Freemasons and all that. He just had this great take on things and I felt, 'He's perfect. I'm going to use him as a kind of narrator but I'm not going to say he's a narrator. I'm going to shoot stuff with him and get him to help the film along,' and he was the glue that held it all together.

Have you ever shown a film to someone that you've interviewed where they've hated the bit of the interview that you've included, or they've not liked what you've done with it?

I prefer it if people like what I've done. Or if they don't like it, they at least can see it is honest. When we made *The Club* we showed the film to the committee members before it was broadcast. They loved it. Doubles all round! Some of them were even talking about making me an honorary member of the golf club, despite the fact that I can't play the game. But it was a very different story when the film was broadcast. There was a storm of protest about the attitudes and behaviour on display at the club, particularly a scene where the committee rounded on and bullied one of the members. Which just goes to show that people's perceptions of themselves and the way they behave doesn't always coincide with the way other people see them. I never got my honorary membership.

Also, after *Sylvania Waters*, Noleen made a huge fuss and said that she'd been misrepresented, culminating in a frankly spectacular session at the Edinburgh Television Festival where she publicly attacked myself and fellow director Kate Woods, saying we'd ruined her life. So it was funny that half an hour after the session she gave me a big kiss and said, 'Let's make a second series.'

Generally, I think that, no matter how good it might be for your film, you do have a duty or a responsibility to your subjects. I always say to people, 'Look, I'm not going to change things if you just say, "Oh, I don't like the way I look in that, or I look a bit fat, or I could have said that better." I'm not going to change that. But if it's factually incorrect I'll change it. And if you tell me it'll cause you real distress and cause you trouble then we'll talk about it.' But, generally, I've never had any problems with it. Generally, people are fine with it. But that's because I'm not going to stitch people up anyway. People say to you at the start – all the time people say, 'Are you going to make me look like a fool in this film?' And I say, 'No, I'm not. You might make yourself look like a fool, but that's your responsibility, not my responsibility. I'll just be filming you so you need to think about how you behave.'

I think you can see in the interviews in all your films that your contributors trust you. Are you surprised at what people tell you in interviews?

I used to be. I used to be really surprised at what people would say. But what I've realised over the years – and this is not just about filmmaking, it's about people – is that if you approach people in the right way and if you ask the right questions, and if you're open and give them a bit of yourself, then people will start to give you stuff back. So I quite often reveal things about my own life. If there's something in an interview that I might have had an experience of, I might say, 'Oh, yeah, well, that happened to my granny,' or whatever. Or 'I know what you're feeling because once when I was a kid ...' blah, blah, blah. Having a bit of life experience can help you there, because there's more for other people to relate to. You're the first audience for that person telling their story, and, if they think that you're the kind of audience that is sympathetic and is going to try to understand them, they're much more likely to tell you stuff, much more likely to be open.

You definitely get the sense that your contributors are part of a relationship, because you can see them relaxing. But it's interesting that you're not in your own films very much, in terms of asking questions. Some people make films in that Nick Broomfield sort of way where their questions are all over it. I think in The Club *there's one question from you and that's probably just there to help make sense of the answer.*

Yeah, and we had to re-voice even that. We thought when we were cutting the film that it didn't quite make sense so I had to go in the sound booth and re-do it. I don't want it to appear that I'm criticising other people and the way they make films, because that's up to them, and some people seem to like that style, but I personally don't want to be a character in the films that I make. And I don't want my personality to be very obvious. I know that in a couple of films, recently, there have been more of my questions, but that's not any desire to have people hear my voice. That's just how it's worked out with that particular kind of film. Also, I've narrated a couple of films recently and, again, that's not something I particularly enjoy or want to do, but I felt that in those particular films getting an actor in to narrate it wouldn't have been the right thing to do. In the film I'm making at the moment, the Mark Kennedy film, I've found that he is a character who has to be pushed a lot, and that he likes to talk around subjects rather than giving direct answers. That's not a criticism, that's just the way he is. But it has forced me into a more prominent role in the film than I'm comfortable with.

I am not the most outgoing type. But, when I have a camera there, I feel much more emboldened to ask people all that stuff that I never would ordinarily.

It gives you licence, I think. It gives you a certain kind of legitimacy and a licence to ask questions that you wouldn't otherwise ask. I think also that, sometimes, in really difficult situations, it can be a shield and a buttress to stop you getting freaked out. Like when I was filming *Slaughterhouse*, I found the whole experience quite difficult and sometimes disgusting. Animals being slaughtered in front of me in their hundreds every day. But because I was there with the camera it didn't bother me as much as I thought it would. I am quite squeamish; I find it quite hard to watch *ER*. And being in a slaughterhouse watching death every day and animals having throats cut and the pigs ejaculating when they die, it was just like, 'Fucking gross.' But with a camera I could deal with it. Similarly, when I made a film called *Pornography: The Musical* and I filmed at a *bukkake* party, which is the grimmest thing I have ever filmed, the fact that we were there with a camera made it all okay. Well, sort of okay. It was still a very difficult thing to be present at, even with a camera.

Do you think it's true that interviews, maybe more than anything else, set the tone of a documentary?

Yes, that is quite interesting actually. I think documentary, excluding wildlife and stuff like that, is about people's lives and people's responses. I try to remember all the time that documentary is a visual medium. (You should pay great attention to how a film looks, which I think a lot of people just don't, really don't.) But if you are making a film about people and people's lives, then, yes, what they say is probably the most important aspect of it. And if that is the case, that what people say is the most important aspect, then the way you get them to say that, i.e. how you interview them, is probably the most important thing that you, as a director, are doing. So, in a sense, yes, I would say it does set the tone.

Did you do interviews in your working life before TV?

Yes, yes. In the '80s I worked for Greenwich Council. Greenwich was one of those radical Labour authorities that was trying to offset the worst excesses of Thatcherism. I worked in this team called Community Affairs. There were about thirty of us and I worked in the Welfare Rights Unit. Mainly my job was trying to get people to claim benefits that were going unclaimed and that the DSS weren't telling them about. I used to represent people at social security tribunals. You do spend a lot of time interviewing people, and I spent a lot of time talking to people about their lives. So that has kind of carried on, I guess. It is just a straight through-line. You have to be really interested in people and you have to be interested in people's lives to make decent documentaries. And not everyone is interested in other people.

Interviews are quite often like therapy, aren't they, for the people you're talking to?

Absolutely. I think people do regard it as therapy and the most obvious example I can think of, in a film I've made, is when I made a film about Robbie Williams. I went on tour with Robbie for six weeks for a film called *Nobody Someday*. Right at the start, I said to my crew that when we were making this film we shouldn't treat Robbie any differently to any other documentary subject that we might be making a film about. That is what we did and he responded to that amazingly, because he is surrounded by people who try to anticipate his every wish, who just kiss his arse all day long. He falls for that and kind of plays along with it, and starts to think he is God, whereas we became like mates to him. He just wanted to hang out with us the whole time, even to the extent that one night we were travelling to Paris ... We had been travelling most of the day and we had arrived in Paris in the evening and we had checked into a hotel. I said to the crew, 'Right, we are off the clock now. Let's go and get some dinner in Paris.' We were just in the bar having a drink prior to going out and Robbie's assistant came down and said, 'Robbie wants to do some filming.' I said, 'No, we are off. We are going out for dinner.' She kind of turned white because the thought of going back up to Robbie's suite and saying, 'They don't want to film you' was just like, 'How the fuck is she going to deal with that?' I liked her so I said, 'Look, I'll go up and I'll have a chat. I don't want to get you into trouble.' So I went up to his suite and I said, 'What's the problem? You want to do some filming? Is it something really urgent that won't wait?' He went, 'No, no. I just thought we could have a chat and film some stuff.' I said, 'Well, we want to go out for dinner, you know? The lads have been working all day.' He went, 'Yeah, yeah, fine, fine.' Really, he just wanted to hang out with us and talk to us. I said, 'Come out for dinner with us, that's fine. Don't worry about it.' And then, every time we turned the camera on, he would just pour out stuff, pour out stuff, pour out stuff. It is partly because he felt that we were friends. I wasn't somebody who would be kissing his arse, so he felt able to talk to me in that therapeutic role. He would seek us out all the time just to talk and talk and talk.

And what Robbie is saying really sounds like therapy, doesn't it? It sounds like he is in therapy.

Yes, it does. Sometimes you talk to people and you realise they have done therapy, and perhaps they have done a bit too much therapy. And you just think, 'Ah, actually this isn't very good because this is therapy speak.'

Did you think that was going on with Robbie?

I don't think that so much with him. I just think Robbie is incapable of self-censoring. I think he just blurts everything out. If he feels comfortable with you, he will just spew everything out. So, we were supposed to be on tour with him for six weeks, and after about three weeks I was thinking, 'I can't get anything else out of this guy. He has said everything. It is just too fucking easy. I don't have to dig around.' I just go, 'Robbie, tell me about your childhood,' and bleurgh! He spews it all out. That might sound as though I'm complaining or being critical. In fact, I'm doing neither, because I've also experienced the other kind of interviewee, the one who is tight-lipped and buttoned up and doesn't want to tell you anything at all. Give me someone like Robbie any day!

By contrast with Robbie Williams, someone like Cliff in *The Not Dead* was much harder to interview, but it was much more satisfying, in a way. Cliff suffered terribly in the Malayan war. He did some things that he was extremely ashamed of and saw some things that deeply, deeply upset him. He had lived with this for fifty years and nobody was interested. Nobody wanted to talk to this old man about what he'd been through: 'He's just a boring old bloke going on about the war.' When I met him I started talking about it and we did this really moving interview over a whole day in a hotel in Blackpool. It was one of the most satisfying but significant things I have ever done in my career. It was just amazing, and it was this very intense day where Cliff and I just forgot about everything else around us. I forgot about the crew and, you know, they had to tap me on the shoulder and say, 'We need to change the tape.' This was the first time Cliff had been properly allowed to tell his story to somebody. That was proper therapy for him. That was a great unburdening. The significant thing was that somebody was actually taking him seriously and wanting to hear his story, and was willing to allow him that space to do it. That really was therapy for him. It was brilliant. I was so pleased we did that.

It is amazing sometimes that you can get 'flow' when you are doing an interview – you can lose track of time, and find yourself totally immersed in it.

The time just goes, yes. It is great for them and it is great for you, I think. It really is the most satisfying part of my job, doing a great interview like that, and then to feel utterly wrung out at the end of it. It's great. I love it.

Do you feel with Robbie that he was offering you so much that you needed to challenge more? It's almost like there is so much apparent honesty that you start wondering whether it is honest.

Yes, yes, is this all a kind of smokescreen? Is there other stuff buried deeper? I don't know. I just couldn't get to that stuff. But, interestingly, I met Robbie recently, because I was going to do another film with him. And I was going to do this second film in a different way. It was just going to be his audio and we were going to illustrate it with pictures and archive. I went to LA to spend a week with him, just interviewing him, just talking about his whole life. Then the plan was to edit that and give it back to him and he would re-record it. I wouldn't add anything to it, but I would just take repetitions out and turn it into a script. We spent the first day talking and it was very intimate. He talked about his childhood and he said some things that I don't think he's talked about publicly before. Then the next day I was arranging with his assistant to go and see him again up in his house. She said, 'He doesn't want to do it any more.' I went, 'What do you mean? I have just come five thousand miles to do this.' She said, 'I know, I am really sorry, but he doesn't want to do it. He does want to do it but he doesn't want to do it now. If he does it with anybody it will be with you.' I knew he had enjoyed seeing me. She didn't say this, but I think what happened was overnight he had just thought, 'I can't stop myself.' I think he had said stuff that people genuinely hadn't heard before, stuff that was quite deep and quite dark.

You felt like you had penetrated through that layer of therapy speak?

Yes, it felt really honest and he was telling me quite interesting stuff – I mean brilliant stuff actually. I think he just thought overnight, 'I can't do this because it is going to damage so many people.'

115

It was too raw?

Yes, and I was pissed off, obviously, because I had travelled all that way and I had thought, 'Fuck me, if he carries on like this we are going to have a sensational film.' But that is how it goes, isn't it? And actually he deserves and needs the same amount of consideration and respect as anyone in any documentary. Perhaps it was right that he pulled out then rather than further down the line.

He seemed like quite a tricky character in Nobody Someday, *because he is playing up so much. It's like everything is a bit of a performance. You are never quite sure what is genuinely him and what is the Robbie Williams persona.*

I know what you mean, but I do think he is generally pretty honest, or as honest as he knows how to be. The first day I met him I said, 'If we make this film what is off limits?' He said, 'Nothing.' He said, 'You can ask me about anything. You will never be denied access to me. You will never be stopped. If anybody tries to stop you, you just come straight to me and I will tell you anything.' And he was pretty true to that.

Have there been any interviews that you felt like you didn't nail?

Oh, yes, loads. I mean, loads of occasions where I've spent time with people in films and interviewed them and then looked back at it and realised it's just not interesting, or not usable, or not as usable as I thought. I think that, personally, I'm never really satisfied when I look back at something I've made. I've never made a film and gone, 'Yeah, that's it, that's perfect, couldn't be any better.' Either in the photography or the way we've used the music or the character selection or, you know ... there's always room for improvement. 'If only I'd got this out of that person ...' I remember Cliff, when Cliff came to the viewing of *The Not Dead*, and we were in a taxi afterwards and he was quite moved by seeing it and he said, 'Oh, good job I didn't tell you about all the other stuff that we did.' And I went, 'What stuff?' And he started telling me these things. It was fairly hard-core stuff that had happened in the war. I might not have used it, but it was very interesting material.

How did you do the interviews for True Voice?

I am very interested in those areas where there is a film crying out to be made, but you can't take a documentary camera there. You can't take a documentary camera, but just scripting something isn't going to be very satisfying either. So, what I did with *True Voice* was find people whose stories we wanted to tell, but we couldn't tell them for legal reasons or for personal reasons or whatever. Like in *The True Voice of Rape* film where the two women had been raped, but people had never been convicted, so you can't go and openly tell the story. So, we had this idea that what we would do is take the stories, alter names and dates and give them to actors to perform. The stuff that you hear in the film, the actors' monologues, is mostly verbatim, but not absolutely verbatim. I just sat and talked to people: 'Tell me the story about when you got raped. Tell me the story of when you murdered your husband.' You know, I just talked to them like you would in a documentary, but we did it all on audio and then I edited it. I got them transcribed and then I went through and I edited. I was cutting out repetitions and stuff that was off the point, but never added a single word. I would cut some stuff out and rearrange a few paragraphs, just to make it flow better. People don't always talk in the most logical or natural way to tell a story. Then we gave them all back to the people and said, 'Is this okay? Are you happy with this?' Then, if they said, 'This is an accurate and fair description of my feelings and this is what I said, and this is true,' we went ahead with the drama bit.

They're interviews but in the form of monologue. Did you think about re-creating them as interviews?

No. It wasn't difficult to attract really good actors. I thought just to re-create an interview would be to waste the talents of those actors, really. I thought I should let them put something into it; you know, let them play with it and let them interpret it. So they didn't change the words, but they could pause and make it their own. I really loved doing those. I thought they were really fantastic. I would have loved to carry on doing more.

The songs are like interviews in your musical documentaries. What is the relationship between the actual interviews and the songs? How did you work it out?

Well, it's really tricky. It's a really tricky balance to get right. We – not always me, sometimes the researchers – will interview people at length about their story.

Then those interviews go up to Simon Armitage and he listens to them and he writes stuff based on what he is hearing. Some of it is factual or an interpretation of what they are saying about their life or about the situation. Some of it is him listening out for speech patterns and certain ways of talking or phrases that they use. He writes it and then we give it back to them. If they agree, then the composer comes in and we record the song. But then it becomes – and it has always bedevilled us – this thing about how much information are we giving in that song or that poem that we don't want to give in the interview. But if we don't cover some of that same ground in the interview, will the song be understandable? Will it tell you something about their life? It is best if you don't repeat any of it really. It depends how literal his song is and how interpretative it is, or whether it goes down some kind of metaphorical route.

So in *Drinking for England* there is a song for Jane called 'Sherry and Me', about her love affair with sherry: 'Sherry and me we are all on our own', and so on. That was something which just reinforced the factual stuff that she had said. In something like *Feltham Sings* where we had this kid called Terell Thuesday who was a car thief, there is a certain amount of overlap between his song and him talking in interview. I didn't think that his song really gave you enough information. But it is really tricky, because you don't want to bore people by repeating it the whole time.

What has been added in the transition from interview to song?

It doesn't necessarily add much in a literal sense to the information you are getting. I think what it adds is a few things that aren't immediately apparent. I think it makes an audience view the character in a very different way. I think that no matter how liberal and well meaning you are, no matter how much of a kind of *Guardian*-reading leftie you are and how tolerant you think you are, when you hear some crack-head burglar talking about houses he has robbed and stuff like that, you think, 'Well, he is just a crack-head burglar.' Very tragic about his upbringing and all that, but you dismiss him, really. But if you hear that kid singing about his life, I think it gives the kid another dimension. It gives you the idea that they have got some creativity about them, that they have something redeemable about them. I think that is really important. And that is actually one of the main reasons why we do the musicals, because both Simon and myself genuinely believe that everybody has got some kind of creative impulse that just needs to be tapped into. It's not really for the screen, but I also think that that experience can really change people. It lets them know they have a talent. I am not saying everybody who has been in one of our musicals suddenly turns their life around and becomes a different person, but I know of at least two people it really has made a difference to – the fact that they said, 'Fuck me, I can sing. I can do something. I am not just a worthless loser.'

It makes you listen to the content in a way you wouldn't so much in an interview?

Yes. I think it makes you listen to the content and it makes you think differently about them. I think the other thing that you get out of doing the songs is that the characters feel more involved in the process of making the film. I don't think they feel just like a subject of documentary. They feel like genuine collaborators and that they are having a creative input and they are involved. It's really satisfying when it works, really satisfying.

The way interviews are shot goes through periods of fashion: very tight in, very wide, on tracks, down the lens. You're known as an innovator in interviewing. So what's the next turn of the wheel, in terms of the way interviews are done?

I don't know, really. In terms of a visual style, I'm about to start making a film and I've just been talking to the DoP this morning about how we might shoot the interviews a bit differently and I haven't come up with the right answer yet. And I don't know if I will. I mean, you don't want to do stuff just for the sake of doing something different; there's got to be a reason for it. In *Drinking for England*, we had very odd framing for most of our interviews. We positioned people oddly, you know? We had them looking at the side of the frame that you wouldn't expect and that was because it was a film about drinking and we wanted to make it a bit off-kilter. So there was a reason for doing that. I don't know, I might be really radical and just go straightforward, sit to the side of the camera and talk to people!

Filmmakers don't often entertain different styles and approaches, do they?

No. I was surprised, when I first started making documentaries and thinking a lot about them, at how few visual techniques and how few storytelling techniques people use. You know: 'It's got to be *cinema vérité*, it's got to be pure. It's got to be uninflected and uninterrupted.' And that kind of held sway for a long time. But I just don't buy that. I don't buy that there's just one way to make documentaries. I think, in fiction, people are much bolder in the way they tell stories: narratives that go backwards, multiple narratives all colliding, and so on. People are much more inventive about how they use narrative and whether narrative really matters. I just started to think there have got to be other ways of making documentaries. There have got to be other ways of telling stories, of making a documentary about people's lives than this kind of, frankly, rather dull stuff that we get to watch all the time. It's partly budgetary, but there also seems to be a huge lack of ambition. There seems to be a huge kind of lack of desire to experiment, to make things different and to push the boundaries. It's become a very conservative and risk-averse industry, however much people who work in television and run television like to think they're mavericks. I just wouldn't be allowed to make films like *Feltham Sings* these days. But it's so refreshing when you see a film that does push boundaries, because at least the director's having a go, even if the film is not entirely successful.

I think documentary, really, if it's going to thrive and be exciting and attract audiences, has got to change. Because I think too many people watch documentaries because they think they should do. Like eating broccoli. I've always thought that you've got to make a documentary entertaining. You've got to make it interesting to look at. And I think too many people, particularly in America, think it's enough that you're just there. You're there witnessing some event that's important. It doesn't matter that it looks like shit or that you can hardly hear it, as long as you're bearing witness. I think that's a great disservice to documentary.

Those sorts of documentary, in the vérité style, very seldom have interviews in them. And I think they often feel like they lack depth because of the absence of interviews.

Yes, it literally lacks depth because you're just getting the surface of what's going on. I mean, if you're lucky enough to get the kind of things happening where an alert audience will spot other layers of meaning, then great. But often you're not. Often you're just wondering what the fuck's going on and it's all happening on the surface. And I much prefer to make films where you can go beneath that, and you can present another layer of meaning. And interviewing is one of the main ways you can do that.

It's interesting the way interviews and actuality relate to each other when they're both present in a film. In The Club, *for example, is the actuality teeing up the interviews, so that they are the really telling bit? Or is it the other way round? Are the interviews teeing up the actuality to really nail what the film is about?*

That's an interesting question. I think one of the joys of making documentaries is the way stuff reveals itself to you. Sometimes it's frustrating as well. But the joy, for me, is you start making a film and suddenly you're in the cutting room and you go, 'Oh, *that's* what it's about!' And it's to do with the juxtaposition of images and actuality with what people are saying in interview, and you suddenly start to get a deeper understanding. I don't know what's the most important element, though. It's all about the mix as you go deeper into the film. Which is the most revealing element varies.

Do you do much interviewing as part of actuality?

It certainly has its place and I have managed to get some really nice stuff doing that. It can be a bit quotidian: 'What we are doing now? Where are we going?' It is a bit descriptive and a bit tedious sometimes, and it can be difficult to get long, meaningful answers about something important. But you can sometimes get really telling, off-the-cuff comments.

In *The Club*, I didn't do that many big sit-down interviews. A lot of it was just actuality and me tossing in the odd question. I got this really nice material, just people looking for their ball in the rough and they would just come out with something, just a small statement but in its way as telling as anything else, really. The good material that you get in that way is much less digested, less thought through, more spontaneous. Sometimes you get something really revealing, because your character is more focused on doing or thinking about something else. You can't ever tell. You can't ever legislate for those things. I wouldn't want to do a big interview like that, but I like sometimes to just throw in the odd question, and get a quick off-the-top-of-the-head answer.

They're very speculative, those sorts of questions – fishing, really?

Yes, I think they are, and that is the great thing about that kind of observational filmmaking. It is the great thing, and also it is sometimes the really frustrating thing. It is speculative and a lot of it yields nothing, but sometimes you get little gems and those little gems are just as important as the long, considered, thoughtful answers. I wouldn't discount the element of luck in good documentaries. I think there is a certain amount of luck and a certain amount of serendipity. You can say that you create your own luck. But I do think that sometimes you get lucky for no reason. Sometimes you stumble on the stuff that really makes your film.

You're known for being committed to making good-looking films, like Climate of Change. *Have you ever shot your own film?*

I've actually just made a film which I shot myself. It's the first time I've done it. It's about a child contact centre: you know, when a couple split up and it's so acrimonious that one of them takes the kids, usually the mum, so the dad has to go and see his kids once a week or once a fortnight in this neutral ground, for just a couple of hours. And it's the saddest thing. It's awful. Because of the length of the schedule we had, and the tight budget, I thought I'd better shoot it myself, which I didn't particularly enjoy doing. It's not bad. But I couldn't hope to achieve what a proper cameraman could have achieved. So I don't think it's something I want to carry on doing.

How was it doing the interviews when you were self-shooting? Did you find it distracting?

Yes, it wasn't ideal. I would have preferred not to have had a camera on my shoulder. Inevitably, it has to be distracting because you're worried about focus and exposure and, you know, you've got to think about all those things. I don't think anybody really does it especially well. Morgan Matthews is the exception among the new breed of self-shooting directors. He does it better than most, probably because he does it so much.

What makes an interview really memorable?

When I'm choosing characters, I just ask myself, 'Would I want to sit in a pub or a restaurant and listen to this person telling me about their life?' If I would, then I think that probably makes them a good character. Because I don't think as an audience I am that different to most people. I think I probably share similar interests to the vast majority of the population, and like the same kind of things. I've got fairly broad tastes so if I find something interesting there is a pretty good bet that somebody else will. And then, once you have thought, 'Yes this person will be interesting,' it's really just a question of getting the best out of them. Maybe it's old-fashioned now, but my idea of doing an interview is to get as much as I can out of the person I am interviewing, to get them to talk about stuff that they maybe haven't spoken about before. That's what makes it memorable for a viewer – the sense that you are hearing something that's fresh and unrehearsed, that's being aired for the first time. And that's often just a matter of allowing the unexpected to come out – the stuff you don't know about. And if it is surprising to you it is going to surprise your audience. I think you have to give people that space to feel relaxed.

I think that what made Cliff in The Not Dead *so striking as a character is that he seems to be thinking aloud, and surprising even himself with what he's saying at times. He's sometimes overwhelmed by his own memories as they occur to him.*

Cliff had told his story before, but he had never told it in such detail. When I first met him, I only spoke to him for about twenty minutes and he started telling me some extraordinary things. And I said, 'Don't tell me now,' because I knew then that I wanted him for the film. I said, 'Don't tell me now because it would be nice to capture it on camera, so that I'll be hearing it for the first time when we come to film. That way it will be more interesting for me to try to dig it out of you, and more interesting for you to tell me.' That, I think, is why it felt like it was the first time he had told it. I am sure he had told bits of it to doctors and to his wife and to friends over the years, but I don't think anybody had ever sat down with him and heard it all. He was a very genuine chap, and he wanted to tell his story in his own way, in his own time.

Do you think of your films as portraits?

I suppose they are portraits; like *Slaughterhouse* is a portrait of white, working-class men. I think of them more as kind of shining the torch in the murkier corners of the world. I do like to think that they give a voice to people whose voice wouldn't normally be heard. (Albeit I've done a film about Robbie Williams, whose voice is heard all the time.) But, generally, the films that I make are just about regular people whom you wouldn't necessarily hear from. They're about ordinary people with something to say about the world and about their own world that can strike a chord with other people. That's important to me. Interviews are only a part of that, of course. But if you are serious about understanding a person or a phenomenon or an issue, then you have to give weight to the interview, you know? You have to hear from the person who's at the centre of your story. Other people can make films however they want, but, personally, I find it more satisfying to sit down and talk to people.

Are there any questions you always ask?

No. No, I can't say I do, because everybody is different and every film is different, and every character in every film is different. You've got to feel your way.

7 Emotion
Louise Osmond

Louise Osmond is an expert storyteller, and the director of a number of feature-length documentaries, including: *Deep Water* (2006), the extraordinary story of Donald Crowhurst, an amateur sailor who enters a single-handed round-the-world yacht race in the hope of winning a cash prize to aid his failing business and help support his family, quickly running into trouble, with tragic consequences; *The Beckoning Silence* (2007), the story of an unsuccessful attempt to scale the sunless North Face of the Eiger in 1936, told by Joe Simpson, the hero of *Touching the Void*; *Killer in a Small Town* (2008), the story of the fastest serial murders in British criminal history, told from the point of view of the victims, and their friends and families; and *Lost Abroad* (2010), a film about the agonies suffered by parents of grown-up children who have died in mysterious circumstances while living overseas.

Osmond's films are carefully crafted and sensitively handled, exhibiting a fine judgement of emotional tone, which makes them very moving and absorbing to watch. As one reviewer wrote of *Lost Abroad*, her work is always poignant, powerful and heartfelt.

Louise Osmond, on location in 2012. Picture by Uli Hesse.

Big emotions, like those in Lost Abroad, *need to be handled with care and respect.*

Yes. I think there were definitely times during *Lost Abroad* when I felt slightly overwhelmed by the emotions in it. They seemed to be too big to get close to. You're dealing with overwhelming grief. In *Deep Water*, the grief was part of the context of the story, but in *Lost Abroad* it was absolutely front and centre – a present, living reality. There was nothing else, in a sense, for those families. It was driving them completely. And I know there were moments in the edit when we felt almost like we didn't know how to handle emotions that seemed that big, and that raw. We had to find light and shade in it, in a way, to make it accessible to the viewer, so it wasn't just, 'I can't bear to go on!' That's the worst thing that I could possibly imagine feeling. We had an interesting viewing where we realised that we had to give much more of a sense of what the families had lost in order for the viewer to properly empathise and understand the depth of the emotions involved. What we tried to do, I think, was to show what they'd had that had been shattered, and then slowly build to a full understanding of the extent to which it was driving them to the edge of despair as the obstacles unfolded before them.

There weren't many tears in that film. I think, oftentimes, the biggest emotion comes from things unsaid or unstated – just expressions or looks, or an air of defeat. Emotion has got so many levels and layers to it that it's not just the moment where somebody cries. It's all the infinite shades that lead you to that.

Less is more with emotion, do you think?

I think almost always, yes. I think the thing is to be absolutely ruthless about sticking to moments that feel true. By that I don't mean that the interviewees are ever dishonest. They're obviously always being themselves. It's more about what the viewer can relate to, something that can bridge that gap between the interviewee and the viewer. And sometimes when you're making a film, the things that bridge that gap, that really touch you, are not the things that appear to be the big, obvious themes of a film. For example, in *Deep Water*, with Clare Crowhurst, one of the things I found almost unbearably moving was, on the last night before her husband set sail, how much went unspoken between them, in this very English kind of way. It was her sense of: 'Perhaps I should have asked him not to go. Perhaps I should have said all these things.' Perhaps he didn't want her to, or perhaps he was begging her to and she didn't. Those are the kinds of unspoken things that go on in any relationship. But that's something which haunted her, because I think she had come to the conclusion, after the event, that perhaps he was begging her to tell him not to go.

One of the things that I found moving was the fact that when he went to sea he was wearing a tie. That says it all about him. It's very expressive about who he is, and what his values are.

Yes, I think there are so many layers to emotion in a film. That's a really important one – trying to give people a sense of the characters through tiny, specific details, so that you come to understand the characters and the relationships between them in a very precise way, and so that you feel like you understand them. That's something I learned on that film, to let viewers understand people in the film as individuals and really work hard to let viewers hear that person's voice, their distinct voice, because in a way we're trying to get inside Donald Crowhurst's head.

It's interesting what you said about making sure to give the audience an entry-point into intense emotions that might be a bit foreign to the average person, because it seems to me that there's a theme in your films of family, of families under enormous pressure in these extraordinary situations. And family, of course, is universal; it's a great way in.

Yes. The themes in the films are to do with families, siblings, relationships between children and parents, loss. I'm sure every director, in their own way, is expressing things they're interested in or feel an empathy with. I think of documentaries as being about finding an idea or story that, just for some reason, fires a trigger in you. And then it's all about expressing that thing. It's like you're a frustrated musician, struggling to play a new instrument. Somebody once put it to me – they were asking me about what I did – and they said, 'Oh, so it's like you've got to get into their emotions, get behind them, understand them and then find a way to bring them to life.' And I thought, 'Well, yes, exactly.' It had taken me about fifteen years to work that out. But I think that is exactly what it is about. And then you're struggling, through the way you tell your story, through the music, the way you shoot it, everything. You're trying to bring your characters and their story to life. You're trying to tell the story in a way that will take the audience into this world and let them understand it, let them feel what it's like to *be* the characters at the centre of it. It's quite personal as a process.

Is that because there is a big emotional investment from you?

Yes, I think so. I always feel tremendously involved. Some people would say less flatteringly, 'You might be slightly obsessive!' I go through lots of ups and downs about it.

Some directors feel very much that when they're making a film they're engaged in a technical process. They're shooting it with all the gear and making choices and solving problems, and they just don't feel huge amounts of emotion. But others, myself included, go through an emotional wringer every time. Especially when you're making a film that has very emotional interviews in it, or it's very intimate and people are revealing quite personal things ... your characters get a lot of catharsis out of doing the interview, and they feel good at the end of it, but you don't really, as a director.

I think films are always emotionally all-encompassing, and normally you kind of drop out of them feeling quite flat, and it takes a long time afterwards to come round. Is that a good thing or a bad thing? I don't know. It's just become a habit. And it's not just about the emotion of it; it's partly the endeavour of trying to tell a story well. You want it to look good, you want to tell the story properly, you want the music to be right. You're collaborating with people perhaps you've never met before. It's quite an intense and intensely felt process. But I think that the joy of it is working with the DoP and the editor, so that you can share your pain and all that you love about a story and all that you find difficult to convey about it. And I talk a lot about it ... probably too much! Before we go and shoot anything – I have been shooting with Jeremy Hewson for quite a while now – I'll make up a book of images: some of them might relate to the landscape we're going to, and some of them are just things I like. So there's a book of stuff, and we always discuss it, and he always very politely flicks through and looks at it. But it means that, when we're filming, there's something to refer back to, so we know where we are.

It helps you set a mood?

Yes, so when you're filming, you're filming with a purpose, or filming with a view to the story that you want to tell. The idea is that, in the shots that we design and choose and put together, we'll create an atmosphere that suits that particular emotional moment in the film.

I think that's one of the very striking things about your films: that the emotional mood and pitch always seem to be so finely crafted.

I have to say that you can run into trouble with it. There was a moment in Ipswich when we were doing *Killer in a Small Town*, when the soundman that I've also worked with many times, Ollie Astles-Jones, who's always a great sounding-board, said, 'I think you might be filming Ipswich as if it's Baltimore in *The Wire* – and it's just not like that.' But still, what you're trying to do in building an atmosphere is to give an emotional sense of place to the area where the story's set, and in that film really more so than ever ... Ipswich had just ripped its own heart out through its planning. It had torn up all the old buildings around the water and had put up all these glass houses, many of which were still being built. And they were entirely empty. Nobody in Ipswich could afford to live in them. They'd created them with the idea that it was going to be this waterfront commuter town for London. It seemed a telling fact about what had happened during that period. In a sense, everybody's eyes had turned towards this smart new idea that they had of themselves. And in the meantime, this thing happened. The women kept getting moved from up-and-coming Ipswich into darker and darker areas as their 'allowed patch', if you like, until they ended up in this really sinister area around the football stadium. And, as anybody knows, the empty streets around a football stadium, when there's not a game on, are really dark and deserted and shadowy. I wanted to make sure we captured that, and conveyed the world the characters lived in through the way we filmed it. And that's where the book of images helps. I guess the book becomes a bit of a bible for me, and we keep looking back at it.

So it's a bible of images, but also of emotional states?

Yes. For example, it seemed to me that the women at the centre of the story lived and died while the world passed them by. And we tried to make that into a visual theme. The striking thing about that part of the world is that almost everywhere there's a road in the distance. So you can play that idea of these women who were right there, in the heart of this tiny town, and yet they were falling away and disappearing. People were passing them by. It was part of their decline. And then the actual murders themselves happened without any witnesses, and yet there were always people there, in the distance, getting on with other stuff.

One of the things I like best about your films is how calm and considered they are. There's a sense of stillness, and then an escalating feeling of emotional intensity.

I came to documentaries by a weird path, which was that I started in news. I joined ITN straight from university. It was a brilliant learning ground, fantastic in terms of problem-solving, deciding what you should film and what you should give time to. But when I came to move into documentaries I felt like I was somehow trying to catch up with this profession, and sort of understand it. Julian Ware was the guy I first went to work for. He was a brilliantly patient teacher, and he would say things like, 'Pictures as words', and things that really stay with you. I went off to try to learn about the visualisation of films, the way films use images and storytelling. And as I started doing that I got really passionate about it. I love the visual side of making films. I think the danger of it is that you can create over-designed and over-controlled films that are somehow slightly detached, you know? Too controlled visually. Not inhabitable somehow, because it's too designed and nice-looking and distant, and not going with the flow and not really the absolute truth of it. So when you say 'calm', 'calm' is a dagger to my heart! I don't want my films to be calm or controlled. I don't want them to be smooth or elegant. I want them to be true, and I want them to be just absolutely accessible. And now I find – perhaps it's age! – I'm starting to loosen everything up and I'm trying to do things in a much more simple and immediate and fresh way, and I'm starting to think about filming some stuff myself.

Having said all that, I do think you also have to seduce people, to draw people in. You're trying to evoke feelings and moods. You're trying to bring alive emotions, with not necessarily a huge amount to work with, so I think you've got to try to do it visually. And I think that images shot to deliberately express or underscore an emotion can help get inside somebody's feelings and express them and bring them to life, and complement the words in the interviews. I do feel, sometimes, that a spell is broken if you're using a shot that doesn't have atmosphere in it, and if you can build atmosphere through the shots, you're kind of creating a mood, and that's all part of creating the emotional intensity of the film. I love the idea that you can watch a film with the sound off, and still have a pretty good sense of its emotional temperature, and what's going on in it.

Is the idea that it is more honest if it is just happening, and you're not cutting it very much, you're not producing it, you're not lighting it? Do you think that makes those films more emotional: the wobbly, hand-held, not-lit, not-considered approach?

I think the idea is that in the world of documentary all you should be doing is just observing with a lens. You should be right there just watching, like *Grey Gardens,* and it should just be unfolding before you. Those films are brilliant, and they're so moving because there's no artifice; there's nothing in the way. It's just this person in front of you, exposed as they're undergoing something, filmed in moments that unravel the circumstances of their lives. But if you're mixing past and present elements, you're automatically drawn down a slightly different road. You've got to tell your story, maybe without archive or dramatic reconstruction, so you're having to develop a style of images which evokes something. And that leads towards something that's a little more styled and considered.

I have to say, sometimes I sniff a degree of bullshit when you go to documentary festivals and people are talking about 'absolute freedom' and 'let it flow' and 'purity of the spirit' and 'I only go where the river will take me'. And I think, 'Really? Are you absolutely sure that's what you do? Or are you actually paddling intensely hard below the surface?'

Like most directors, I'm constantly trying to re-think the way I work. But I guess the problem is the things you like, or at least the things that move you, will stay pretty much the same. You don't often get the chance to have conversations about this sort of stuff, about making films. There seems to be a shortage of those discussions where you talk about these challenges and issues. Where do you go? There should be a Samaritans phone line for documentary directors, where you could call in and say, 'I'm struggling with the issue of artifice. I worry my shots are over-designed!'

It seems to me that emotion has become a cheapened currency in documentaries, especially on television, because people cry all the time in factual television now, and I think that the danger when you watch is that you end up not feeling anything. The tears are so ubiquitous that they don't really mean much. Your films seem very moving because there's tight control over the amount of emotion and the way the emotions unfold.

I think the moments you're looking for with a documentary are the moments when you just recognise there's a fellow human being. You just think, 'Oh, God, I know that! Shit! I recognise that. That sounds real. I can imagine that's exactly what it would be like.' Moments that appear to sum up in some way what is driving your characters, or what has haunted them all these years, or whatever. And often there are no tears at those moments. They're often really quiet.

When you're filming, you're gathering these moments, and then you throw them on the editor's desk. I've been amazingly lucky with the editors I've worked with. The best ones have a real human understanding. They see a lot of people pass before them and they have a great eye for what's true and what isn't. But they also know how to manage those moments. You mustn't burn through them too quickly, because then people will find it hard to empathise. And you mustn't be emotional too early, or let someone be too angry or too emotional too early. It's amazing how quickly you get used to anything; it can be panic, fear, high emotion, deep joy. Those things are one-hit wonders, after which you're on a kind of downward path of familiarity.

You've got to lead the audience through the film, emotionally speaking?

In the end, you're almost trying to make the viewer live the experience that your character or subject lived. So, like in *Deep Water*, you're dealing with the highs and lows of Clare thinking her husband's coming back as the most famous man since Francis Chichester; 100,000 people going to meet him on the dock, and the kids are getting fêted at school because their dad's a hero. Then the next call is that his boat's been found and he's not on it. You're trying to unfold a narrative that the audience can place themselves in and think, 'Oh, God, no, yes, no, yes' – the highs and lows. But I think sometimes your characters are not in a position to unfold that narrative for you. The film is about those people and their lives because that's what's interesting, but I think you're creating this support structure around what they experienced in order that you can translate, in a kind of amplified way, what they experienced. I mean, sometimes, obviously, the people who are speaking to you are quite quiet or withdrawn, or kind of torn by grief, and might have become slightly hardened or perhaps bitter. That's all absolutely real and human, but sometimes, in the structure of the story, you need to amplify the sensations that they were experiencing, and if you want to amplify the sensations, then you've got to plan quite carefully how you're going to film it. Certain images do that, I think: powerful, telling, visceral images. And the way you structure a film ... you have to feel that you are on that ride. You're on that journey.

In terms of people identifying with the story, the appeal of the underdog can be an amazing way in, can't it? It seemed to me that Erica's a bit like that in Lost Abroad *and also Don in* Deep Water. *It's easy to go along with them because you're rooting for them.*

Yes, I do think that's probably why, in the first instance, those stories resonated with me. I'm sure that in some ways it's very personal: I probably feel a bit like an outsider myself. I suppose I have empathy for people who are set against things, or on the edge of things, or on the margins of things – trying to make sense of a world or deal with a world that, momentarily or even over decades, is making no sense at all. And they are trying to find a road through it. I just feel automatically immensely engaged in the stories of people like that. Like Erica, for example, in *Lost Abroad*: she found herself in that situation accidentally. Actually, Erica is an amazingly ebullient, social, charming person who found herself caught up in this thing, having to battle the system. I suppose I just instinctively find those people enormously appealing.

I do love my job. I love my work. I love the people in my films. When I don't, I can't operate at all, which, I suppose, is an illustration of how much filmmaking is driven by emotion. Almost the unhappiest I've ever been at work was, briefly, going down to the City of London to look at doing a story about bankers. At that moment in time, they were suffering tough times, a terrible collapse. I went down there to Canary Wharf and sat in the lobby of Lehman Brothers, who were right on the edge of collapse, and just saw all these people ... and I just thought I couldn't make a film about this group of people if it was the last subject left on earth. I just felt, 'In my soul I have nothing to say about this place.' I just thought, 'I'm not interested,' and that's a terrible thing to say because you always should be interested. I just couldn't do it, and I'm sure it's because they were very much of the world and part of things, and I was wanting to find something different or marginal.

Until you find your way into a story, and a way of getting some purchase on it, it's very hard. And then, when you do find it, that helps you decide what the story really is. Like in Ipswich, you think, 'There's something fascinating here, the idea of it happening in this small town,' and that somehow, beneath the surface of the town, there is this other world. But you don't know what's going to bring it to life for you, and you go and you search and search. Then, halfway through filming, Tom Alderton, who's Anneli's brother, replied to an e-mail we'd sent a long time before and said, 'Why don't you come up to Norwich and see me?' So, I drove up one Saturday morning and had a coffee with him. He sat down and explained how he had been in the extraordinary situation of watching his own sister's demise while being a drug counsellor to people exactly like her in the city of Ipswich, and that ... it just brought the whole film to life. And Tom was another underdog. Absolutely.

When Tom loses his composure a little bit, it's incredibly moving.

Tom was actually angry for much longer – he was really letting it out. He was smoking a cigarette and looking pale and about two stone lighter. By the end, we were all reeling and shell-shocked. In the first assembly, we put it in quite generously. But in the end, we just pared it back and pared it back and pared it back and pared it back, until you'd think he was angry for two sentences. Because the minute he was angry a little bit too much, your reaction to him changed. It's such an extraordinary and delicate process bringing this thing, an emotion, to the screen. If you cross that line, suddenly you're feeling pummelled and hectored: 'Don't rant at me!' You're suddenly feeling intruded upon in a weird way, as a viewer. There's just a moment with Tom when it's a kind of licensed loss of temper. You're protecting that moment, so when it comes the audience meets it in the right way. You have to be able to share his anger. Otherwise, it would just work against you. It's really interesting that you can have an intense and powerful four-hour engagement with someone you're interviewing, but the key moment in the scene, the bit that's going to really resonate and drive the film forward, will probably only last eight seconds.

It seems to me that you really earn emotion in your films in the sense that you're inviting people to invest. We get to meet characters. We're given information. We're coming to understand the world that they're living in. And then the emotion is so much more intense and keenly felt because it's been earned ...

Yes, and I do think that's important. I think the truth of emotion is that there are so many different shades to it. You've got to calibrate the emotions in a film in a kind of ascending scale. In the end, there are probably only four moments in a film that really *make* a film, and they've got to be judged very carefully. So everything else is building towards them or leading away from them. In *Lost Abroad*, it was Erica's terrible frustration in that small town, and then maybe Bill in Tokyo handing out those leaflets about his daughter and the man who killed her. That was the world he was living in. There was a terrible sense that the one person who might know where his daughter's killer was might be the next person coming up the escalator. It was torture for him.

I think there's a theme in your films of traps or binds: people getting themselves into, or finding themselves in, situations which are impossible. So, you've got

Toni Kurz stuck on the mountain in Beckoning Silence *in a physical way, but you've also got Don Crowhurst, who's got himself into a no-win situation on his boat. You've got Erica trapped in this situation where she can't stop but going on is incredibly painful as well.*

Again, it's the things that resonate with you. You think, 'God! Oh my God!' you know? Very few of us will ever live through such extreme circumstances as any of those characters, but in our daily lives we're all experiencing shades of these situations. I just find those things completely compelling and fascinating and deeply human. You're thinking, 'Would I have had the courage in the situation that Donald was in, to turn up in the face of all that attention and say, "Actually, folks, it was all a lie!"?' It's that element that makes those moments emotional.

I think it's very moving when characters seem to be thinking aloud and expressing their emotions quite freely, like Tom in Killer in a Small Town. *Joe Simpson is interesting in that context because he's very articulate but he doesn't let much slip.*

Joe's an interesting guy. When you meet him, you understand why he survived. He's private, and he's very self-contained. He's very tough and he doesn't need people around him. He's quite happy to sit in the corner, nursing a pint and smoking a roll-up. People who are guarded or reserved can often appear cold on screen, or even unlikeable. But the most powerful characters in documentaries are people for whom large amounts remain unspoken. Something about a good documentary allows you to see that sort of character in a light which enables you to recognise that, and understand what's going unspoken, and then you feel very moved by it. *Beckoning Silence* was a difficult film to make because the way we told the story was quite detached. Joe was telling a story that had moved him, but he wasn't there on the climb. The story of the climb was just actors on a mountain. So, in a way, the emotion in that film came from Joe talking about why the story moved him. It was small moments – quite understated. It was no *Touching the Void*, and I think it suffered a bit from that. On the other hand, I thought Joe told the story really well. He's a brilliant storyteller.

It's interesting that his insights are quite psychological, and I was wondering whether psychological insights are actually the opposite to 'being emotional', because they explain too much?

Yes, that's really interesting. I find myself having really fascinating debates with editors about whether you want to hear any insights, or do you want to just let something be. And most often I find that the insights come out of the cut in the end. The insights that stay, the ones that work best, are the ones that are personal insights from a friend or relative. So in *Lost Abroad*, Erica's mum is uniquely placed to deliver an explanation for Erica's motives, and it's probably the furthest the film ever goes in that direction. It's only okay because it's her.

One thing that I found very touching in Killer in a Small Town *is the photographs of the girls, the victims, when they were young and innocent.*

Yes. I felt like I didn't know much about their lives. I had read the papers like everybody else when it was happening, and they were only ever called 'prostitutes'. But it was just one step left of life, do you know what I mean? You never really think about how they get there, but then you realise that the way they get there is incredibly ordinary: literally something as tiny as liking the bad guy in class – something that small. You fall in with the wrong crowd. Their family photos show their lives before they diverged, when they were just the same as us. Gemma worked in car insurance, and she looked like this incredibly beautiful, happy girl. You could imagine her in a comfortable house with a handsome husband and two kids. She just looked so healthy and happy, so that was incredibly poignant. You see her growing up in those pictures, and you keep waiting for the picture of her in a wedding dress.

Yes, it's their ordinariness that's so moving. It's the same in Lost Abroad, *with the Hawkers. In fact, I think the dad says at some point, 'We are just an ordinary family,' and then heartbreakingly he says, 'We didn't think that we'd done anything wrong.'*

Yes, there's a common theme to almost all of my films, which is the idea of ordinary people who find themselves suddenly caught up in something that is completely beyond their control, and that is taking them into completely foreign lands, where you have no reference point, no means of negotiation. The Hawkers, one Saturday, are an ordinary family who have always done right by their daughters. And they are all doing brilliantly, going to university; they are all beautiful. And then, by the end of Monday, they have got five hundred snappers outside their door and three helicopters over the house and no one to help them, no one to advise them, and no one to protect them. You can completely identify with people as ordinary as that. It could be you. It allows you to go on the journey because you think, 'Oh my God, that could be me, that could be my daughter, that could be my neighbour.'

In terms of generating and expressing emotions, what role does music play?

A huge role. Again, that is something you should work on quite organically with the editor. It will just suddenly start to emerge from bits and pieces and moments in the film. There are rules I try to follow, like that music shouldn't lead the emotion. It should follow on from the emotions that the film generates, rather than force the pace of the mood.

Do you think that if music is working well emotionally you don't really notice it?

Not always. In *Lost Abroad*, in the scene where Bill goes out on to the streets in Tokyo giving out flyers, the editor, David Hill, cut it as though Bill had done this for hours, saying the same thing over and over again, and it was absolutely desperate to watch. It just felt like it needed music – something big and agitated and that was an absolute expression of what these families go through. In that instance, the music was very noticeable, part and parcel of putting it all out there in this powerful, pivotal, set-piece scene, where normally you would be much more delicate with it.

You were announcing that scene as a big emotional moment?

Yes. There was another big moment in the Hawkers' story that we used drums for, and that became my favourite thing musically in that film. The Hawkers are just about to go into this news conference, and they are sitting down and they are so nervous with all of the press in front of them. They had prepared that morning and thought, 'Right, sod it, we are going to stand up and say what we feel honestly now, enough is enough.' You know how you give little tags to chapters? In our shorthand it was a scene about letting loose, the family going out on the warpath. That is how the drums came about, traditional Japanese drums that have a sort of war-dance feel about them.

I think with filmmaking, you are building and building and building the tension, and then occasionally you need to let off steam a bit before climbing to the next thing, and music is immensely important in that, and important also sometimes in just giving you breathers, just a moment when no one is going to talk to you or tell you anything difficult, and you can just rest for a minute. During the editing process, I'll often listen to my composer's music on my iPod. I'll listen to the music that's been written for a particular section of the film because I find it a great way to think about how to tackle a particular sequence. Music can fill your head with ideas about things you might do with a particular scene. It's really helpful.

In Lost Abroad, *there are quite a lot of drones which I thought was interesting. The whole film is vibrating with emotion and the drones are sort of a representation of that in music.*

Yes, that is interesting. We used them in places where it wasn't a big confrontation or a big set piece, but another small moment of frustration. Drones are good for making you feel a bit uneasy, and for conveying intensity and keeping the tension alive without trying to force emotion or impose a pace. Just kind of keeping a chill in the air, or some kind of turbulence.

How does narration relate to emotion?

I think that the function of narration is never to take the place of emotion, and the interviewees should never take the part of narration. So, you don't burn up a minute's worth of your interest in the interviewee by getting them to say something that you could say more economically in narration. I think, in an emotional film especially, the cooler and more factual the narration, the more it works as a counter point, so that the interviews and sequences can be more purely emotional. Obviously, I love to do films without narration, but they are hard and, in today's world, I think oftentimes it's a wasted effort trying to do away with narration in the edit. You know, not many films get through nowadays without it.

Do you think that you need a certain sort of personality to be good at handling emotion?

Well, I sometimes think the more people think you're a loser, the easier it is to interview them! It depends entirely on the character of the person you're speaking to, of course, but I think, if you bring too much personality into the room, it's unhelpful. I don't know. I think interviews usually work best if you're just listening. I think, typically, in the moments that are really strong or moving or powerful you're not saying anything. You do see big personality documentary-makers who have a fantastic way with interviews, so I'm sure it's just about different strokes. I'm quite shy. I don't find it the easiest thing to be social or around people, and I suspect people know that. People are very perceptive. And I think sometimes that can help you because people don't feel challenged by you, and so, in a sense, they're almost helping you to get the interview done.

Do you think it helps if you're making films that deal with strong emotions to be experienced in life?

Yes, yes. I think, if you haven't felt on the wrong side of stuff, you might not recognise it when you hear it. If you feel you've been in situations not too dissimilar, then you're kind of in the mix with them as opposed to judging them as 'characters'.

It's making people feel like they can relate to you partly, isn't it? You've been in love and had your heart broken. You've known frustrations, had highs and lows, fallen out with people, lost things ...

I don't think you can fake it if you haven't really lived through it, if your interest is just academic. Most of the people I've ever filmed with, because of what they lived through, they have very strong antennae, and people can be very sensitive to the idea that you're judging them. I know that I would find it difficult to talk openly and honestly to someone I thought was judging me.

Crews can help create the right mood and tone for an interview, I think.

Yes. Often by the time you do an interview you've spent lots of time with your characters, and the last thing on earth you want is, when the filming begins, for it to be a sudden break in that relationship, and for it all to suddenly be about wires and machines and boxes of kit, invading their home. You try to keep that spell of trust. The crew I work with are very sensitive to the process and they're very solicitous to the people, and they're very calm. I can't stand the kind of hyperness that can sometimes be injected into sets unnecessarily – the idea that filming needs to be agitated. I think it should be the opposite of that: just calm.

I reckon you know whether a film will work or not when you first meet your characters. I think you can tell in seconds if they're going to give you good emotional scenes, and then you know you're on to a winner …

Yes, you know immediately when someone's going to be good, and I think it's partly about that person's ability to project their feelings. That means they have a way about them, they have a turn-of-phrase, they have an ability to articulate emotion. It's not just that they're emotional, it's that they have a way of making you understand the emotion. So that, for example, you could ask fifteen people something completely banal, like on *Killer in a Small Town*, 'Do you remember when you heard the news of the first murder?' And you'd get fifteen different answers, and one would just be electric and immediate and would really take you back to the moment. What you're looking for is a combination of intensity and a kind of openness, or, if it's a closed-ness, it's an interesting closed-ness. It's a kind of closed-ness that you can peer into. And an ability to explain richly and in a quite complex way all the emotions that they might feel, so as to really bring those emotions alive and get across the complexities of the life they're living.

For example, you meet Jade in Ipswich and Jade is just unbelievably articulate. She's hugely emotional and angry, full of grief at the loss of her friend. She's led this incredibly hard life, but is unbelievably articulate. So, suddenly, you have a person who can bring a world alive to you, who can bring home a world which is as far away as you're going to get from most ordinary people's sitting rooms. She'll bring her world alive for you. You have to really search for people like that, and that's when having amazing people-finding APs makes all the difference. Jamie Balment, the AP in *Killer in a Small Town*, spoke to a lot of people before he found Jade.

I often find people's faces the most moving thing about an interview. Watching TV, I kind of zone out quite a lot. I feel like, 'I get it, I get it.' When I feel really engaged and touched and moved by a documentary, it's quite often someone's face.

Yes, do you know, that's really interesting. I think some people have a way of expressing themselves ... yes, absolutely via their face. I think that may be to do with honesty. I'm not saying people aren't usually honest. I'm just saying that with some people there's a kind of directness about them that you feel immediately. When you meet people for the first time, you're often trying to assess them. Are they being friendly or are they just being polite, and so on and so on. I think in some ways, in television, you need people who are going to cross that boundary quite quickly if they're telling a story. Or, if they're not crossing it quite quickly, that's got to be part of the film, so that it becomes intriguing to unpeel the layers of this person. They've got to have something to pull you in, something that's pretty compelling, I think, to make you want to follow them and understand them and what lies beneath.

I sometimes think that, despite your best plans and hard work, the emotional tone and pitch and quality of a film only really become clear at the end of the process, just as you're finishing it.

Yes, I think that you choose a film because it appeals to you. And being the person you are, you'll normally choose an idea that has lots of 'crush' in it, lots of layers, and it's got something in the treatment when you first read about it that made you feel moved. Then when you're filming you have a sense of the way you're trying to tell the story, and you're trying to focus on those moments in a story when things seem to coalesce or the plot turns. Those moments in the story where, again, something about them fires you or moves you. There's a weird process in the edit when you're trying to pull it all together, and sometimes your big emotional moments just don't work. They can all be completely flat or misfiring.

Like when someone's telling you a joke and it's just not funny and they say, 'Well, you had to be there.' Sometimes filming something can feel emotional – it feels like there's real emotion and tension in the room – but it doesn't translate on to film. The editor's saying, 'It's just not what you think it is.' Maybe because when you filmed it and you felt the emotion, you were tired or stressed or excited, or just willing it to be emotional?

Exactly. I think that's absolutely true. Good editors can help filter that stuff out for you. They have a really interesting perspective on it all, because they haven't been out filming and encountering the characters. They're just responding to what happens on the screen. It's an awful feeling when you realise that something that you thought was going to underpin your film is just a phantasm, just not going to work. But then you always find something else. And then, yes, it's in the edit that the film really comes alive. I often feel like you make a film four times over. First, you respond to the story, and then you have an idea about how to film it, and then you go out and film it, and then you go into the edit and it remakes itself again. You often end up back where you started with your first vague ideas. But each part of the process in between is informing and shaping the film. I think the exciting thing about the edit is this strange alchemy that occurs whereby the better a film gets – you're getting a deeper understanding of someone and the journey they've been on, or you're describing it more clearly – the more emotional it becomes. And then there's suddenly a moment where a film that's not been moving you or anyone else has sort of found itself, and *is* powerful and moving. And often it's not until the final viewing. By the rest of the film working better, it releases the feeling.

The guiding thing is storytelling. I think that's what it's all about: telling the story in a way that is actually engaging people, so that they're able to see the humour in it or the pathos or the emotion. It's just storytelling. When you see a film that you don't find emotionally engaging, you think, 'Is that the temperament of the person who made it? Or were they deliberately not making it emotional, maybe thinking that's a manipulative thing to do?' Or was it because in some way you weren't understanding the characters and their motivations? And it's a weirdly hard thing to fathom why a film, particularly a good film, can sometimes leave you cold. Nothing frustrates me more than not feeling emotionally engaged by a film. But I think, when you *are* engaged, it's usually for simple reasons: the characters are true, and the story's straight, and you're just on the journey. You're just in it somehow.

8 Making a point
Kim Longinotto

Kim Longinotto is a prolific British documentary-maker with an international reputation and a large number of prizes and awards, including a BAFTA, Best Single Documentary at the Royal Television Society awards, and the World Cinema Grand Jury Prize at the Sundance Film Festival. Her films, shot in a calm and unobtrusive *vérité* style, often centre on victims of discrimination and oppression, and tell the stories of strong female characters who are fighting for justice and change.

Longinotto's filmography includes: *Shinjuku Boys* (1995), about the professional and personal lives of three women who live as men and work as hosts at a club in Tokyo; *Divorce Iranian Style* (1998), a gripping observational film set inside an Iranian divorce court; *The Day I Will Never Forget* (2002), a feature documentary about female genital mutilation, following (among others) a Kenyan woman named Nurse Fardhosa as she takes a stand against the practice; *Sisters in Law* (2005), about two women who work in the judicial system in a small town in Cameroon, focusing on cases involving violence against women and girls; *Hold Me Tight, Let Me Go* (2007), about a school devoted to children suffering from emotional trauma; *Rough Aunties* (2008), about a group of women who care for neglected and abused children in South Africa; and *Pink Saris* (2010), the story of Sampat Pal, a woman devoted to protecting lower-caste women from injustice and abuse in northern India.

Kim Longinotto (left), during the filming of The Day I Will Never Forget. *Picture courtesy of Kim Longinotto.*

What is a Kim Longinotto film?

I don't think of the films I make as documents or records of things. I try to make them as like the experience of watching a fiction film as possible, though, of course, nothing is ever set up. I mean, you are watching something, a story, unfold in front of your eyes. For me, that is the magic of documentaries – something will happen in front of you that you couldn't have imagined. In fact, it's usually more extraordinary and gripping than you *possibly* could have imagined. That's why I'm in love with documentaries. I remember being in a police station with Manka Grace in *Sisters in Law*, and her family was all there. And the perpetrator, the woman who had beaten this little girl, kneels at her feet and asks for forgiveness, but you can see it's theatrical. You can see that she's putting it on, because she's afraid of the family. The family wants retribution, but the little girl looks awkward and embarrassed. As I was filming it, I remember thinking, 'This is what documentary can do.' I would never have written that into a script. People would never believe it, and yet it was real and I was there.

I'm not trying to put across my view of the world. I'm not trying to say what I think. I'm going on a journey and I'm following a story as best I can. The story will amaze me and make me see my own society and my own life in a different way. You know, when I'm filming scenes like the victim meeting the perpetrator in *Sisters in Law*, I'm thinking that this is a good thing that this is happening, and that we should be doing the same in Britain. There are things we can all learn from each other, so I am going there as a witness in a way, witnessing what's going on so that the rest of the world can see.

Your films have a very definite style. They're very recognisable as Kim Longinotto films, even though you don't narrate them or even ask questions in them.

Yes, I suppose the style is ... I'm trying to let the audience feel that they're where I am, experiencing it how I am. I try not to zoom in hard. I try not to pan too much, or if I pan I try to make it as if you are looking and the camera is going where you want to watch. So I'm trying to be the eyes for the audience. You're being part of something. You're watching something unfold.

Your style is very pure in the sense that there is not much voice-over, if any, and no formal interviews, not very many captions, and not much incidental music.

I wouldn't have described the style as 'pure', but I see what you mean. It's trying to make you feel like you're there. I don't want you to be thinking about me, and I want you to feel the confusion that I feel. And that is why I don't like to use voice-over, because when you say something in voice-over you're framing it and you're asking people to see it the same way as you do, but often I don't know how I feel about things. I can see the same film several times, the same scene, and I can see it differently every time. Did you see *Hold Me Tight, Let Me Go*? When I was making the film at the beginning, I felt one way about children and families, and then in the middle I had a crisis where I started to doubt everything I thought about my own childhood and my relationship with kids. And then I changed again towards the end. So what can I say in the voice-over? There's a storyline with a mum called Donna, and Ben, her son. When we're with Ben, you realise how much he misses his mum and wants his mum, and he says, 'My mum says I'm boring and she doesn't want me.' And then you meet Donna, and she's doing a course and wants to change her life. And when you see Ben on her lap, you can tell she wants to go and get on with her life, and I'm thinking, 'Yes, go get your life together,' but also Ben wants her to stay, which is heartbreaking. I'm seeing it from all sides, you know? And so what am I going to tell people in voice-over? Some people will watch the film and they will love Donna like I did. And some people will watch the film and they will see it from the little kid's point of view. What voice-over tends to do is to lock you into a certain way of seeing things, I think. It closes things down. I just feel so ambivalent about everything. I joined the Socialist Workers Party, but I only stayed a couple of weeks, because I kept agreeing and then disagreeing with them. I would think something, and then I would think something else, and then change my mind again.

What are you hoping to achieve when you make a film?

I want the audience to fall in love with the characters. I want them to fall in love with the people I have fallen in love with. Because I think that is what films can do. You can make this jump into someone else's experience. You are living through this person. And by living through them, our lives are being changed. I'm not looking to simply document things. What I'm looking for is change. I'm looking for people or situations where, when you are watching the film, you will be changed by it. You will see something changing. That is why Vera and Beatrice were so good in *Sisters in Law*, because they are trying to start a little grass-roots revolution. They see everything as human rights issues, in a battle against tradition. There is a very strong feeling in me against authority and against tradition. It seems to me that authority in a culture keeps you back, and holds you down, and kind of destroys you. And so I admire and love people that are fighting against it.

I think, on the whole, the films we make are very much to do with the kind of people we are. And I think the *way* you make films reveals a lot about who you are. My first film, which I made about my old boarding school while I was at the National Film and Television School, is similar to how I make films now. I was always very clear, even then, that I wanted to operate the camera, so that, if I messed up, it was just my fault and no one else's. I had a problem as a kid of not really liking adults, and not really feeling comfortable around grown-ups, so I would find it very hard to tell people what to do or to ask people to do things, and I think that's why I like to just observe and let things flow. I'm trapped in who I am and how I make films. I think that you just naturally make films the way you are.

Your films seem to share a common purpose or agenda.

Yes, they all do. They celebrate rebels – people that are trying to change things around, often in a small way, or sometimes in a really big, painful way. In *The Day I Will Never Forget*, it's this extraordinary thing that has been going on for four thousand years. In this country, until very recently, people were saying, 'We can't do anything about it. It's culture,' and that was why I really wanted to make that film. Change was needed. And also a close friend of mine told me it had been done to her. I had known her for some time, and then she told me that it had happened to her, and she said that it had ruined her life, on lots of different levels. It made her distrust the people she loved the most. Your mother and your aunts do this thing to you that means that you will never be whole again.

What is the agenda? Is it about justice? Or outsiders – people on the margins?

It's both of those. It's about outsiders definitely. The people that I seem to relate to have grown up through their childhoods feeling like outsiders. I suppose the reason why I am drawn to these people is that, when I was a child, I felt that I was always in the wrong place, and I didn't like anyone around me. I didn't like where I was. But I didn't rebel against any of it. I was always trying to conform, to get through in the least painful way possible. The people I admire are the people who are trying to fight oppression and change things, people struggling to break out of tradition and the sort of role that has been written for them. When I was making *Shinjuku Boys*, it all became really clear to me. The people we were filming had been filmed a lot by Japanese film crews and had been made to feel really bad, and mocked. These heterosexual men would come up in their vans and would film these women that were living as men, and have a great deal of distaste for them. Then, when three really scruffy women came over from England, suddenly we were very close. And they would say, 'At last, you have come!' It was the same with the little girl in *The Day I Will Never Forget*. I remember her saying, 'I have been waiting for you.' She was fighting against female genital mutilation, and it was the first time people had ever agreed with her and thought that what she was doing was good.

Would you say your films have a feminist point of view?

Yes, I think they do ... if feminism means that we are all equal. They're feminist if only in the sense that it's still, weirdly in the twenty-first century, rare to have women as the heroes in films.

You seem a bit wary of the word. 'Feminist', as a term, has quite bad PR at the moment?

Well, they are clever how they do that. The Right tries to make everything that's right-wing seem mainstream and normal, and anything they find threatening, anything that is asking questions or trying to shine a light – especially anything that seems overtly feminist or socialist – as weird and outlandish. I'm trying to make films that are subversive and challenging as well as accessible to a mainstream audience.

Across your films, is there a single point that you're trying to make?

I'm just trying to follow people's lives – amazing people, usually – and to take the audience on a journey that will hopefully change them. That's the dream. I want them to identify with the people in the film, who are usually very different people to them, people who they would never normally meet. Not necessarily people who live in Cameroon or South Africa, like in *Sisters in Law* and *Rough Aunties*. It could be teachers in plain old Oxford, like in *Hold Me Tight, Let Me Go*. But I want the audience to think, 'That could be my mum,' or 'That could be my sister,' and make that imaginative leap.

And the films are sort of like children; you nurture them and they grow into something. The way I make films is very controlled and thought through as a process, but, at the same time, I'm trying to be as flexible as possible and go where the journey takes me. For example, in *Pink Saris*, I thought the main character, Sampat Pal, was going to be wonderful, like Mildred in *Rough Aunties*. But then, very soon after we started filming, I realised that she's so edgy and damaged that she's actually, potentially, quite a dangerous person, in the way that damaged people often are. The people at the centre of the film would be the girls she's helping instead. So the film shifted. They always do that. So it's not like I go in saying, 'I want to say this or that.' I go into a film like *The Day I Will Never Forget* just wanting to be part of a groundswell. They are the ones who are brave and really doing something worthwhile. I'm just a witness to it. And, through their brave actions, I'm hoping to change the way people perceive female genital mutilation and become more critical of it. So I am trying to say something, but I'm not forcing an agenda on to the people I'm filming.

My first real obligation is to give the audience an experience. I want them to sit in a cinema and absolutely *feel* the film. I'm not going in with an agenda, a list of points that I want to make. I have a real problem with most of the documentaries that I watch. I don't really like many documentaries (I know this is an awful thing to say), because I often feel slightly bullied or like I'm being told what to think. I find most voice-over really intrusive and unpleasant. I'm not trying to say anything from me to the audience. I want my films to take them on an emotional experience, full of ups and downs like a rollercoaster. I don't want them to be bored for a second. I want them to be on the edge of their seats. It's a voyage of discovery, rather than me trying to say something.

What is it that you want the audience to discover?

For each film it's slightly different. Whatever it is, I want them to discover it with me, as I'm discovering it. With *Rough Aunties*, you're watching Mildred change her life in front of your eyes and become someone else. She's been a child slave. She's had to fight for everything she's ever had. And then she leaves her husband, to take control of her life. That's what I want people to see.

What conclusions do you want people to draw?

Conclusions are very tricky things. Things that I thought I was really sure about, I'm no longer sure about at all. So I don't want my films to have conclusions. The best films I've made (and seen) are films that have really made me question things, and made me ask more questions than they've answered. I suppose with *Rough Aunties* the conclusions are, if I'm being really bald, and because you're pressing me, that there's hope for the future in South Africa and elsewhere, with black and white women working together. And that a culture of silence can only be bad. I've been raped, like Mildred in the film, and a lot of the other women I know have been, and we shouldn't see ourselves as victims but as survivors. We should be able to talk about it, and not feel ashamed. There were so many realisations that occurred to me making that film that I'm hoping that people watching will get from it. They are not conclusions. They are more like emotional realisations of truths that we already know.

Your body of work is so consistent in terms of subject matter and themes, it feels like there surely is something you're getting at. What do you want people to take away generally? Is it empowerment?

That's a good word, thank you. My dream would be for people to come away from each film feeling a stronger person. That's how I felt meeting Mildred. She's been such an inspiration to me. She was brought up with nothing, and yet she's breaking all these barriers and changing her life. When I was growing up, my mum stayed with my dad, and they were miserable. There was a horrible atmosphere. She should have left him. In *Rough Aunties*, Mildred has so much less, and yet she's leaving to make a life for herself. That's a real image of empowerment. I suppose the reason I'm being a bit cagey is that *I'm* not saying it; it's coming through what you are watching. *Rough Aunties* got criticised a lot for a lack of context and statistics and information. But the context I'm trying to work with is much broader and more exciting. It leaps across barriers. I want people to apply what they see to their own lives.

You are saying, 'You can change.'
Exactly. Exactly.

They are quite complicated, your films. I always thought they were feminist films, addressing feminist issues, celebrating women. But when I re-watched them it seemed to me that they are that, but not only that. Anyone can watch them and feel inspired. There's a larger message: you're not stuck; you can change your life.

You see! You do it much better than me! That's exactly what they are trying to say. When you said 'feminist', I was pleased you said it, but, if you look at them, they're not purely or strictly or always that. You know, in *Hold Me Tight, Let Me Go*, the male teachers were a real shock to me, because I still had the idea of teachers being the enemy from my childhood, and I never wanted a father. I used to say to one of the kids – he would say to me all the time, 'I want to find my father, and for my father to see this film and come and get me' – I used to say to him very gently that I grew up with a dad and I felt nothing but fear of him, and I would have loved him to have disappeared, and maybe sometimes fathers aren't what we want them to be. I knew by chance that the boy's dad did know where he was and just didn't want to see him. And then you see these wonderful young men being so affectionate and gentle, and putting up with all sorts of abuse from the kids. You know, Charlie has a breakdown in the film, and he's hitting Pete the teacher, and then hanging on to him, and Pete is like this ideal man/woman parent – just the most extraordinary man.

'Feminist' just feels a bit old fashioned. I suppose that's why women don't like to say they're feminists. It has all these negative connotations. It's limiting. Also, I hate to put labels on things, because I find words in general so slippery. So you say to me, 'Are they feminist films?' and, as I'm saying they are feminist films, I'm also thinking that something is always what it's not as well. That's why I was so drawn to Japanese culture, when I was making *Dream Girls*. They were able to see something as one thing and also as another, with both having equal validity. You know, 'I'm a housewife. I love my husband. I love Anju Mira. She gives me an electric shock. I know she's a man, but I also know she's a woman.' We don't do that in the West. I like meanings to be open. I think that's in a way why I don't have commentary. And I've only just realised! It's so nice to talk about these things. We so rarely get the opportunity, as directors, do we? What I want people to do when they're watching a film is to feel lots of conflicting things, because I think that's how we are as people. That's certainly how I am. I find it really hard to judge people and take a definite line on their actions because I've made such a mess of most of my own life. I've done terrible things in my life and really let people down, you know? Like when I was sleeping on the streets, and I used to steal all the time. I couldn't have lived otherwise. So I do find it quite difficult to feel the moral certainty that other people seem to feel. Everything seems to me more complicated than that. So that's why I struggle a bit when you ask me, 'What are you trying to say?' It's more layered than that. I want people to go through a journey and feel all sorts of different emotions, which will depend partly on who they are.

I get that on the level of an individual film. I watched Divorce Iranian Style *and thought it was very complex and open to interpretation. You're never sure how you feel about the judge, for example. But, in terms of your body of work, when you put that film by the side of, say,* Runaway, *your film about a refuge for girls in Tehran, your films have such strong similarities that it seems like you must be getting at something.*

I am getting at something, it's true. But I think each film has so many different messages, and also the messages in the films are going to change depending on who you are. I'll give you a perfect example of that. At the end of *Divorce*

Iranian Style, we didn't want to end the film on Maryam saying, 'I want my children, my children need me, can't you see?' and sobbing in that awful hiccupping way. So I said, 'Well, we'll put something on the end,' and what we went for was a scene of the women praying. To me, that last scene is showing how there's a few women in the back of the mosque and it's a very small area and they're kind of jammed in, and they're praying and they're looking very submissive. It's a really different image of how women are in Iran, because you've seen all these strong, powerful women struggling against Sharia law and child marriages and demanding change, and then you have these veiled women praying. They're separated from the men only by a flimsy little curtain, a tiny little bit of material, and the camera can go round it, and then you see a huge area, which is the rest of the praying area, and that's where the men are and the judge from the courtroom is there. You see the difference between the world of men and the world of women; it's very big, but it's also very small. It's only a tiny curtain separating them. There's also something quite beautiful about the way the women are. There's a sort of calmness and comfort to it. So Ziba, whom I made the film with, will watch the film and say, 'Oh, that was a very soothing scene at the end.' Others will watch it and see a polemical message. And others will watch it and see only futility and a reinstatement of the status quo. You can take from it what you want. Do you see what I mean? That's why I love documentary.

What draws you back to the same sort of subject matter? I can see that you want the meaning of a film to be open. But why do you keep coming back to the same themes, like women fighting for justice in the courts?

Well, courts are a good place to film because they're like theatres. What I'm looking for in all the films I make is stories and settings where you'll be able to watch events unfolding in front of your eyes. I don't want stories about things in the past or the future. I want you to be gripped. When I was younger I got into trouble a lot and I was up in court a few times, so I know what goes on and what the emotions are. There's real drama there. In *Sisters in Law* and *Divorce Iranian Style*, people are going in front of the judge and they're trying to get the judge to give them what they want, with everything in their power. So the little girl, Ziba, in *Divorce Iranian Style*, will be tricking the judge, and telling lies, then telling us the truth. It's compelling.

153

As for why my films are about women so often, it's very straightforward. When I was making my films about Japan, the women were the ones who were open. They were where all the emotion was, and where all the fun was. The men wouldn't open up. It was the same with the films in Iran. Before we went to Iran, people were saying to us, 'Oh, nobody will talk to you in Iran. It's such a closed society. Nobody's going to open up.' But the women were so happy to be filmed! Women just let you get close, and their lives are more dramatic and extreme and full of struggle. In places like Africa, where change happens, it's usually through women. And yet all these women are not normally given a voice. So, from a filmmaking point of view, it's an obvious choice. The feminist thing is almost a diversion. We're filmmakers, and we just want to make good films and tell good stories that have good characters in them.

Your films get quite a lot of academic attention, with academics interpreting your work and saying, 'This is what it actually means.' How does that make you feel?

I'm always very impressed! I honestly don't know what my films mean. I'd love to know. So I read that stuff and I often go, 'Wow! Is that what they mean?' And then I read something else ... I know what they're about, each separate film, of course. But I couldn't put it in a sentence. I'd have to talk through each whole film, what I'm hoping people will get from each scene, and how the scenes overlap and support or contradict each other.

You don't like the idea that your body of work stands for something?

No, I'd love it to! I'd be very happy if it did. I'm just not at all sure what. Sometimes they're about me, you know? I mean, the first film I made was very autobiographical, about my boarding school. And when I went back to school to make that film, I had all the same feelings I had being in school: the hatred of adults and of authority, and the hatred of class and being told not to notice the people working in the kitchens, the hatred of the parents, you know? Everything. It was a revenge film. Others aren't about me at all. They're about all sorts of things.

More than any other filmmaker I know, when you look at all your films together, there seems to be something or a set of things that you really want people to get, something that you really want to say. And it's consistent over a number of films.

Yes. I really do want there to be something.

What, though?

This is the dream: for a homophobic man to watch *Shinjuku Boys* and come out and feel differently. You know, my dad was an extreme racist. I would have loved him to watch *Rough Aunties* and be changed by it. I could never say anything to him. I was almost mute around him when I was growing up. I was on the receiving end of so much hate and racism and homophobia – all these horrible feelings. I didn't know any good feelings. What I would have loved is for him – he's dead now, thank God – for him to watch *Rough Aunties* and just suddenly see Mildred and feel affection for her. You see, that's what I want. And once it happens, then all sorts of things are possible.

Is that the thing that you're driving at: openness to ideas and different ways of living?

Yes, that's it. I'm so lucky I live the life I do and I have very close friends who are gay and from different cultures. But I grew up with people who had such a fear of outsiders and 'the other'. If people have those fears, I want to help them to overcome them. When I was a child, I wasn't really allowed in my parents' bedroom. But I remember one day going through my dad's cupboard, and I found these magazines, called *Man Alive*, and they were all these more or less naked men with muscles. There was a whole stack of them in his bedside cupboard. I can't remember much about my parents from my childhood, but I remember that. I never mentioned it because I knew it was not fit to mention. I think all the bad things that people feel are based on not knowing. I think that prejudice is really based on fear. I wouldn't normally talk about this – I usually let the films speak for themselves – but, as you're pushing me (very politely), I'll try. I think a lot of my dad's anger came from his fears. He was always on the verge of explosive rage. You know, he would talk about black people in such a kind of violent, pent-up, sexual way. And it only occurred to me after I'd left home a long time later, that everything he said was sexual and that maybe it was connected to his own ambivalent sexual feelings that he was ashamed of. Now if he could have seen and appreciated *Shinjuku Boys*, it might have made a difference to him.

So if I'm harping on any theme, it's the need to make an imaginative leap into someone else's life and understand them and love them at the end of it. I want people to see the world through someone else's eyes. I think it makes us better people. I lived my childhood through one way of seeing the world. And I saw how it destroyed my parents. It destroyed our childhoods. At my boarding school, there was a terrible fear of outsiders. You were made to feel you were better than other people. But at the same time, nobody showed you any love. So I've lived through, both at home and at school, what it's like when you live with people that have absolutely no love and are frightened of everything that is not within their realm of experience. My mum was from a mining village in Wales, and she took elocution lessons and wanted to be posh. My dad was a fascist, a proper one. Look, this is the only thing I have of his [*shows me a district officer's badge for a British fascist organisation*]. And the two of them were against pretty much everything, and gave back almost nothing. So I suppose, in a way, if you're asking me what I'm really trying to do with my films, I'm hoping they're a sort of antidote to that, the opposite of that. So they're inclusive and non-judgemental, and they invite you to use your imagination. They're a response to hatred and fear. They're saying, 'Be open to change. Things can change. You can change.' I never rebelled when I was younger. I never dared stand up to my dad. I was terrified of him. I tried to avoid trouble at school. Then I went and lived on the streets. I wanted to die, really. I didn't want to be or do anything. I got very ill. And then film school and filmmaking saved my life. I suppose that is what it's all about. I don't really want people to know about it, but all the people I film are so honest, I suppose I should be too.

Who are your films aimed at?

I suppose I'm aiming them at the widest possible audience, and that's partly why I try to make them as accessible and dramatic as possible. That's why I'm trying to make them like the experience of watching a fiction film, because I'd like them to get big audiences.

Is there a danger with films like yours and someone like Michael Moore – films made according to a certain mould – of preaching to the converted? I'd say you, more than most directors, have committed fans of your work.

I don't think you can worry too much about that. When I'm filming a scene and maybe thinking, 'Wow, I'm really glad I'm filming this because people are going to see it,' I'm thinking of my friend Tony or my friend Colin. I'm thinking of people I'm very close to. I think that's all you can do. And you do your best to capture what's happening in front of you. The other thing to say is that my films get seen on television as well as in cinemas, and television brings films to a much wider audience. I meet people who say, 'Oh, I was just channel-hopping last night and I watched one of your films ...' Or they might watch a film like *Pink Saris* because they've got a next-door neighbour who's Indian. You know, people can casually come to a film, rather than having to make a conscious decision to watch it, as they would in the cinema.

Are your films conceived as international films for an international audience or are you aiming to bring the world back to Britain? I think your message, if it's okay to call it that, is quite universal: 'Open your mind. Things can change' – it's a very humanist sentiment. It could be meaningful for people in pretty much any country.

I just want my films to be seen by as many people as possible. *Rough Aunties* was sold to loads and loads of TV channels around the world, which was great. But again, I don't think you can be worrying about whether your audience is mainly British or international when you're making a film. You just have to make as honest a film as you can, and be prepared for films not to travel very well. You can quite easily tie yourself in knots when you're making a film, worrying about too much. You just have to do your very best. That's all you can do. That said, if the way I make films means that they work across boundaries and different cultures, then that makes me very happy. *Rough Aunties* just went out on TV in Britain, and it got criticised for lack of information about South Africa, which I did find a bit hurtful and upsetting. You know, you put so much into making a film, and then you feel like you've failed. But if that lack of information makes it more of a universal story, so that more people can apply it to their own lives, then that's a good thing from where I'm standing. If I'd filled *Rough Aunties* with information about South Africa, it would have been about South Africa, rather than being a universal story about people helping others and fighting for change. I hope the way I made the film allows you to apply it to your own life.

In academia, everything that people write is a contribution to a debate. Is that true of your films? Are you aiming to contribute to a debate or a discussion?

Well, Ziba, whom I made *Divorce Iranian Style* with, she's a lecturer in Sharia law, so she uses the film. She teaches every year at NYU and she uses *Divorce* and *Runaway* as part of her course. And I'm really happy that she can do that. She'll show them excerpts and say, 'This is what this is saying and this is what that's saying.'

But do you feel like that's what you're doing when you're making films – contributing to a debate about human rights or women's rights, or whatever it might be?

Yes, I suppose so, in a broad way. But I can't say I follow discussions on the subject of human rights. The films are all about human rights but they're stories first and foremost. The films I like least are the ones where you feel there's an agenda, which you have to follow and probably agree with. Fiction films like *This is England* or *My Beautiful Laundrette*, both of which I think are brilliant, subtle films, don't do that. They make you *live* the film, and they get to you that way. They're *exploring* things, through stories. I'm trying to do the same.

What's the difference between you and Michael Moore, say?

I have things I want people to take away from my films, whereas he's different because he's got things he wants to say. With *Bowling for Columbine*, for example, he has a definite agenda. I watched *Bowling for Columbine* and I went on the ride very willingly. I loved his agenda in that film. It was an important film. He was dealing with really specific, important things at a specific point in time. He was conducting a campaign and mobilising an argument. And, of course, doing it in a really funny, entertaining way. It makes you feel strong to laugh at what you fear. You can feel it in the audience when you go to see one of his films – everyone feels stronger for watching it. All of his films are like that: *Capitalism: A Love Story, Sicko*, all of them have an agenda. And that's what makes him completely different. I would say he's the complete opposite of me. But don't get me wrong, he's one of my heroes. There's so much news coverage now that it's just baffling. They give you all these facts but you don't know what the fuck is going on. It creates a thirst for perspective, I think, and Michael Moore caters to that. He tells you how it really is. I know he can be a bit grand, but I don't care if he stays at The Ritz with his entourage. I don't care if he has a publicist and twenty other people following him around. He's a hero for our times.

I can see that Michael Moore's films have an agenda. But don't Sisters in Law *and* Runaway *have an agenda as well?*

I suppose they're saying that women should have rights, but that's a pretty obvious agenda. That's not really an agenda.

Isn't it?

Not really. I think *seeing* that something is wrong is more powerful and effective than being *told* that something is wrong. You really can't change people by just telling them to change. *Experience* is what changes people, not being told things. Like with *Pink Saris*, you're *seeing* the caste system in action, and what it really means in practice, in people's everyday lives. You get lost in the story, and then you're *living* it. The film isn't *saying* anything. The film just shows it. I'm not saying what the film's about or what the message is. You're *seeing* it, and *experiencing* it. That's the difference.

Are you not saying it by recording it (albeit in a very quiet and patient and unobtrusive way) and editing it and organising it into a film?

Yes, yes, yes. But, you see, what I'm against is people saying things to me. I generally don't want somebody hammering a point home to me when I'm watching a film, and I certainly don't want to do that myself. Personally, I think it's a less persuasive and impactful way of going about things. Michael Moore is in total control with his films. He writes a script and he sets things up. He makes arguments and he appeals to your intellect. I want to appeal to your emotions. I want you to watch my films and for little bombs to go off, maybe in the cinema or maybe much later when something triggers your memory. Michael Moore uses people almost like conduits for ideas, and he does it brilliantly, of course, whereas I want the characters in my film to be what the film is all about, so that people can identify with them and get to know them. I want my mum to watch *Divorce Iranian Style* and think, 'That's me! That's what my life is like.' By getting people to identify with my characters and live life through them for a short while, I'm trying to open little doors in people's lives, and get them to look at and think about their own lives slightly differently.

159

I can't think of many other directors who have assembled a coherent, meaningful body of work like yours. Why is that, do you think? Is it getting harder to do?

It certainly is hard, but it always has been. It took me two years to make *Divorce Iranian Style*, and that was all I was doing. We were just doggedly hanging on to raise the money, and maybe a lot of people can't afford to do that. It seemed like an impossible film with impossible access, and I'm not very good at selling ideas, because they'd say, 'Is it about this?' and whatever they said, I'd say, 'No, not really,' and drive them mad like I've been driving you mad. And then when we did eventually get the cash, the only reason was because Peter Moore was just about to leave Channel 4 and he said, 'Oh, go on, then. If it'll shut you up.' I was really amazed, and he said, 'Get out of my sight, before I change my mind.' I didn't have kids to support, I was sharing a flat, so I was incredibly persistent. I think if a film really is the most important thing in your life, and you give everything else up to do it, then you can make sure that the film gets made.

I think also the reason that not many people make the sorts of films I do is that most directors are trying to make films they think that commissioning editors want, and commissioning editors are very risk-averse these days. They want films to be frothy and light and have a happy ending, and they're quite suspicious of any film that has a point to make or sounds too worthy. Or films like mine, where it's very hard to make promises about what you're going to come back with. I suppose there's always the possibility that you might come back with nothing. I go to a place and find my film when I'm there, which is scary, of course. I usually don't sleep for the first three weeks and my heart's going and I'm thinking, 'Why am I doing this? I hate this! Why am I putting myself through this? Where are the stories going to come from?' It always feels impossible. With *The Day I Will Never Forget*, even the people I was working with kept saying, 'You know we'll never get any access, don't you? Because people are so secretive about circumcision. It's just not possible.' When I think of it now, I think I must have been mad. But you hold your nerve and you have a bit of luck, and away you go. I've made my life very much so that I've only got myself to be responsible for. So every film that I want to make, I don't stop until I get it commissioned and get it made. I just don't give up, you know?

Do you think films are always better when they have an agenda or something they want to say?

I think it can be so painful and stressful making films, and you go away from home for months, and it's often physically quite tough, and emotionally as well, and you're giving up so much ... I wouldn't want to make a film and put myself through all that without there being something in it that people can relate to. It's only worth doing if you can send your audience away touched and maybe changed by watching it. It has to mean something. There are so many documentaries you watch and you think, 'Why am I bothering?' The ones that stay with you are the ones that are really about something. Like I think Nick Broomfield's best film is *Aileen: Life and Death of a Serial Killer* because he really has got something to say in that film. And that's because he was really changed by what happened when he was making it, getting sucked into the legal processes of someone (someone he knew and cared about) waiting to die on death row. I know Nick really well, and I've lived through all his films with him. *Aileen* shocked him and changed him and made the films that came after much more engaged and less flip and playful. The great thing about it as a film is that it has real clarity of purpose because Nick cared so much. It's impossible to watch that film and think the death penalty is a good idea. It exposes the whole system by which people are put to death as corrupt. It's devastating as a film, and you're swept along by it.

I feel when I'm making films that that's when I'm really alive. I feel absolutely alive – when you're in the moment, and it's a special moment, or even if it's a bad moment, you just feel totally alive. I feel full of purpose. I think making the films I make is the whole point of me. If I weren't doing this, I sometimes think there wouldn't be any point in me at all, you know?

9 Thinking in pictures
James Marsh

James Marsh is the director of the Oscar-winning feature documentary *Man on Wire* (2008), the story of 'the artistic crime of the century', Philippe Petit's wire-walk between the Twin Towers in the World Trade Center in 1974. The film draws on footage shot by Petit and his co-conspirators, stylised dramatic reconstructions and still images of the climactic wire-walk itself.

Marsh's other films include: *Wisconsin Death Trip* (2000), a hypnotic black and white documentary that brings to life an extraordinary collection of photographs and local newspaper reports documenting the harshness of life in the remote city of Black River Falls, Wisconsin, at the end of the nineteenth century; and *Project Nim* (2011), about a chimpanzee named Nim Chimpsky who was the subject of a landmark study in language acquisition, and the various humans he came into contact with. Marsh's films are distinguished by their polished, crafted feel and memorable, carefully designed imagery, in marked contrast to the prevailing documentary aesthetic, defined by improvisation and hand-held observational camerawork.

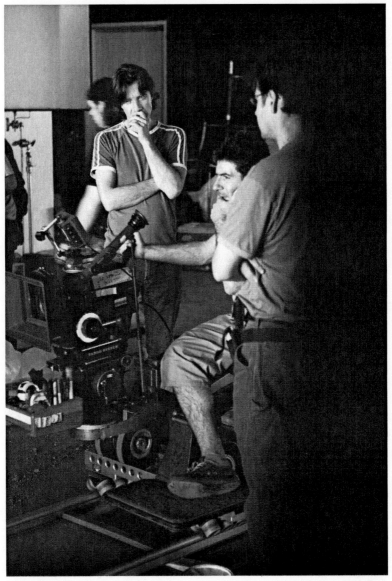

James Marsh (centre, standing), during the making of Man on Wire. © Dave Dilley/Red Box Films.

I wondered if we could talk about the 'look' of documentaries. It struck me, watching your films, that they have incredibly strong images in them that are quite often beautiful, in a way that Paul Watson's films, say, or Kim Longinotto's films, or Nick Broomfield's, are not. Those directors sometimes seem to go out of their way to be not very interested in the way a film looks.

That's a very interesting question and observation. I think by the act of shooting anything you're mindful of the texture of the image you're creating, whether you're shooting on a very cheap domestic format or shooting on 35mm film. I think each of those filmmakers might well take issue with you on that observation, but to take Frederick Wiseman as an example, who works very much in the observational mode of documentary filmmaking, I find his films incredibly beautiful and very strange and unsettling, because the framings and compositions are so well chosen and suited to what he's doing. So I think everyone who is working in manufacturing or capturing visual images is aware at some level of their aesthetic quality, even if they choose, as you say, not to be overtly concerned with it.

Because I largely make films that you could call constructed – there are observational elements in some of the work I've done, and one whole film that's observational from start to finish, but generally they are constructed around elements like archive film or photographs – it's always felt to me from very early on that you should create images yourself to serve your story and help you expose what you think the essence and the truths of the situation are. I suppose, because what I do is very constructed, I'm coming at filmmaking in a much more detached way than a director who's observing a story as it unfolds before them. I've done that, and I actually found it very hard. I wasn't suited to that form of filmmaking. Instead, what I do is write a fairly detailed outline of what I think the story might be, being very mindful that as you talk to people and go deeper into the story it's almost certainly going to change. I definitely have in most subjects I choose a thought or idea for organising it before I shoot anything. I'm dealing with stories that in a sense already exist and I'm like an archaeologist; I get to try to expose what the building was, and then in a sense add to that building – make it more complete. In that respect, I've always been very concerned about the creation of images that I think serve the story that I'm telling. It goes way back to some of the earlier work that I did at *Arena* at the BBC [the broadcaster's flagship arts strand], which is where I started out as a director – the idea that you could go and shoot reconstructions, or images that were definitely yours, that you were creating to help tell the story. And if you're going to create images, it always felt to me that you need to make them memorable and appropriate in equal measure. If something is memorable and striking, images can stand for a lot more than just themselves. They are my way of illustrating to you what the story is.

So, for example, when I approach a film on the level of reconstruction, I try to do it so that it's not just random cutaways to cover up the absence of other images. I try to approach reconstruction so that it can stand alone. If you look at the reconstruction in *Man on Wire*, for example, they're proper scenes. They're not just an image to cover up the absence of any other imagery. There's something much more intentional about them. Lots of documentaries use quite vague imagery, quite generic imagery, and often generic archive too. My view is that I like to be very precise in what I do. If I'm going to create an image, I'll think about it a lot. A lot of my reference points aren't other documentaries. I guess I try to work with a lexicon of the whole of cinema, not just documentaries. My interest has always been in the whole of cinema, and I've made fictional films, as you know – features – which only tends to reinforce my approach to documentary: that they're very constructed and that they're composed of imagery which you make yourself.

There's one film I made called *Wisconsin Death Trip*, which is in a sense defined by my attempt to create moving imagery based on a photographic world – these very interesting glass plate negatives and black and white images. That film was a very aesthetic undertaking. I knew that the film had to have a very powerful visual element and be very seductive, in a way, because there was no form there. It was a film without much structure. So the idea was to create a film that was a cinematic experience. You'd sit and let it happen to you, kind of wash over you, as opposed to it being based on information or a linear structure. It was a very impressionistic film, and therefore it did have a strong aesthetic that we tried to be consistent with, so that the film has an overall aesthetic integrity.

Wisconsin Death Trip *feels very dream-like and hypnotic.*

That was very intentional. The state of dreaming is the nearest thing we have to watching a film in a cinema. And the filmmakers I like, including Frederick

Wiseman oddly enough, do feel very close to the state of dreaming. I love David Lynch's films for that reason: you feel like you're in someone else's dream. The very act of watching a film in a cinema is dream-like; you get into a different state. The lights go down, it's dark, and you have this kind of mind's eye projection that you can enjoy. In a sense, that film was trying to create very potent imagery that was only going to work if it came together like a kind of visual dream; it wasn't going to work if it was very dry and just photographs. You can compare *Wisconsin Death Trip* and a film by Ken Burns [director of archive-based documentaries such as *Baseball* (1994) and *Prohibition* (2011)], where he uses some of the same sources that I might use – historical photographs and records of whatever period he's dealing with – but he handles them in a very different way than I do. I would much prefer, personally, to pursue something that is visually richer and more interesting and more *aesthetic*, if you like, than the rather drier and more straightforward approach of someone like Ken Burns.

It's quite descriptive, isn't it, the Ken Burns approach? Very show-and-tell.

It's very predictable. You know what you're in for. There'll be still images; there'll be some fiddle music on the soundtrack; and there'll be a sonorous voice reading a historical document for you. And that's about it. All his films seem to be variations on that technique. It's no surprise that he was adopted by corporate sponsorship and PBS so easily, because he's no threat to anybody with what he does. He's just reinforcing America's mythology.

The individual images in Wisconsin Death Trip *have a pronounced dream-like quality. What was it about the way you filmed them that give them that feel?*

We went into that film with very clear intentions, and some of those were based on technical choices. The whole of that film was shot at thirty frames per second, not twenty or twenty-four. It was shot on Super-16 and all shot in black and white, but we shot it all slightly off frame-rate, so there's something odd in how you regard that, even though you get used to it. Some of it is overtly slow motion, but the whole film is shot at thirty frames per second. It feels like you're slightly fogging time like that; you're controlling time in an odd way, and that's one of the reasons why it feels like a strange experience to watch.

The whole look of the film was based on these extraordinary photographs, these huge glass plate negatives. Our job was really to create a film where what we shot was going to absolutely blend with the existing source materials and feel like part of the same aesthetic, so we often used quite wide shots as well in that film. Generally, the idea was to make them like dioramas. So it wasn't acting – it was figures moving in a landscape. It was more like a silent movie, and indeed it was all shot mute. There was no dialogue in the film at all. In a sense, by the nature of the challenge, it created a very interesting aesthetic that was quite unusual for any film, let alone a documentary.

Were they filmed on a track as well, the images? They often feel like they're drifting.

Yes. I guess in some respects I was being a little indulgent. Some of them are really quite ... not showing off exactly, but they are really. That was the first time I had the means to do that stuff, even though the film was a very low-budget movie. We knew we had to create something that was striving to be cinematic, and in that respect I was creating shots that were really quite elaborate.

It's remarkable, I think, in that film but also in Man on Wire, *how long you can look at a still image. Actually, when you go beyond a certain point, the longer you look at it, the more mesmerising the image becomes.*

It becomes something else, and that's true even when you're sitting in the street looking at something. If you keep looking and looking, something will change. And it's not just time that's doing that, it's the way you process something. This comes out of a fairly deep obsession I have with still imagery, generally. I've studied it and looked at it. Again, *Wisconsin Death Trip* was a very important project in that respect. It really turned me on to the power of the single image, and how one image can be so powerful. Again, if you ponder an image and behold it for long enough, you begin to project something on to it. The viewer begins a relationship with it. You let people look at something long enough to lose themselves in it. With *Man on Wire* that became a very important consideration, because there was no moving footage of the main event of the story. We had a film that was constructed around this amazing event and we had no means of really showing it to you apart from still images. I trusted, from my experience with *Wisconsin Death Trip*, in the power of still imagery to

167

tell you a story, and to tell a story emotionally and dramatically, not just descriptively. A still is a description of an event; it's a freeze frame of one twenty-fourth of a second. But in the climax of *Man on Wire*, some people think they've actually seen moving images in that sequence. But there are none, trust me.

Because they're animating it in their minds?

The walk was difficult. You had to appreciate how high the stakes were. It was high up and it was scary. There was talk of how we were going to do this; were we going to do it in CGI? (We had quite a big special-effects budget.) Were we going to have him against a blue screen? All those ideas felt very foolish, in a way, because there's no way you can re-create that walk. We thought about it, and I flirted with this idea and that idea, but very quickly realised that even trying to re-create it would be a silly thing to do. The best thing we had were those little fragments, those little moments that had been caught on still cameras.

But, before I could show those stills, I knew I had to create something that was really going to raise the stakes for this whole sequence. And, in the end, all the special-effects budget I had I spent on one shot, this shot that creeps over the side of the World Trade Center and looks down. It's all a big CGI special effect and it didn't last for more than five seconds in the film. But that shot created this illusion that people had that there was moving footage in the sequence. More importantly for me, it made everyone go, 'Oh fuck, that's really a long way down, and he's going to go and dance on that! Oh my God, that's pretty terrifying!' Then you've created a sense of fear. I'm terrified of heights so I'm the right person to design one shot to show vertigo. I really am very uncomfortable high up. That was why the film was interesting for me, because I've often had dreams where I'm high up and I'm flipping out. That one shot allowed the still sequence to work in a really quite different way.

It's all about structure and technique, how you achieve what you want to achieve. Often you do it in ways that are very manipulative, if you think about it. But they have to be. You want people to trust you as a storyteller and feel that they're in capable hands from the moment the film opens, that you're in control and you're going to lead them through this story in a way that's emotionally powerful.

What is it about the images of the wire-walk that gives them their power? Because they do have amazing power – they stay with you.

You know him so well at this point. You know this character, you know what he's like, you know what's at stake. And I never had any question in my mind that what he was doing was artistic in a very profound way. It's a transformation. He's taking these two huge buildings and humanising them, making them something different for the forty minutes he was on the wire. I always saw it as a very beautiful and subversive undertaking, and I think the images show you that. They show you the beauty of it at least, and that's the main thing. I found what he did very beautiful. It's at the limit of human possibility to do something like that. He's just one little guy out on a tightrope. That felt to me like one of the bravest things I've ever seen in my life, and indeed one of the most beautiful.

I think that what makes the images so powerful is that his walking between the Twin Towers reclaims them, and transforms them from this symbol of destruction into something very positive.

That's what we now think. What's interesting is that the film invites the viewer to reinterpret their perceptions of something. The buildings have an immediately tragic connotation now, and yet, at the same time, if you enter into this story which happened in 1974, you kind of take the curse off, just by following one person and their obsessive fixation on these buildings, and their plans for it, which are beautiful plans, not destructive plans. I think the subtext of that film is enormous and impossible for me to control, so the best thing to do was not to go there, and tell the story as best I could, knowing that every single person who was going to see the film, almost without exception, would know about the fate of the Towers. It's a very interesting relationship that every person will have with that film, even if they don't really care about the Twin Towers. Everyone is aware of that abiding fact about them. Because you can't control how people respond, and because everyone is going to have a different response, it felt to me that the right thing to do was not to confuse the two issues, and allow everyone to have some kind of subjective response. Every film you make is completed by the person who is watching it, in my view. It's not complete until it's been watched: that's the point of it. Even if only one person watches it, that's fine, it's completed at that point. That film, in particular, I knew was going to be completed more profoundly by the viewer.

The reconstructions in Man on Wire *become quite impressionistic, as they get closer to the climax of the film.*

Indeed, that was very conscious. As the reconstructions unfold in the timeline of the film, they become less and less realistic and more and more fantastical and fairy-tale-like. By the end of the characters' journey to the Towers, when they're up on the roof, it's like they're on the moon at this point. So I was very consciously trying to reflect that, so that the film becomes more and more cartoon-like, and more and more fanciful, as what he's doing becomes more and more real. It felt like a very interesting tension. It was also a way of embracing the given situation, that we don't have the Twin Towers any more. I couldn't film them. I couldn't film inside them. It felt to me that they became much more ghost-like as the story unfolded, and that we embraced that to some extent.

Your new film is about dreams. It sounds like it's going to be full of imagery.

Well, it's an attempt to use some of the thinking and ideas that I had in *Wisconsin Death Trip* in something with a much more definite structure to it. It's a film that is proving hard to get going, both financially and creatively. It needs time for it to really work, but the basic idea is very simple. I came upon a dream diary that's actually warehoused with a bunch of other dream diaries at an academic institution in California, which is devoted to sleep research. I got in touch with them because I found out about them and wanted to know what they were about. The professor there recommended one particular dream diary to me, which was by an old Jewish man who is still alive and lives in Toronto. He'd recorded every dream that he'd ever had of the woman that he was in love with throughout his life. If she was in the dream, he'd write it down, and this goes across maybe thirty-odd years of dreaming. So what you have is a series of 165 dreams, all of which have the same person in. And because they span quite a chunk of his life, and they go on after she dies, you can construct a kind of love story out of the dream diary. You can lay out a sequence of dreams that show the course of this affair, this obsession he had. Sometimes they're very fragmentary. Sometimes they're very funny and sexy, and sometimes they're just weird. But they have great emotional resonance and I organised them to be like a love story, with a beginning, a middle and an end. It starts with dreams where clearly he's infatuated with this woman though he doesn't quite know who she is. There are dreams where they actually get married, and have children, then he has an affair with somebody and the dreams start reflecting this estrangement, then they reconcile and there are dreams that show their reconciliation. When they reconcile, she has a terminal illness, and that plays out in the dreams too. Then she dies and that plays out in the dreams. The whole film is a kind of tender, doomed love story constructed from real dreams.

Whether it's a documentary or not ... I've no fucking idea what you'd call it, what genre it is. But it's image-based, and I'm going to appropriate this man's dreams – with his consent, his encouragement, in fact – and dramatise them to show you this love story through the unfiltered subconscious of dreams and dream imagery. They're real dreams, they're written down, and we'll hear them, probably read out, in the film in some shape or form. But the film will be a very impressionistic, visual journey into this affair. Now whether this is ever going to be watchable is another matter altogether. I don't know. But, emotionally, it has an architecture that is strong enough to invite you into this dream-world. The film will have to be very dream-like, I guess, and visually very strong for this to work. It's a tough film to sell, even to a viewer, because the cliché is true: other people's dreams are kind of boring. But if I manage to organise them in the right way, and I'm rigorous about the emotional journey you can go on with these dreams, I think it could be a very interesting project.

It's one that I have to do, but I don't quite know how to do it, and that's always a very good starting point for a film – that you're intrigued, but you have no fucking clue how you're going to pull it off. I have to be potentially defeated by a subject in order to want to do it. *Wisconsin Death Trip* started that way. I had no idea how I was going to make that film. But I knew there was something I could get at. This is the same thing, this dream film, if it happens ... I can't die without it happening, so it'll get done.

There's a sense in which the climax to Man on Wire *is quite dream-like as well.*

That's very much what we were aiming at, in terms of the way it was scored and the way it was offered. If you were fortunate enough to be walking downtown on that morning, what the fuck would you think? You'd think you were tripping. There's a guy so far up, walking not just once to show you he can do it, but giving you a performance in the air, at the top of the World Trade Center. It's absolutely like a dream. The fact that he created something so brilliant and so visual that it's like a dream is part of the reason why I loved the act itself so much. I loved it not only for how he did it and what it now means, perhaps, but just for its own sake, in a way. That is the definition of art: he does it only for its own sake. There's no other reason behind it. You wouldn't ask a painter why he painted or a musician why he made music. That's why the questions after the walk were so funny and so pointless. If you're going to ask the question, you're really missing the point. But, yes, it is absolutely trying to create a dream-like experience for the viewer, because I'm sure that's a quality it had at the time as well.

Man on Wire has this kind of heist structure, and the story of the undertaking is very compelling. But is there a sense in which all of that story is there just to set up this transcendent, dream-like finale?

The heist structure of the film was really the first and probably the only idea of how to structure it, and how to organise it. But that's how Philippe regards it himself, and that's his character. He would watch TV shows and movies that were about robbing banks and stealing things. So the heist structure was there because that was what it was like as far as he was concerned. It did involve essentially a criminal conspiracy between people to do something that was illegal, and the brilliance of it is that they're not going to steal anything. They're going to *give* something. No one is going to get hurt. Nothing is getting stolen; it's a gift. That's just a brilliant inversion of a heist movie, because usually it's about stealing from other people and taking what's not yours.

The structure of the film also allowed me, more importantly as a filmmaker, to take an event where you pretty much know what the outcome is and make it surprising. The poster of the film both in the UK and the US was he's on the wire, there's no issue there, and clearly he's alive the moment you see him. So then it became one of the challenges of the film to try to dramatise the process to make the result seem uncertain. And, by God, when you look at the minutiae of the story, it absolutely was. There were so many points where it could easily not have happened. The structure also allows you to consider his life in a different way. It seemed to me that you had an obvious structure where you could create a very dramatic entry into the film by saying, 'This is the day they're going to do it, and this is going to unfold, and things are not going to go the way you think they're going to go.' But within that structure you can very easily flash back to the way in which this came about in the first place, both in terms of his wire-walking career, and in terms of how this event came into being. Then when he finally goes out on to the wire, it's a huge relief, and also, I think, you feel properly invested in its success as well. It's a proper climax. And you can lose yourself in the dream as well.

The way around not having footage was to allow you the point of view of those that most cared about what was going on, i.e. those that had helped Philippe. They all became very emotional – every single person who remembered and talked about it was very tearful. They had a big investment in what was happening, and it's very proper to let them purely recall. Everyone was looking up when they were talking in the interview, which was really quite charming and amazing, to see everyone unconsciously look up as they were recalling the event.

It seems to me that a lot of people who work in documentaries are suspicious of imagery, because they see it as being slippery.

Indeed, or somehow dishonest, and not appropriate to what the medium should be about. I have absolutely no suspicions of created imagery or image-based filmmaking. I have some sympathy with the point of view that somehow I'm being more manipulative that way, or I'm imposing an aesthetic that is my own on to my subject matter. But we're all doing that, really. The moment you make an edit, everything changes. I'm not sure I'm aware of any documentary film that runs in one single take, though I would say that some of the best scenes in documentaries, in observational films, tend to give you a very full idea of what the time frame is of the scene. I think what I do is to construct films around stories that are pre-existing, and it's my pleasure and my duty to create compelling and appropriate imagery. You want to give the audience, the viewer, an experience, as well as lay out a story for them. What I'm not doing is making arguments; I'm not making a political argument. You could argue that that's way more of a manipulation than what I do. I'm just trying to tell you the story the best way I can.

So I don't think any of us should be criticised for embracing imagery. But I would say that I reached the limits of that with a filmmaker that I hugely admire, and have been influenced by, Errol Morris. I thought that *Standard Operating Procedure* [a film about an infamous series of photographs taken inside

Abu Ghraib prison in 2003, which revealed abuse of prisoners by American soldiers] took what I do, and what he does, into a realm I was actually very uncomfortable with. I wasn't at all comfortable with the imagery that he created for that film. I think he's a brilliant documentary filmmaker in the same genre as I'd like to see myself in, but that film was one where the existing imagery was so powerful, so truthful and so revealing that to create aestheticised versions of it didn't work for me very well.

Do you set out to make films that are beautiful?

Well, I think I'm mindful of the medium's aesthetic possibilities, to put it in a florid way. I'm mindful that, if someone gives you a camera and you have resources, that you can use them, if you like, to create images that you find potent and appropriate and powerful, and that can exist really for their own sake, and *Death Trip* has quite a lot of those sorts of images in it. It feels to me that it's a privilege. If someone gives me a 16mm camera, I'm going to try to make a film look as interesting as possible. I'm not sure how many of us in documentary filmmaking are interested in cameras and lenses and film stock. But I'm absolutely fucking fascinated, obsessed by them, and their properties and possibilities, and I make very clear choices about what lenses I'm going to use, and what cameras and what film stock.

And, for me, it's always a huge collaboration with the DoP on all of my documentaries. You know, we watch films together, we talk about ideas and visual strategies. A very, very important part of how I approach a film is how it's going to look. That look could be very artificial. It could be very personal to me. But it has to be one I feel is appropriate to the subject. It feels like part of the joy of what one can do as a director – how powerful and seductive your images can be.

Black and white photography is something that you keep coming back to – it's in both Wisconsin Death Trip *and* Man on Wire. *What is it about black and white...?*

That's a great question. It's just a personal interest of mine: photography and imagery and the great photographers. And photography is a medium that flourished very much in black and white, as much as in colour. There's a purity about black and white. I mean, you learn a lot from black and white about composition, because composition is incredibly important in black and white photography. It's a big consideration, which is different when you're shooting in colour. So it's very much born out of a personal interest. *Wisconsin Death Trip* was the project that turned me on to the power of photography generally, and I studied – endlessly studied – all the great photographers. I like the photographer Atget who shot Paris at the turn of the twentieth century, sort of ghostly images, really amazing. And Koudelka I love, who is a Czech photographer. So I studied photography, and, of course, anything that you're personally obsessed with and enjoy is bound to have an impact on your work.

When I say studied, I would sit with a beer and photographic books and just love them and lose myself in them, and try to understand how the aesthetics of black and white cinematography worked through black and white stills and studying the great masters. Photography and visual imagery became a real resource for me as a filmmaker, a way of nourishing myself and sort of refreshing myself all the way through a project. *Wisconsin* became very much a homage to my own interest in black and white photography. And that, I guess, was played out again in *Man on Wire*. There's an aesthetic choice involved too. You're not offering up something that is completely realistic if you are working in black and white. You're creating something that is already becoming not real. Because the world isn't black and white, it's colour.

Do you think documentaries that are more interested in images and the aesthetic part of filmmaking are more long lasting?

That's a very interesting question. I'm not sure so much that they are or they aren't. Certainly, a film that has very strong aesthetics has that going for it; there's a whole other element to it that you can respond to. But I think that any excellent film in the documentary genre – whether it's *The Thin Blue Line*, which is very constructed, or a Wiseman film which is based only on raw footage – if a film is excellent, then it's going to survive.

There are definitely image-based films that don't look nearly as clever as they did when we first saw them. One of those films, actually, for me is *Koyaanisqatsi*, which is an interesting and beautiful visual poem. It doesn't interest me nearly as much as *The Thin Blue Line* still does, but certainly they're both films that are still on our radar. I think there's no superior version of the documentary. There's no version that we should all be aspiring to, and that will endure or survive. If a film is good, it will survive. It will keep finding an audience.

175

Your films are all very original, not least visually. Are you looking for original subject matter, material that will allow you to make very original and visual films, when you're looking for projects?

I think so. I mean, I think you're always looking for something that's going to be formally challenging on a level of technique. With *Wisconsin Death Trip*, there was no reference point for that film, no precedent, or at least nothing that I was aware of. There was nothing that I saw and felt, 'It's going to be like that,' though one film that was important to me was a Russian Soviet film called *Man with a Movie Camera*, which is a sort of symphony of imagery that just hits you and rolls you over by the power of its editing and the power of its images. So I wanted *Wisconsin Death Trip* to be original. And it was, on my part, a conscious effort to really enjoy image-making and the resources of cinema, if you like – the tracking shots and crane shots and how cinema can be so powerful as an experience.

The way I came to want to be a filmmaker was going to movies when I was a child and just being so excited by the idea of it going dark, and that something is going to fucking happen on this big screen, and it's going to be amazing and you're going to feel something. I used to always try to find films that had lots of sex and violence in them because they were taboo. We were all trying to see films that had lots of nudity in. So, in other words, I'm really stimulated by the visual image. I'm a voyeur, essentially. I'm very aware of my voyeuristic tendencies, and I'm voyeuristic in life to some extent, too. I love sitting down in a café and just watching people, or in a bar – just observing body language and little glimpses of conversation.

They're quite hard to define, your films. They're quite hard to pin down.

The bane of my life has been that every film I make feels like it's self-contained; it doesn't lead to the next one. So I have to start all over again, which may be a by-product of trying to do something, each time, that challenges me and is trying to be, in some way, original. That has sometimes been a struggle in terms of work. Actually, every film I've ever made I've always felt very, very unsatisfied by. There's that moment when you sit back and watch it in the final part of the filmmaking process, usually the sound mix, and you sit back and you think, 'Oh, there's another one I've fucked up.' I get quite embarrassed by the work at that point, which is why you keep doing it, and trying again and changing things and looking to improve. If I felt that I'd made the perfect film, I'd probably just give up.

Other top directors will tend to make the same film over and over, like Kim Longinotto, for example.

Well, I think that that has real virtues for a director, to understand what you do and then just find very interesting areas to explore. Like Wiseman – you could say that he's the best example of a director who knows exactly what his method is, but it's endlessly applicable to the subjects he chooses. And similarly, Michael Moore ... Personally, I think you have to challenge yourself, while being very aware that you're making something that you want people to watch. Every film should teach you something. You should learn something, both intellectually and morally perhaps, but also technically. Every film should refine part of what you do. But that's just for me, that's how I work. That's why none of my films really looks like another I've made.

Your films are unusually quite complex in the sense that there's a lot going on in them; they have a lot of levels.

There are definitely layers, both to the filmmaking and to the narrative structure, that are quite complicated to achieve. The idea is that you make it effortless to consume. *Man on Wire* was actually quite a complicated structure, even though it came across as simple. To achieve that really wasn't easy. You're working with images you create yourself; you're working with photographs; you're working with archive; you're working with sound design. I'm in the middle of a film right now [*Project Nim*] and it's really fucking difficult. It's about a chimpanzee that's taken from its natural chimp mother when it's born and given to a human mother, and the objective is an experiment run by Columbia University to teach the chimpanzee sign language. Essentially, the film is the life story of a chimpanzee who is always under our control, and the chimp goes on this extraordinary journey in human society, and meets lots and lots of different people who look after him, or who don't look after him or whatever, and he ends up in a very bad place. It involves about twelve people, all of whom had a strong relationship with this chimpanzee, and recall him in different ways. With *Man on Wire*, I felt like I was juggling three or four balls – elements in the filmmaking structure – and I would get them up in the air and I could keep juggling them. On this one, I feel like I've got twelve on the go, and I keep dropping them. It's proving quite difficult. I'm in the cutting room as we speak and I'm struggling to get this one under control, though it's showing signs of life, finally.

There's complexity in terms of the filmmaking. But they seem to me to be complicated in terms of what they're about. Like Wisconsin Death Trip: *is it a film about a period of history? Is it a film about insanity? Is it about America today?*

Some films you make, you have a clear idea. What they're about is the story. So *Man on Wire*, that's the story of a French tightrope-walker who has what appears to be an impossible objective, to do the ultimate tightrope-walk, and does he do it or does he not do it? That's simple. *Wisconsin Death Trip* was an attempt to make a collage out of history, to show you little fragments of forgotten history, and to create a kind of impression of what life would have been like in that time and place, to show you how people thought at that time – what their concerns were, what their fears were – as revealed through small crime stories in a local newspaper. It's trying to give you a snapshot of that time and place. There's no real narrative there. The narrative is organised around a seasonal progression, which is an artifice that I created. It's supposed to echo the lifecycle. So it became a question of making sure that the stories were sufficiently weighty to reveal this whole state of mind of living in the last decade of the nineteenth century in a very remote part of America.

That was the intention of the film. But it was a film that had no money behind it, so it became this kind of personal obsession for everybody who was working on it. It wasn't just me; it was the producer who worked on it for three, four years. We shot it over two years and it was really difficult and we were improvising a lot with money and equipment, and borrowing this and stealing that and whatever. We were shooting in the worst kind of weather conditions, and then we couldn't finish it, and so on and so on. That became its own thing after a while, and in a certain way I lost sense of what I was doing, and got caught up in the doing of it, and the fact that it became an impossible task. So when I got into the cutting room I had to rediscover the impulse behind the film. I'd lost that impulse by being too caught up in the means of doing it. So to cut that film was really difficult and the film relied only on rhythm, not on linear progression or narrative structure. It was a rhythm I was going for, and that's the hardest thing of all to achieve. And it took a long time to put together. If it works, it works only on that level, I think.

Thematically, Man on Wire *seems very complex. Although on one level it's the story of a man doing this extraordinary thing, it also seems to me that it's about freedom and faith.*

Well, here's the thing: I think what a film is about is revealed only through its narrative, the story. It's not about those things for me as I make a film. I'm aware of those bigger ideas (and in this chimp film, for example, the ideas are as big as they get; they're about evolution; they're about the meaning of life, ultimately; they're about what we are like as a species). But what *Man on Wire* is about is none of those things and all of those things. You're just trying to tell the story as clearly and as evocatively and as wittily as possible. And if you do that well enough, then the ideas that you are talking about will emerge, but they're never at the forefront. They're always what the story will generate for you if you get it right. So it was only when I'd finished the film that I was really able to understand what those ideas were.

For me, there's a very obvious idea in the film about trying to do something that's impossible, and what kind of a person does that. And also, on a purer (and maybe more pretentious) level, the film is about the nature of art itself and what it is. I felt that this was as artistic as anything else I've ever encountered in my life. Whether it's Beethoven's Fifth Symphony or a Van Gogh painting, this act of wire-walking felt to me like it was up there with those great artistic experiences I've had. And the other thing about that film which very much appealed to me going into it, and which I hope it's about, is subversive thinking. Because I found Philippe to be very subversive, but not in a destructive way, and that's what I loved about him and what he did. It wasn't destroying something. It wasn't about some kind of cause he was trying to advertise. It was subversive by taking these imposing and not terribly aesthetically pleasing buildings and making them beautiful for forty minutes and showing again the limit of what it is possible for a human being to do.

But all those ideas came by getting the story right. And the same is true of this chimpanzee movie I'm doing now. It's a very interesting story and, if I'm telling it correctly and making the right choices, then there are very, very big ideas in this film. But, for me, they should never be discussed. You tussle with producers sometimes, when they say, 'Why don't you make this more overt? Why don't you have some discussion about language and what it means?' Well, I don't want to do that. It's not how I make a film. If people in a documentary start telling you about things and articulating ideas for you, I get a little bit wary. I don't want to deal overtly with the realm of ideas. I want to deal with the realms of narrative that will *expose* ideas. So you can respond to *Man on Wire* very differently, depending on who you are.

Your films are quite playful.

That's probably the biggest compliment you could pay the work that I've done, if by 'playful' you mean that they are always looking for the absurd detail, or the revealing absurdity, but hopefully not in a cruel or unkind way. *The Burger and the King,* for example, is ostensibly a very frivolous kind of idea that we approach with great gravity and seriousness of purpose, which is to use food to understand Elvis' background and what he was like and where he came from, and how he ended up dying the way he did. But it's played out on a level of black comedy, because what he chooses to eat is so weird. And we show you how you too can cook that food for yourself; we have recipes in the film. Generally, I don't really like earnest and po-faced filmmaking. Absurd and funny detail can speak volumes for the story you're telling. I genuinely love absurdity and strangeness. That's why I like documentary so much. You could not make up *Man on Wire*. You couldn't make up this chimpanzee film I'm doing, either. It would be impossible to make that up. They wouldn't believe you. My favourite filmmaker of all time is Buñuel, whose films are awash with playful, absurd detail and how preposterous we all are. But he's very forgiving; he doesn't condemn people, Buñuel. And I hope I don't either.

Is documentary an art form?

No. It's a medium. It's a medium that can occasionally reach the level of art and become an art form, but not often, in my view. I think it's a medium of storytelling and emotion. But it's not necessarily, or by definition, an art form. And that's true, I think, of all filmmaking – that there are certain directors and certain films that cross the threshold into truly artistic and revelatory experience, in the way that a novel can do, or a painting or whatever else. But I'm not sure that there are any – or there are very few – documentary films that can truly be regarded as works of art. I'm also quite wary of very strong self-expression in documentary filmmaking. I try to be very anonymous in terms of how I make a film, although I have certain stylistic interests that, I guess, are idiosyncratic and personal. There's only one documentary filmmaker who I think makes art, and that's Frederick Wiseman. He's the first person to say, 'What I do is reality fiction.' He doesn't call it the truth, or honesty, or reality. His films consistently seem to create a view of the world by the way he films things and the way he puts his films together. There are other filmmakers who make very artistically interesting documentaries, but, generally speaking, I think it's not a useful aspiration for a documentary film. I think the aspiration should be somewhat more limited, and perhaps more prosaic. Perhaps if you do your job well enough you might create something that other people could label art.

Is that what you want for your films? Do you want them to be art?

No. I really wouldn't say that. What I want is to work in the area of feeling, and for people to be able to feel things – strong emotions – when they watch a film. With *Man on Wire*, for example, I wanted people to feel the joy and the thrill of the story. It's the same with *Project Nim*. I want people to experience it and feel it and go on a ride. I really don't strive for any kind of artistic statement, or for my films to be meditations on a subject, or to achieve some kind of level of artistry where I think, 'Oh, that's now a work of art.' I wouldn't presume to do that, nor do I think it's a very useful objective. I think film is a medium that is very powerful in the right hands, and I enjoy the resources of filmmaking that a documentary allows you. But you should never forget the collaborative nature of all filmmaking. I think most of us have to acknowledge the importance of an editor and editing in what we do, and often the importance of a cinematographer. Most of us rely on other people to collaborate with, even if that collaboration is only with your subject or the characters in your film, like *Man on Wire* was a collaboration with Philippe. So it's not a single vision for me, in any film. Even if you're Stanley Kubrick it's not, or indeed Frederick Wiseman. We all need and thrive on collaboration with other people. It makes our work better.

10

Telling past-tense stories

Kevin Macdonald

Kevin Macdonald is the director of *One Day in September* (1999), the Oscar-winning story of the kidnap and murder of a group of Israeli athletes at the 1972 Munich Olympics. The film draws on an extraordinary fund of archive material, as well as vivid testimony from some of the people involved, not least an exclusive interview with Jamal Al-Gashey, the last surviving member of the Munich terrorists.

Macdonald's next film was *Touching the Void* (2003), the story of a disastrous attempt by two British mountaineers to climb Siula Grande in the Peruvian Andes. The climb almost resulted in the death of one of them – Joe Simpson, who would later write a best-selling book about his experiences, and his almost miraculous survival. The film won the Alexander Korda Award for Best British Film at the 2004 BAFTAs.

In recent years, Macdonald has shifted towards directing feature films, such as *The Last King of Scotland* (2006), about a young man who travels to Uganda and is made personal physician to the dictator Idi Amin; and *The Ninth* (2011), an historical adventure story set in the second century AD. He retains an interest in documentaries, however, and recently directed *Life in a Day* (2011), utilising footage filmed on the same day by thousands of people around the world, providing a snapshot of their concerns and preoccupations at a single moment in history. He is the editor of *Imagining Reality: The Faber Book of the Documentary* (1996), an authoritative collection of writings exploring the history of documentary filmmaking.

Kevin Macdonald, during the making of Touching the Void. *Picture courtesy of Kevin Macdonald.*

Is history a passion?

I'm interested in history, I suppose, to the same degree that a lot of people are. I'm not a history buff. I'm interested in the past as a mysterious, foreign place – particularly the recent past – and in trying to understand the present through looking at the past.

A lot of people I've met who make documentaries are nosy people, interested in asking a lot of questions. And that's a sort of prerequisite, I guess, for working in documentaries: you have to be interested in people and things. You have to want to ask questions and want to find out what happened or find out what someone is like, or what motivates them, or whatever it is. Stick your nose in; be nosy; be difficult.

Is history a source of stories?

For me, it's a great source of stories. But I also like the idea of rediscovering the past and changing people's perceptions of it, so that you're turning things on their head. I did a documentary about Klaus Barbie called *My Enemy's Enemy*. It was kind of flipping people's notion of what happened to the Nazis after the war. The idea of the film was to show – I even thought of subtitling it *How*

183

the Nazis Won the War – how immediately after the Second World War, even before the war was finished, the Allied powers decided that the real enemy was the Communists, and that now that they'd pretty much won the war against the Nazis, actually they realised that the Nazis had more in common with them than the Soviets did. So the Allies planned to co-opt some leading Nazis into their world as spies and scientific experts, in order to fight communism, and any sense of moral judgement about what the Nazis had done really took second place to those preoccupations. So it was a kind of reversal of the generally perceived notion of 'We won the war! Fascism is defeated!' Actually, fascism was co-opted. That was the thesis of the film.

And Klaus Barbie was the great exemplar of this. 'The Butcher of Lyon' was his nickname, responsible for killing women and children, torturing, horrific crimes, and he was known as somebody who sadistically took pleasure in his actions, which I think makes his crimes seem even worse. And yet, after the war, he was first of all on the run, like a lot of Nazis, but then was working for British Intelligence, then American Intelligence. American Intelligence denied knowledge of him to the French. They then helped him escape from Germany and got him to South America, effectively, I think, so that he could become a CIA agent in South America. And then you go to South America and you start researching the Nazi circle there, the real-life *Odessa File* kind of thing, and you realise that all these people were there and they were all working, in one way or another, for the Western Secret Services, either for the West German Secret Service or the CIA, and they were also helping prop up the right-wing regimes. That was really their purpose: to prop up the right-wing regimes in Latin America. So that's a long way round of saying that to look at the past and flip or reverse or radically subvert people's notions of what they think they know about the past – that seems to me to be a very interesting thing to do. And I think in *One Day in September* we did the same thing – take a very well-known event and say, 'Actually, you think you know what happened but you don't really.'

But the other thing is, you know, I think of myself above all as a storyteller, as somebody who likes to tell stories simply. Even as a kid I loved writing stories and I loved telling stories. Most documentarians are storytellers, which comes as a surprise to people who don't think about it much. They think, 'Oh, you just go and film a lot of stuff and put it together and it's not really telling a story.'

But, of course, it's like journalism. Journalism is storytelling. You have to take facts and somehow find the story in there. You have to find the almost fictional thing that binds all these facts together, because a bunch of random facts is meaningless, and what we do, as journalists or documentarians, is to give order and meaning to the chaos around us in one way or another. That's the sort of pretentious, grand way of looking at it, I suppose. But I like to tell stories, and if you tell stories about the present the risk is so great that you start off making the film and you don't get anything good. And I think there is a part of me which is maybe more conservative and actually quite likes the idea: 'Okay, so I can research and find out about the past and then I can tell that story.' It's a surer and maybe easier way of doing documentaries.

You know when you're on to a winner.

Yes, you sort of know you're on to a winner, more or less. I mean, the risk factor is part of what's attractive about documentaries. In observational film, you start with nothing, really, except the people in front of you and you have to make a film. And there's a huge amount of just accepting luck as it comes to you. And of course some people are good at creating luck and some people aren't.

But in the kind of documentaries that I've made, there's still risk. In *One Day in September*, I had to persuade a lot of people to talk, and then that becomes the thing that's hard. I spent, you know, months, years persuading them to talk, and, if you don't get them, well that's it: the film's not really going to work as well as it should do. And so in that film, there are various police officers who initially refused to talk and then eventually did. Also Mossad agents, and the one Palestinian terrorist who survived that whole thing – it was a big deal to try to get him to talk.

So it doesn't cancel out the risk but at least you know what your story is, to an extent. And because that's the way I think about documentary, that's why it was relatively straightforward for me to move into fiction filmmaking, because I generally have a script in my head, a story that I want to tell. I don't know the details of it, but I know I want to hit particular notes and I know where I want it to end up. I'm not someone who sits and writes a forty-page script for a documentary, but I know the main emotional beats of the story, and that's an approach to documentary that's more similar to fiction filmmaking than the way a lot of documentarians work.

Do you think that documentaries are a good way of doing history?

Yes and no. You can get less information across in a documentary than you can in a newspaper article. Documentaries are not great, necessarily, at facts. There are better ways of getting facts across. Like all film, documentary is really about sensation and emotion, I think, and storytelling. And so the skill in making documentaries about the past and history, and using archive and that sort of thing, is to not get bogged down in too much detail. You need to know what the pertinent detail is, and what the details of the story are that you need to tell, because actually you can't go into that much detail. In my experience, you do end up simplifying things to such a degree that sometimes you worry, you know, 'Am I actually lying? In order to make this story more straightforward, am I simplifying it to the extent of almost erasing it?' I think that, because they don't get bogged down, documentaries are a great way of popularising history and a great way of telling the stories of history in a narrative sense. But they're not necessarily good at being analytical. They're good at being provocative; at being radical, possibly; at telling a good tale about the personal, about the emotional: those are the things documentaries are good at. But they're not good at the detail of things, and I guess real history is about detail.

They can show you a lot, though. Like in One Day in September, *the archive is extraordinary.*

Yeah, there's great archive in that film. There's a lot of pleasure to be had in just handling archive; in getting hold of great material. Looking for it and finding it – it's like a kind of archaeology. And there are always so many surprises in it – those little moments, private, personal moments, that were maybe on the end of a newsreel which didn't even get used that you find and think, 'Wow, that's great.' It's not the big famous moments that are usually the most telling and the most interesting. One of the reasons why I'm doing this *Life in a Day* project is that I'm trying to make a whole film like that, a whole film which is about a big issue – 'What's the world like today?' – but through the small details. We're collaborating with YouTube and I suppose what we're trying to do is create our own archive. It's like archive in the sense that I don't have any involvement in the shooting of it, and I'm trying to be hands off about, and as non-prescriptive as possible about, what the material should be like.

Have you seen Adam Curtis' films? The Power of Nightmares *and* The Trap?

Yes, I think he's brilliant. He's a genius at finding archive, and finding *significance* in archive. In a way, there are some similarities with what I do, but he makes very different kinds of films. I think his films are far more brilliant than mine. He does something where he chooses a pair of spectacles: 'I'm going to look at this period of history through this particular pair of spectacles. You thought everything was rose-coloured, but actually it was all shit-coloured.' And that's fascinating, reimagining the past in that way.

Archive is just so revealing. I think it's incredible how much even the quality of the format, the medium that something is shot on, can tell you about the time. Of course, when video came in, everyone was like, 'Oh, video's not as nice as Super-8 that all '60s and '70s archive was shot on.' But, of course, looking at it now, video again has some quality of the past about it, a texture that tells you about the past and gives it a romantic quality.

It seemed particularly striking, the archive in One Day in September, *because it made the film feel present tense, even though it's a film about something that happened forty years ago.*

Yes, and I think also one of the things that was important to me about the way that we told that story was to go against the prevailing documentary television attitude, which is you put the best thing that you've got in the film first, so that you basically give the story away. Well, my attitude was: I'm going to treat this like a fiction film and edit it like a fiction film, dribbling out the information as it occurred in real time and telling the story in a way that, hopefully, is suspenseful. And I think that, with both *Touching the Void* and *One Day in September*, my aim was to make thrillers – to tell a really suspenseful story but using reality, like *In Cold Blood*, if you've read that?

You know, we've all sat spellbound while someone who's really good at telling a story tells a story about something, in a mainly chronological order, and you sit there and you're like, 'What? What happened next?' And it's exactly the same goal when you're telling a story in a documentary. I think that was one of the things that worked best about *One Day in September*, and I think it was the most surprising thing about the film for people in a way, that it did manage to release information in a suspenseful way. The perspective of the movie, at all times, was very much in the present tense, following all the developments in the story and the twists of fate, and using that newsreel footage accentuated that feeling.

And because you're in the present tense, it has those amazing moments, like when everyone thinks the athletes are fine but they're not. And then you see the news anchor who says, 'They're all gone,' because he doesn't really know how to phrase it, because it's happening live and he's announcing it ... Very powerful.

Yes, it is powerful, because it's new to them and because you're seeing as a viewer would have done at the time, with the added privilege that you're seeing it from all around the world, with bits of archive that not everybody could have seen at the time. Really, *One Day in September* is an incredibly simple film in its conception. It's just that we stuck rigidly to that notion of telling the story in that way.

Something else that struck me when I was watching it is that there's something very modern and very recognisable about the archive. And it only occurred to me afterwards that it's because it's rolling news, of the sort that we've become very familiar with. So that the terrorists know that the police are making moves against them because they see it on TV.

Yes, it's constant coverage. It is remarkable that the terrorists know that the police are planning a move against them because they're watching TV themselves, and they can see it unfolding.

Absolutely every angle is covered, isn't it? I wonder if the Israeli athlete hostage crisis might be the very first example of this sort of coverage?

I think you're right. Certainly, at the time when we were doing it that was what we said to people: 'This was the first event of its kind', where a huge news story broke and there was satellite TV and therefore things were broadcast on video around the world. Because, prior to that, what would have happened is that it would have been filmed and then taken back to a studio and then clips of that would have been shown on TV, whereas this was actually shot on video cameras and broadcast simultaneously, all the American footage in particular. It was the first satellite Olympic Games, and in some ways the first major event that dominated world headlines in a live, unfolding way.

There's a shot of the outside of the window and nothing's happening. A guy sticks his head out, then goes back in. And that builds the tension, because you're there, in the present tense, knowing that something's going to happen, even though you're looking at nothing very much.

Yeah, even though you're looking at nothing. One of the problems that we had with the film was that you can't actually get inside the room where it's happening. And, I guess, what we tried to do was to make that into the point. It's the classic trick, isn't it, when you're structuring any documentary: the big problem you've got, you try to turn that to your advantage and make that the point of it. And that's what we tried to do, so that you only go into the room once, which is when outsiders do go into the room, and the head of the German Olympic Committee, whose name I forget, goes in, and you see these photographs of what it was like inside. And other than that you're always on the outside, and you're always taking the perspective of what the onlookers could see, which was basically not very much – the very end of the longest lens, and it's a wobbly, blurry shot.

I haven't seen the whole film for a very long time but I've seen bits of it and I think there are certainly a lot of things I would do differently now. I think there were some really good decisions that we made, but I think there were also some decisions I would make very differently now.

Which ones?

Well, one thing that I'm always guilty of in my films is using too much music. And I think that film, particularly, has too much music in it. That, again, was a reaction against the norms of documentaries. I wanted the film to be constantly in motion, but I think in trying to achieve a sense of momentum and motion in the film we overdid the music. But there are things I do like about it still; I think that the use of music from the period and particularly the kind of heavy rock tracks – there's a Led Zeppelin track in it and Black Sabbath – they work brilliantly. The interesting thing was everything from the early '70s is so revoltingly sentimental and twee. And we were listening to thousands of songs, going through the charts of every week and trying to see what was going on musically, and there was so little that had any bite. And then we thought, 'Actually, the way to do it is to go hard rock,' which was so against what you would imagine. But that was the era of those bands, and I think it works really well.

They're very moving as well, I thought, the images that went along with the hard rock: the sequence of athletes' faces, in particular.

Yeah, that's brilliant. And I have to say that that sequence in the film is really entirely the work of the editor. We'd sort of discussed, 'Let's have this sequence where we see the games going on,' and then I went away on holiday and I came back and she'd done it, and it's probably the best sequence in the film.

One of the great experiences for me in making that film was that I worked for the first time with some really talented collaborators. With previous documentaries that I'd made, I'd been in the position where it's frustrating, where you're working maybe with an editor and thinking, 'God, I can do this better,' and telling them everything. There's nothing worse. What you want is for somebody to come in and for you to go, 'Oh, yeah, let's do this,' and for them to go, 'No, no, no, it'll be much better if you do this.' And even if you then disagree with them and something else comes up, a third way, that's even better. *One Day in September* was my first experience of that, and I had a great time with the editor, Justine Wright, whom I worked with for the first time on that. I've worked with her on pretty much everything I've done since. I think, in documentaries, the roles of the director and the editor are not interchangeable exactly, but the creative responsibility of the film is almost as much the editor's as the director's. And I find that, when I work with Justine, she will come up with some great ideas that I hadn't thought of at all, and it's a great creative collaboration. And that's one of the things that I really love about documentary: that it's made in the cutting room in a way that feature film sort of isn't. You sit there with another person and you say, 'Let's try this, let's try that,' and that's always a lot of fun.

How did you decide when to go away from archive? It doesn't happen very often. There's a bit of road imagery and a Kalashnikov being fired and a light bulb exploding.

Well, I wanted it all to be archive, but there were things we couldn't illustrate. It was just a matter of 'Where don't we have archive?' I didn't want to use archive of people just walking in the streets or whatever. I suppose, also, probably the biggest influence for me in documentaries has been Errol Morris and specifically *The Thin Blue Line*. And, although I was quite purist about documentaries and really didn't approve of reconstructions, I so admired his films, his coolness of approach, his stepping back a little bit to allow the audience to make up their own minds and to figure out the story for themselves without being told everything ... The decision to use those – they're not exactly reconstructions, but maybe we'll call them that – came out of *The Thin Blue Line* and seeing that film and the stylised nature of those elements. So I suppose I was doing something that was a more simplistic version of that same idea – things that are relevant but not literal – because I think that's always the death of reconstruction, isn't it, when you try to be literal? When something is symbolic or pictorial or metaphorical, it can work.

Interestingly, of course, having said that's what I thought – and it probably still is what I think – the next feature documentary I did was *Touching the Void*, which was mostly made up of pretty literal reconstruction. And actually, I battled furiously with myself thinking, 'God, can this work? Can you do reconstructions? How bad is this going to be?' But you can talk yourself into anything really, can't you?

Always with TV documentaries, the discussion with execs is about narration: how much do you use and how much signposting should you do? How did you decide when to use it in One Day in September? *I imagine you'd got most of the narration points covered in archive, if you'd wanted to go that way?*

In my opinion, these days – not always, but almost always – there's far, far too much narration. And it's treating the audience like idiots. There are two sides to your brain: there's the right and there's the left. The left is the rational, literal side that hears voice-over and thinks, 'Oh, well, now I know what's happening I don't need to be empathetic, to use the right side of my brain. I don't need to put myself inside the characters I'm watching. I don't need to invest in the same way. I don't need to think about it and invest imaginatively in what I'm watching. Here's this voice-over guy who's got it all in hand.' Once you put that voice-over on, you might as well do radio; the pictures are just illustration, like the news.

But voice-over can be incredibly useful at times. In fact, I just executive produced a documentary on Ayrton Senna [*Senna*, 2011] – another historical subject – where I was the one fighting to put voice-over on, because you didn't know what anything meant without having a certain amount of information, and that was the only way to get that information across. If people are looking at the material and not actually understanding points which are going to increase their enjoyment, then I think voice-over is essential. Or some form of information, whether it be captions or whatever.

So it's finding the right balance of those things. You need to give people enough information that they can make sense and enjoy what's going on. But not too much so that actually it all becomes a left-brain activity and you're thinking, 'I'm going to be told everything and therefore I don't need to engage with it.' Directors often think it's a failure of storytelling to have voice-over, but I think it's a necessary evil. Generally speaking, I've become less purist in the way I think about filmmaking now: 'By any means necessary' is my philosophy. I think, 'Yes, don't have too much voice-over, but if that's the way the story works the best and that's the way that you're going to get pieces of information across, then do it. If there's another way then do that.' I think it's great to see an elegantly produced, lyrically made film, but if you don't understand what's going on, and you therefore have less engagement with it and less enjoyment, then ultimately the film has failed. On *One Day in September*, we cut it first of all without voice-over, and there were a few key areas where people didn't understand the story. Then there were a number of other areas where it felt like telling the story through the archive would take a lot longer and I was very keen that the film should move along at a good pace. If it was going to take a minute or two minutes of extra archive I thought I'd rather cut it tight, and have a very terse line of narration. And I tried to keep the narration – as, I believe, most of the time you should – factual and objective and simple, so that it wasn't giving opinions too much, just giving the facts that you need to know in order to move on. Whether or not we succeeded in that I don't know. I mean, the reason we had Michael Douglas was purely because the producer wanted to sell the film in America, and felt it would help if we had a movie star.

Did you direct his voice-over record? There's a certain tone to it. It's rather sad and very grave.

Yes, I did. It was meant to be very flat, very factual and as an actor that was not necessarily how he wanted to deliver it; he wanted to give it more emotion. But I think that was one of the things I learned from Errol Morris, who said you should step back, let the audience invest, let the audience be sucked into the story by not pleading with them and saying, 'This is going to be emotional.' Let them get to that themselves.

You can see that a lot of research went into One Day in September.

One source of inspiration for the film was *JFK*, which, I suppose, operates as a kind of investigative thriller. It's very complex, and full of unanswered questions and theories. You're piecing together the story and finally Donald Sutherland at the end sort of reveals the truth. I think that any good piece of investigative journalism is kind of like a thriller, in that you're putting one thing on top of another on top of another. I mean, that's why the detective story is so exciting, because to be in the shoes of a detective who's piecing together the mystery is fascinating. And so, I suppose, what we wanted to do in *One Day in September* was to put the viewer in the position of discovering everything along the way as we the filmmakers discovered it. So you don't give away anything at the beginning; you don't sort of lead with your headline. You just let it come out bit by bit by bit by bit, drip-feeding the information, which is how we went about researching it.

You know, I think every documentary involves sleight of hand, in that you have to create a story out of the chaos of the rushes. And there are all sorts of tricks and techniques from different genres that you can use to tell your story. We chose the thriller because that naturally fitted the process that we had gone through ourselves, with German secret police interfering at the time to keep the truth from coming out, and a real sense that a wall of silence had been put up around the story.

Were you doing the research for the film yourself?

Absolutely, yes. There was lots of stuff that we uncovered for the first time. Like a lot of these things, you get conflicting points of view. So you'd look at the newspaper articles from the time, or documentaries that have been made before about it, and they all had slightly different perspectives and said different things. And, of course, partly that is the nature of the human mind: our memories are unreliable and we all put our own projections on to reality. But also it was because people had never really pinned down exactly what happened. The story had never been told in its entirety. So we did a huge amount of research – investigative, journalistic research – and we did, I think, pin down exactly what happened. There were all sorts of things which had never been discussed before, whether that was because they had been covered up or whether that was because people hadn't known about them or whatever. But I think also it's in the nature of very complex events that at the time it's very hard to know exactly what happened. It takes a sort of forensic investigation afterwards to really figure out exactly what occurred.

The film made news, didn't it? The front page of a Sunday newspaper?

Yes, it made news. We had quite a lot of press both here and in America and Germany. In Germany, it was because of the accusation that the German government had been involved in the cover-up of the hijacking of this aircraft, which is at the end of the story. And that became a big story in Germany. And in Israel it was a big story, partly because some of the widows and family members of the people who'd died didn't like the film. So there was all sorts of stuff in the papers over there. It's interesting, because that event, the Munich Olympics massacre, if you look at a timeline of the history of Israel over the last whatever it is, sixty, sixty-five years now, that is one of the key events in the history of Israel. Eleven people died, which doesn't seem that many, but it was a key event because it was, I suppose, the tipping point where, up to that point, Israel had been perceived by a lot of the world as this very idealistic kind of place, you know, with its kibbutzes and its socialist ethos, all of that. And I think at that stage things changed, and the security services became really paranoid. And also, in the history of terrorism as well, it's one of the key events that forever afterwards defined the way security happened at big events, and changed the way we all thought about terrorism. So it's a key piece of history which, I suppose, I didn't really know when we started making the film.

It was a real coup to get Jamal Al-Gashey.

Well, it turned out that Jamal wanted to make an appearance with his family and his children to show 'I'm not a monster. I'm an ordinary guy. And it's affected my life too.' And he then began to get slightly cold feet, but also the PLO began to put pressure on and they didn't want him to talk because they thought it would be too controversial and upset the peace process at that time, which was fragile but very much alive. And so there was a lot of negotiating back and forth. And twice he was meant to be interviewed. Once I was meant to go to Tunisia to meet him, and I was all ready, and then it was cancelled literally two hours before takeoff. And then another time I went all the way to Lebanon to interview him, and he didn't show up. We did some other stuff, interviewed various people, met lots of the families and the widows of the people who died, which was fascinating, but didn't actually make it into the film. And then, finally, a meeting was arranged which he turned up at in Jordan. But he was very limited in what he would say, and it was very frustrating, because I didn't really know what he was talking about, because of the language barrier and because it was all done in great secrecy. So it was only when I got the tape back to England and got it translated that I actually knew what he had said. It was very frustrating because there were so many great questions I wanted to ask him and I kind of felt that we didn't have enough and it was very slight, but we managed to draw it out. And I think, in a funny way, it's just his presence there, even if the things he says are not so revelatory; it's his presence that has the strongest effect.

Was it quite late in the process when you interviewed him?

Yes, very late, very late in the process. And always, of course, I was thinking, 'This is going to make the film work or not; it all depends on this.' I'd started trying to get him right from the very beginning and I think it took a year to persuade him. So, yes, it was a big coup to finally land him.

It's a great film, but would it have made such a splash without Jamal, do you think?

No, probably not – although, in a funny way, I don't know if it made that much difference to the film. But it certainly made a difference to the sort of publicity factor. You know, it was one of the things that people talked about: 'There's an interview with this guy who's the only surviving terrorist and he's never spoken before.' When you're making a documentary, you're at the mercy of who you can interview and what footage you can get, what access you can get, and so on. And you don't really know when you start off what you're going to end up with. With *One Day in September*, the film probably wouldn't have had the attention that it had without that one little interview, which came good so late in the process.

The images of the dead at the end of the film are very memorable.

Yes. We debated a lot as to whether or not to put those in. And it was those images which upset some of the Israeli family members, which, you know, we are regretful of. But at the same time we felt that the reason they were there was because other family members had said to us, 'Be as powerful, as strong as you can.' The photographs were important to me personally just to ram home the human loss and the horror of what had actually happened. It's okay talking about it abstractly, but I think, without those photographs, it doesn't have the shock factor. As any documentary filmmaker who's done anything like that before would say, you're crossing ethical lines every step you take. And you have to make the decision yourself as to whether or not you feel comfortable with it, whether or not you feel that it's the right thing to do. And, in that context, we all felt that it was. We got those images from the lawyers who were representing the German government in the case which the families, the Israeli families, were bringing. You think of Germany as being the most sort of straight-laced and incorruptible country in the world, but you spend any time there dealing with them, like we did on this documentary, and you soon realise that that is just a veneer. I have never met anyone more corrupt than the Germans, more liable to bribery, and, not to put too fine a point on it, we basically bribed somebody to give us the photographs and various other documents, particularly ones connected to what had happened at the airport. There were documents going through what had occurred at the airport minute by minute, you know, from the original police investigations, but none of that stuff was ever released. I remember we had two days to look at the documents in an office and I had a translator because my German is pretty lousy. And literally she just read it out and we had a tape recorder. I leafed through, found the bits that were interesting, and got her to read those out into the tape recorder. There was no other way of doing it. And then we arranged to photocopy various documents. It was some edgy stuff.

Touching the Void *is a very different sort of film to* One Day in September. *It's almost the opposite in that there's no archive to draw on at all.*

Yes. The only thing they have in common is that they're both about something that took place in the past, and they're both very suspenseful stories. After I had finished *One Day in September*, I really wanted to make another film. I wanted to make another feature documentary, but I couldn't find a subject, for ages and ages. I couldn't figure out what to do. Then I was sent Joe Simpson's book by my producer, John Smithson. I don't mountain-climb and

I didn't know anything about that world but I just read it in one sitting – absolutely fantastic! I thought, 'God, I'd love to make a film out of this!' And then I thought, 'But how do you do it?' You can't do it without actors, really, because there isn't anything to show unless you actually dramatise. And so that was, for me, the big decision about whether or not to go ahead and try to do that film, knowing it needed a degree of literal dramatisation and feeling that I generally don't like that sort of thing. That was always my big worry: 'How do you do the drama so that it lives up to the documentary?' That's always the thing about dramatisation in documentaries; it's usually so lame and so lacking in resonance compared to the stark reality. Inevitably, almost all dramatisation feels sort of cheesy and lightweight and inauthentic, particularly because you are usually doing it with actors who aren't particularly good.

So the concept was: 'Let's take two actors and let's put them through what it must have been like.' That was sort of how I tried to sell it to myself, I suppose, as much as anything else – to say, 'Let's go back to the place where this happened. Let's put these guys, these two actors, through the horrors of what it must have been like. And when they are dangling from a rope and their hands are freezing in the story, they are dangling from a rope and their hands are freezing in reality, so they don't really have to do much acting.' But, again, a constant debate built up about how literal to go and how much to stylise the material. But, of course, in the second half of that film you're confronted with the actor who is playing Joe Simpson, and you're with him and you're with his face, and you have to go with that; you have to go with his acting. So it became a film which unintentionally led me into doing features, because it was the first time I had ever worked with actors. I hadn't really been interested in working with actors or doing fiction or anything like that before, but, when I did, I found I rather enjoyed the artifice and the creativity of actually setting things up. It was a really tough physical shoot, but we always had at the heart of it all this amazing storyteller, Joe Simpson, and this extraordinary story which I think is so resonant for so many people and on so many levels because it speaks to the most profound thoughts that we have about the existence of God, or not, and the hopelessness of life. Is it worth going on? It's kind of Beckett in the mountains; Beckett on ice.

It's mythic.

Yes, it operates on a mythic level, and Joe Simpson was such a good storyteller that in some ways the film would almost have worked if it had just been him telling the story and it hadn't had anything else, just a few views of mountains.

In terms of the mechanics of it, were the interviews very long? Did you have lots of questions?

Well, the book was written around 1988, and it was getting on for twenty years since this thing had happened when we did the film. It was a famous, famous story in mountain-climbing circles. And Joe and Simon had both told the story umpteen times. So that was the big challenge from the documentary perspective. With somebody who has kind of inured themselves to the reality of what happened, how do you get them to relive that reality? How do you get an immediacy that is going to compel an audience to watch, and feel they're in the moment, which is the key to making a film like that work? The audience has to feel you're in the moment, has to believe that there's jeopardy. My theory was, just from observing people and observing myself, my own psychology, that, if something funny has happened to you and you tell the story to someone, the first couple of times you tell it you're rehearsing it to yourself; you're getting your lines right. And then, after that, you've got it down pat and you just tell the story and you do it very much the same way every single time. We've all got anecdotes that we do that with. And I thought, 'Well, with them it must be like that but with knobs on. They really have rehearsed this so many times and they've got their lines.' So I booked them both for two days, and just sat them down with an HD camera, and basically got them to tell the story. And they each told the story in about forty-five minutes each. Then, when they'd told the story, I started to ask them a few questions. We were in an empty studio; there's no pressure on them; the camera doesn't need to be changed very often because it's a one-hour tape. And I tried to get them to go back, in an unforced way, into the immediacy of their experience, just really through the boredom of sitting there. And they both started to – not to be pretentious – but they started to relive it in some way.

They're striking interviews because, as I think is always the case in the best sit-down interviews, they're thinking aloud quite often and they often seem surprised by their own thoughts. So you feel in the moment and still believe, as you're watching, that Joe's life is in jeopardy, even though he's there telling you about it.

Yes, thinking aloud is a good way of putting it. And I think those two interviews really work because they are both utterly honest, and you can tell when they're being dishonest. You can tell when they are uncomfortable with what they are saying, because neither of them is a good actor. There are moments where you really see their discomfort, particularly Simon when he's talking about not looking for Joe the next morning. But also with Joe. They are both open books. It's like a confessional, really, in the end.

Yes, when Simon says that he considered making up a heroic story, that does seem like a very honest thing to say.

A very honest thing to say. I think that they were both very brave in the way that they approached it, particularly Simon because he had been vilified. Also, he was 'the other guy'. He wasn't the heroic one. He was the guy who had done the possibly un-heroic thing. He was the other guy in the *Touching the Void* story. I think that's tough on him, always being reminded of that. He was the other one, not the main one.

So, when you were asking the questions, you were trying to de-familiarise things?

Yes, that's exactly right. I was trying to get them to access their authentic memories rather than trying to just give the pat story. I'm sure that if you and I sat here for two days talking about *Touching the Void* I would start to remember all sorts of things, and things that I have sublimated in some way would start to surface. And I think that's just inevitable, part of what the human memory does and what the human mind does. We try to give order to things, but also we try to hide things that are uncomfortable to us. But, after a while, they come out. It's inevitable. And it was very interesting because I think that Simon, in particular, after that point felt very uncomfortable about the whole filmmaking process. He's quite a shy person and I could tell that he felt he had opened up too much, and that made him really uncomfortable with it all. But what we did with that film was we started with the interviews, because I still wasn't actually sure whether this was going to work. I was really doubtful as to whether or not guys who had told their story a thousand times could be fresh enough to be in a film that was worth making. So I said to Channel 4 and Film 4, who were financing it, 'Give me £15,000 and let's do the interviews and then we'll cut the interviews together and we will see whether we think this will work.' And that's what we did. So before we did anything else, we interviewed them both.

My interviewing mantra was that you want your relationship with an interviewee to be like a therapist's relationship with a patient. And therefore I hadn't met Simon at all before I did the interview. I said, 'I don't want to meet him. Just bring him down,' so he didn't have any sense of me and so he would just talk to me in an open way. We all get prejudices when we meet someone, even for a short time. And also they start telling you the story in advance, then that's it. People only tell the story once really well and after that it's phony. After that, they are telling you as an act. The first time it's real because you don't know what they are going to say, which is an important thing. Joe as well ... I met Joe for half an hour in the pub, and said, 'I don't want to talk about *Touching the Void*; let's just talk about something else.' I think if you set those kinds of artificial boundaries in a way it actually does pay off, particularly in this kind of instance.

So we cut together all the interview material and then we had a two-and-a-half-hour bare-bones movie: just interviewees telling the story. From that, I sort of knew that we potentially had a really compelling film.

People always say, 'Oh, you made a film out of a book,' and I say that I actually didn't. It was inspired by the book, because that's where we found the story. But, actually, the emphasis is very different than in the book, because what I was going on was what they were actually saying and what they were remembering, rather than the literary artefact that had been constructed at Joe's leisure. So there are many differences in emphasis throughout the story because of that.

I loved the fact that the interviewees all looked like the characters that they turned out to be. So it didn't need quite so much establishing who they are. You know, Joe is slightly reptilian-looking, and he looks like he would be a diffi-cult sort of man to deal with. And Simon has those big sticky-out ears and he looks quite friendly and open. And Richard just looks a bit useless and dopey.

That's more or less who they are, yes. I felt, as in *One Day in September*, that you don't need to give people the background. You just start telling the story. You don't need to give people the background of who these people are and why they chose that mountain. And actually it's the same thing I'm just going through at the moment with a film I've just finished, *The Ninth,* which I argued with the producer about. At the beginning of the film he wanted to have everything explained in captions and my feeling was (a) nobody reads those sorts of captions, and nobody really cares when somebody tells you about the background and (b) actually captions make you much less interested in the people, because you're not finding out. You're not curious. You're not trying to take the measure of someone, which is all part of the pleasure of a good film, that actually you're discovering things about the characters. And with *Touching the Void,* it was very much the same. You know, 'character is action'. You discover who they are through what they do, and what they say, not because they describe themselves.

The level of detail in the interviews is very striking, and it made me think that it's probably a characteristic of all good documentaries that they take you into a world.

Into the specific, yes. I think that's true. The general is always dull because we can all imagine the general. We all have some sense of what it's like to climb a mountain. But actually to be told the kind of specifics of what happens to your fingers or what happens to your lungs or what the ice sounds like: that's the stuff we can't imagine because you have to really be there. And I always feel that any documentary about somebody doing their job really well, someone who's really good at what they do, is just totally compelling.

The other thing that struck me about the interviews is that they are quite matter of fact, in lots of ways. Joe is a hard man, and he has a very down-to-earth, terse way of speaking. But in some of what the interviewees say there is real poetry. 'I felt I was part of the rock. I felt I had been there for a thousand years.' Did you coach them to think and speak in a more poetic way?

No. No, not at all. The one idea that I had when I had read the book that I thought was so powerful was: 'This is what it's like to be totally alone in a godless universe.' And that was what I tried to express through the film. And so, any bits where they talked about the lifelessness up there, at 22,000 feet or whatever, and the agedness of the rocks and the stars – that was all the stuff that I was desperately looking out for and maybe I asked questions to elicit that. For me, that was the core theme of the film. It was about the existential crisis that we all face when we realise the emptiness of the universe. And I always had this image of a spaceman cut loose from his spaceship and drifting through space. And I think that's what you feel like when you are in those kinds of very bleak, empty parts of the world, and you're on your own – the pitilessness of nature, the sense of the rocks and the wind and the rain. And the actual place when we went there so embodied that.

I also think that mountain climbers are quite philosophical people. You have got to ask why they do it. Obviously, there's a degree of athleticism about it and a degree of show-off-iness about it. But, really, mountaineering is testing yourself to your limit psychologically, and taking you away from mankind. It's taking you away from the familiar, because those mountaintops are places you shouldn't really be. We can't live in the high mountains, in the Himalayas or the High Andes. We can't survive there. We would die if we tried to live there. You can't reproduce above 18,000 feet, which tells you a lot. So people who go there are kind of existentially questing people somehow. They are looking for something or they are looking to prove something to themselves, or they want to know what it's like to be where nobody else has ever been. So, they tend to be philosophical people and with that philosophy comes a degree of poetry, I think. They spend a lot of time on their own, a lot of time lying in a tent, waiting for a storm to clear for three days. You've got time to think.

Joe and Simon came with you when you went to shoot reconstructions on location at Siula Grande, the mountain where the story takes place. Did you film anything with them?

Yes, we did. I filmed them and made a little 'making of' film. If you've got the DVD of *Touching the Void*, it's on there as an extra. There aren't many 'making of' films that you can say are really fascinating, but I think that is one. It's about what happened to both of them when they went back, and what happened psychologically. When we went back to the mountain, they came as our guides and to show us where it had happened, because they were the only people that really knew. And in some shots they doubled for themselves. In wide shots, they were in the places where they themselves had been twenty years before, so it was kind of an odd thing where the real people were doubling for the actors who are playing them.

How did they feel to be back?

It was hard for them. Both of them freaked out a bit. Joe looked like he had seen a ghost, and had genuine panic attacks. He got quite irrational, like he was tempting fate to go back to the place where he'd cheated death. And Simon went off the rails a bit. He started to become very paranoid, and convinced himself that I was out to portray him in the film as a murderer who had attempted to kill Joe, and that I had an ulterior motive in making the film, which obviously I didn't. I felt that the film was fair to him and not at all condemning because I don't think there is any reason to condemn him. But he got very irrational, and walked off once or twice. So it became very intense. There was quite a poisonous atmosphere at times. It was a very intense experience.

What were you intending to do with that footage? Did you ever think of making a different, observational film instead, because the story was still so alive for Joe and Simon? Or was it always going to be for the DVD?

Well, for me it was always the 'making of'. Actually, the producer, John Smithson, wanted that footage to be in the film, but I never did, and I filmed it just to keep him happy, to be honest. For me, the film was a much purer, simpler thing. I did just want it to be the mountains, the locations, and a limited amount of reconstruction. I wanted it to be much simpler. I think when somebody is in an interview space, in a dark studio or whatever, and there's nothing to identify where they are and nothing that says anything about them, that can really work for you sometimes and help your audience to get lost in the story. I think filming our interviews in a neutral space is one of the reasons why in *Touching the Void* people managed to suspend disbelief and stay immersed in the story: 'What's going to happen? Is he going to survive?' The guy is sitting there talking to them, but because he's sitting there talking to them in a very disembodied, impersonal world they can still ask the question: 'Will he survive?'

Joe and Simon talk to the camera, don't they?

Yes, that was very much Errol Morris. I think that he's the biggest influence on me in *Touching the Void*, as well as *One Day in September*, and I think a lot of what works about those interviews in *Touching the Void* is down to the fact that they're looking at you. You, and people who work in the industry, would notice that but a lot of people who went to see the film didn't. They wouldn't have said, 'This is really strange, because they are looking at me.' It was just that the interviews felt more immediate. It's a strange convention, I think – this is what Errol Morris talks about and I agree with him – that in most documentaries the camera is there, but there's also somebody you don't see whom the person on screen is talking to. And actually, in the kind of documentary where you want people to be very involved in the story, to have the characters looking at you, the audience, makes much more sense because they're telling *you* the story. *You're* the audience it's aimed at. Also, I think it's actually very comfortable for the people in films to talk directly into the camera because, in a way, the more that interviews are de-humanised as a process, the better. That's another one of Errol Morris' great discoveries: that the more you create an alienating environment for someone to be interviewed in – the more you've got a big camera, they've got to look at a picture of you on a screen in front of the camera, and so on – in a weird way, the more they open up and the more intimate they become. So it's a kind of inverse law of intimacy. You would think that 'just me and you' would be better but, actually, human beings are quite intimidating. But, if we're in a situation where we don't really see anybody real and we are just in this artificial environment, it's like lying on the couch and just sort of being yourself. And then, I think, you get people to open up far more, and open up in a different way.

How did you decide what to reconstruct?

Very simply. We did this interview script where we cut all the interviews together, and then we basically said, 'We need this. We need this. We need this. We need this.' And then we tried to go out and film it all, and realised pretty soon that it was bloody slow and difficult filming stuff in the snow, in the ice, in the Alps, in the altitude and all that. So we ended up restricting more and more what we did, and doing it in a simpler and simpler kind of way.

I think that films like Touching the Void *are like really good cooking, in that the fewer ingredients you have the more important it is how you balance them.*

Yes. Yes. I mean, certainly, the simplicity and the purity of the film – that was important to me. I do think that you've got to set stylistic parameters for yourself. Style is partly useful because it focuses down what you have to do. And so you make these stylistic decisions: 'I'm only going to do these interviews with two, three people, and then I'm going to do some drama, filming in the mountains, and that's it. I'm not doing anything else. I'm not having any voice-over or whatever. I'm going to keep it very linear in terms of structure, so it's completely chronological and clear where you are in the story.' Making decisions like that and thinking about making films in that way is very useful, because then you know what you have got to do, and you know you have got to do it really well.

I can't remember with the 'cutting the rope' moment whether one of the interviewees says, 'I cut the rope' or whether you see it?

Well, in the editing that was always a really tricky thing to overcome, the sort of show-and-tell issue. What you don't want in that kind of film is for someone to say, 'And then I took out the knife and I opened it and I grabbed the rope and I cut it,' and then you see that. But, at the same time, there are certain things you want to dramatise because they are exciting bits, and you need to know enough about what is going on to make sense of it and enjoy it, so you need to have the person telling you. So that was always a big struggle, where to have something being told and where to show it. The two elements need to really speak to each other.

Was it trial and error to get it right?

Total trial and error. But, like all big problems, if you are aware of them, which we were at the time, you can try to combat them. There are certainly a few places in the film where I feel we didn't quite get it right, and, for whatever reason, we couldn't get round the problem and we ended up with the two guys telling you and then you would see it, and they would tell you and then you would see it. It's definitely a danger of that kind of filming.

The music was very Hitchcockian.

Yes. It's very dramatic. In some ways, I think the best films are just images and music. And, as with *One Day in September*, part of what I was trying to do with *Touching the Void* was to make a fiction film out of reality, and therefore we needed music which had a theatricality to it or had a sort of scale and a kind of movie-ness to it. It's very much saying, 'This is a film for the cinema, and this is a film I want you to go and enjoy, and I want you to be on the edge of your seat and be compelled by it.'

Touching the Void sort of transcended documentary, in the sense that it won awards for best movie, didn't it?

Yes. I have to say that it was incredibly gratifying to win the Best British Film BAFTA. I think we were the first non-fiction film ever to win the fiction award. That was fantastic and I think that that could only have happened at that time when there was an audience willing to go and see a documentary in pretty large numbers. I think it made like £2 million, which, even now, for an art film is really big box office in this country.

It changed the landscape for documentary quite a lot, didn't it? It's a formula that's all over TV now, whereas in Touching the Void it felt very new.

Yes, that's true. I think the great thing is, even though the formula has been done to death now, actually *Touching the Void* still works. I think, of everything that I have ever made, it's the thing which has affected people more profoundly than anything else. And that's an incredibly gratifying thing as a filmmaker: to make a film which really has affected people and where they really want to talk to you about it. Because the power of the story is so brilliant, I think it still has the ability to do that, even if the style is more familiar these days.

The photographs at the end of Touching the Void remind you that it was all real, a true story. It's powerful, but it's also very subtle, isn't it? Just three photographs.

Yeah. I mean that was the watchword for me: subtle, minimal. Don't overdo it. Don't try to do special pleading. I think, at that time particularly, I was sort of obsessed with style and the power and importance of style. So I was very rigorous, and the photographs seemed to me the way to bring it back to reality. I always love that in movies actually, in fiction films. Do you remember they show some photos at the end of *The Motorcycle Diaries*? It's incredibly moving and impressive when you see that and you think, 'Fuck. He's on a raft. It's just like the raft that we just saw.' And in *Touching the Void* when you see the photographs you see there is Joe on the back of a donkey and he looks like shit and you go, 'My God, it's that place.' It's a great gift you've got as a film director, that you can actually stop people short by saying, 'Look, it's real!' It sends you out of the cinema with that thought, because it's the final thought in the film.

Are documentaries like Life in a Day *and* Being Mick *departures from making historical films? Or a different way of doing history?*

Well, *Being Mick* was a sort of response to *One Day in September*. It was almost like taking a holiday. Having done *One Day in September*, which was a very hard and demanding film, and which was met with a very vociferous political response, I wanted to do something that didn't matter, something that was frivolous. And *Being Mick* just came along. I was phoned up by Mick Jagger's producer, and I thought, 'You can't get much more frivolous than that.' It was tremendous fun to do, and I think that's as good a reason to do anything as anything else.

I do know what you mean about observational films sometimes being a form of contemporary history. Mick Jagger is obviously an iconic, historical figure, and you are trying to get at some sort of truth about him. But I wouldn't intellectualise *Being Mick* in that way. It was just a piece of light-heartedness.

I think that *Life in a Day* is a much more interesting film. It's genuinely experimental, and it's a new departure in documentaries, in that it's using new means at the documentarian's disposal – the internet, disposable cameras, the idea of crowd-sourcing footage. I'm very proud of it, and the way it turned into something very moving and accessible. And I suppose that one did feel more like an historical endeavour. The idea for it came out of my interest in Humphrey Jennings and the films he made, like *Listen to Britain*, which is a lyrical, poetic, non-analytical, non-intellectual attempt to capture a moment – in his case, a day in the life of Britain at war. But I still wouldn't call *Life in a Day* a historical film, as such. I think what it is is an archive film, which is paradoxical. It's a film which is an archive-based documentary about the present. We are used to seeing films that are archive-based about World War II, for instance, but we're not used to seeing an archive-based film about today.

With the kind of films that use archive to tell a past-tense story, like One Day in September, *is it easier to express yourself than with observational films? In that you have more control. Is it more like writing, in a way?*

I think in a way it is. Editing is a form of writing, really. And I enjoy the process of deciding what to include and how to include it, and the timing of it, and what music to play with it, what sound effects to put with it, and suddenly creating a meaning, or creating a tension, or creating a story. That is very fascinating to me, personally. And it allows you to really explore and interrogate some big themes – the lies we tell about our own histories, as countries or societies or individuals. You can explode myths and make people think again about things. You can bring real perspective and clarity, and see patterns and meanings that people missed at the time. When they're done well, historical films can ask really awkward and difficult questions. They can be a really powerful and important kind of documentary.

Making films funny

Morgan Spurlock

Morgan Spurlock is best known as the director of *Super Size Me* (2004), a playful, funny and occasionally shocking documentary, prompted by the spread of obesity across the United States. Spurlock films himself over a thirty-day period, during which he eats only meals from McDonald's fast-food restaurants. The physical and psychological effects are startling.

The film won the Grand Jury Prize when it premiered at the Sundance Film Festival, and went on to become the twelfth highest-grossing document-ary of all time. It launched Spurlock as a documentary auteur and likeable on-screen presence, pursuing ambitious targets with journalistic rigour and a very accessible sense of humour.

His other films include: *Where in the World is Osama Bin Laden?* (2008), in which Spurlock sets out on a quest to track down the Al-Qaeda leader, exploring the rise of Islamic fundamentalism and the impact of the US 'war on terror' as he goes; and *Pom Wonderful Presents: The Greatest Movie Ever Sold* (2011), a film about advertising and product placement in the cinema, funded entirely through advertising and product placement.

Morgan Spurlock, during the making of Where in the World is Osama Bin Laden? *Photo by Daniel Marracino/The Weinstein Company, 2008.*

In the last ten years or so, there has been a real renaissance in documentaries, especially in the cinemas. Is that down to humour mainly, do you think?

I don't know if it is down to humour. I think it is much more down to a desire for information, especially in the States. I think there has been a real bubble put around journalism, in the sense that about five companies control the majority of what you see, hear and read. And I think that independent documentaries are one of the last bastions of free speech. They are one of the last bastions of long-form investigative journalism. Here is a format and a form where you can explore topics for ninety minutes, two hours, sometimes longer. But I do think humour has played a part. I mean, I think the success of Michael Moore's films helped open the door for people like me to get movies put in theatres, and Nick Broomfield. Michael, especially, has been a big influence on me, because he showed that documentaries could have a real sense of humour, and really be about something at the same time. I love the fact that he makes films about subjects that affect all of us, and touch all of us as human beings.

Humour is a very direct way of speaking to an audience. You can make a connection with viewers quite quickly through humour.

Yes. The thing that humour does really quickly is it gets people's guards down. I think the key for me is, through humour, trying to get people engaged in a story. We have a real mantra at our company which is: 'If you can make someone laugh, you can make someone listen.' And I think that, through laughter, people don't realise that they are taking the medicine. They don't realise that they are actually paying attention, that they are taking in information.

There was a great story that a friend of mine told me after *Super Size Me* came out. He was at a movie theatre where it was packed full of teenagers. It was a Friday night and it was playing alongside *Troy* and *Van Helsing*. In a movie theatre in *Texas*, mind you. And after the movie, he said, the kids came pouring out and they were like, 'Oh man, when he threw up out of the car, that was so gross. And can you believe that one in three kids is going to have diabetes?' Literally, they started spouting facts that had stuck over the course of this movie, and one of the biggest reasons, I think, is because the film was entertaining. It was fun.

I've been thinking about what else humour does, and it seems to me that humour gets to the 'human dimension' really quickly. It communicates on a human level. So, if you can find the humour in something, you can find the humanity in it.

Yes, I completely agree. I think that what humour does is to make almost everything accessible. And it is often in the worst situations and the most horrible situations that you *can* find humour. If you can find comedy in a situation, you can try to turn that situation into something that everyone can relate to. You know, throughout history comedy has been used to explore terrible, terrible issues and topics, and I think it allows people to openly have a discussion about something in a way that makes them feel comfortable. Comedy doesn't make it bad and comedy doesn't make it wrong, and it doesn't necessarily take away the seriousness of the issue.

Documentaries, for a long time, have been associated with a very worthy and sometimes dull approach. It's the idea that a documentary, for it to be a proper documentary, has to be gritty and a bit of a grind to watch.

Yes. I think that is terrible! I think there are docs that I watch that are completely depressing and sad and are very hard to watch. I watch a lot of those docs. It is not the kind of doc I want to make, you know, but I watch them. I think there should be an outlet for those films, but I think you start to limit the number of people who are going to watch them. I think it becomes almost like a badge of pride to say that you have sat through a lot of movies like that, to impress your friends and talk about it at fancy dinner parties: 'Did you see the doc on BBC last night? Oh, it was heart-wrenching!' And no one else saw it but you, so you can expound its virtues. But I think, for me, I really want to engage people in these conversations who would never normally be part of them. I want to get people to watch my films who would never normally watch a documentary.

There is an element of preaching to the converted isn't there, with documentaries that are a really tough watch?

Yes. You run the risk of creating something where the only people who are going to go and see it are the people who would go to see it anyway. The question is: how do you expand beyond an audience that agrees with you? That is the harder thing – getting the people who don't agree with you to watch, or who don't like you, and don't like what you do; people who don't really like the *topic*, or people who have *no interest* in the topic. That is a really difficult thing to do.

There's a lot of journalism in your films, as well as entertainment. Time *magazine listed you as one of the top ten journalists in America.*

Yes. People love to think that I just throw them together and there is no work behind them, but there actually is quite a lot of work. *Where in the World is Osama Bin Laden?* – you know, there was a tremendous amount of research that went into that. And with the new one, *The Greatest Movie Ever Sold*, there is a lot of information that we want to convey and in a way that you've never seen before; not pie charts, not talking-heads, not a PowerPoint presentation, although, as we saw with Al Gore's movie *An Inconvenient Truth*, sometimes a PowerPoint presentation can work. I don't know if it would work for anyone who wasn't a former presidential candidate, though. For most of us, we have to try to do something that is a little more, I don't know, rich in entertainment value.

Where in the World is Osama Bin Laden? got some heavy criticism, but it seemed to me that a lot of the criticism missed the point. You were criticised for not finding Bin Laden. But that's not really what the film was about.

Yes. I think somewhere, when we were making the film, a story broke that we had found him, you know, as we were finishing the movie, which I don't think helped when the film came out, because then suddenly there are expectations you are never going to live up to. We didn't put the kibosh on that immediately, which we probably should have. We should have said, 'You know there is a bigger conversation to have besides where is this guy.' Once he was found it was amazing. Suddenly, whereas people were criticising the movie when it came out, now everybody wanted to talk about the movie. Everyone and their brother started calling me to go on news networks to talk about being there. They were like, 'You said he was in Pakistan! We want to talk about your film.' Suddenly, everybody wanted to talk about this because now the film was relevant, and now the film wasn't a joke.

We were criticised for trivialising the issues. One of the things that people often said in the reviews was: 'Well, if you have never read a newspaper or if you haven't read up on anything that has happened over the last ten years as to why 9/11 happened, or if you don't know why we continue to have problems in the Middle East, then you should see this movie, but anyone else doesn't have to.' But the fact is that most people in the States don't have any sense of what is going on in the Middle East.

Do you have an agenda? Is there a 'Morgan Spurlock agenda'?

We don't go into a film with one. When we made *Super Size Me* we didn't go into it saying, 'We are going to show people how terrible this fast food is.' We came in saying, 'Let's see what happens. We know that *these* people all say, "It is terrible," and we know that *these* people all say, "It is fine." My doctor has said, "Nothing is going to happen to you." Great, let's roll the dice and see what happens.' With *Where in the World?*, we were like 'Where is this guy?' 'I don't know, let's go look for him – see what we can find.' And with *The Greatest Movie Ever Sold*: 'Let's see if we can actually get companies to pay for a movie that pulls back the curtain on brands getting involved in the entertainment business.'

So, when I come into a film, we usually have an idea and our starting point of A, and I usually make an outline of how the film would be in a perfect world, if everything worked out amazingly well, and we got everybody we wanted to interview. What would happen in the film? Well, we would try to talk to this person, we would try to go here and there, and it would end like this. So you write this film, and here is this amazing movie and you look at it and you think this is great! And then you start shooting and that gets thrown out of the window because nothing that is on that list ever happens. In *Greatest Movie*, we couldn't get one A-list actor to talk to us about having to hold up a Coke in the middle of a movie and say a line. Not one. No A-list actor would even engage in a conversation about this. And the original idea for the ending of *The Greatest Movie Ever Sold* was, once we have all these brands onside, you see me living in product Shangri-La, like my life becomes a commercial. I am driving my car down the street and the kids are jumping rope in slow motion and the hydrant is spraying water and I get out of the car and Brad Pitt and I cheers Cokes and we take a big swig at the end. And, of course, none of that ever happened, because all your ideas and your best-laid plans in documentary film change.

I got the greatest advice when we were making *Super Size Me*. I had never made a feature-length film and I called a friend of mine up and I said, 'I have never made a movie. What advice can you give me for making a film?' And he said, 'If the movie you end up with is the exact same movie you envisioned in the beginning, then you didn't listen to anybody along the way.' I think that is something that we try to adhere to with every movie, that you have to be open, you have to be that ball in the pinball machine and be willing to go wherever the game takes you. One door may close in your face, but another door opens and takes you in different directions, and you have to be willing to kind of go with that organic process. You can't have that mindset of 'Here is what I am going to prove'. I think that is the wrong way to go into a movie.

That is genuine journalism, isn't it, to start off with a question and not know where you are going to get to?

It makes it a lot harder for a movie. It is real exploration. But, when you are trying to raise money, investors don't want to hear, 'I don't know where it is going to end up.' You know? When you are trying to get a distributor, and you are trying to get it on television, they don't want to hear, 'I don't know how it ends.'

I think that is the big difference between you and Michael Moore. People talk about your films as if they are in the same sort of category, but Michael Moore's films are much more polemical.

Yes. I once heard somebody say that Michael's films are almost like editorials in newspapers, like 'Here is what I think is wrong'. I think his films are still exploring the truth and I think they are still honest in what they show. But I think, yes, he wants to go in and make his case and shake things up. The thing that I love about Michael as a documentary filmmaker is that the minute he makes a movie it becomes front-page news. Whatever Michael talks about becomes the lead story on the television. It becomes the cover of a magazine. It becomes a real talking-point in society. And you want that to happen around your films and around your projects because you hope that in some way they can change the way people think.

If the strength of humour in a documentary is that it helps you speak directly to an audience, and can help you reach new audiences, what are the dangers and the drawbacks?

Well, I think the danger, like with *Where in the World?*, is that people will think that the movie is soft; they'll think that the movie trivialises a topic that shouldn't be trivialised; that it makes light of a serious situation; and that you're not taking the process seriously enough. I think that's the drawback. But what you hope is that people can see that this is a gateway to deeper exploration. What you want to do is you want this to be step one. I like people to leave the movie theatre and come up with their own ideas after the film. I'm not going to tell you what to think. I'm not going to tell you what to believe. But I'm going to give you information on both sides so that when you leave you can make your own decision. Make up your own mind as to what you think is right or wrong. Hopefully, it will create a real debate. I've had people say to me that, if a film is about something we should care about, then we shouldn't be treating it as a joke. That's the way a lot of reviewers have seen the stuff I've done. But I think if you don't laugh at some of the things that happen in this world, then you're going to be crying every single day. You're going to be miserable; you're going to be a miserable bastard. You have to laugh about it just to get out of bed.

Jokes quite often rely on exaggeration, don't they? Do you think there's something inherent in humour that makes things seem overstated or less true?

Well, I think what you don't want to do is you don't want to have humour lessen the impact of a situation, like 'Oh, this is so funny, it's not that serious. It's not that big of a deal.' So you mustn't go too far with humour. You've got to judge it right.

I reckon that something that is genuinely funny is funny across cultures.

Correct. Old ladies falling over and guys getting kicked in the nuts – that works everywhere; works in every culture!

But I reckon also that some sorts of humour can alienate and exclude people. For example, I watched Religulous *just recently. It was funny but, by comparison with the stuff that you do, it's much less welcoming and inclusive.*

Well, I think that a lot of that comes from Bill Maher. I think that Bill is someone who is incredibly funny and really smart, but very standoffish in a lot of ways. I think that if you like him then you can relate to the film, but if you are not a fan then there's already a wall there.

It seemed to me that a lot of the humour in Religulous *is sort of – it's funny, don't get me wrong ...*

Yes, but it's also usually at the expense of somebody else.

Exactly. It's not kind.

Yes. It's not kind. But that's the thing with a movie like *Religulous* – you're going to offend somebody. If you're making fun of all the religions, at some point somebody's going to be offended.

I'd say the humour there limits its appeal, because it's only really funny from a particular point of view – an atheist point of view. By contrast, your films are funny, but not in a narrow way. The humour seems to translate really well, so that they get shown all over the world. So what's the nature of your humour?

What I try to do is I try to let the humour come from the situation. I try to make it situational comedy, situational humour, where I come into the room and I come into the interview and I'm just there being me in this kind of insane world, and trying to understand it and asking questions about it. And I think a lot of the funny stuff comes from people who aren't trying to be funny at all. Like when you're just doing the interviews with people and they say things or do things that are spectacular. Or when a situation is awkward and weird – that's universally funny, and we've all had moments like that. Jokes often don't translate, but that sort of thing really does.

In *The Greatest Movie Ever Sold*, I loved the pitch process where we were pitching brands, and you're seeing these people just kind of shoot me down and say terrible things to me. I don't ever like belittling other people that I'm with, but I'll belittle myself all the time. I think self-deprecation works on a lot of levels. I think it works all the time, and it's something comedians have used for centuries.

It makes a big difference, doesn't it, just being likeable, just being a likeable presence?

Yes. Well, I mean, for journalism I think it's important, period, because you have to come in cold and if you want somebody to talk to you there has to be some sort of a connection on some base level. It can't just be: 'I'm going to ask you questions and you're going to tell me answers.' There has to be a connection. You have to warm someone up.

I was just on a panel with Errol Morris and he basically said he won't interview anyone for less than twenty hours now. So, basically, he'll sit down and interview someone, and he throws the first ten hours out whenever he does an interview. And he goes, 'And then the next ten hours are when it starts to get interesting. And then after twenty is where it gets good.' Because over all of that time he's working on you until you have such trust in everything that he's talking about that you'll just let your guard down. There's become a real relationship there. I think that those relationships are incredibly important in documentary filmmaking.

The kind of humour that you're talking about – from people, and your dealings with people – that has a lot to do with charm, I think.

Yes. You've got to be able to get in there and talk to anybody. I think you have to be able to connect with anyone. For me, when I go into these situations I don't ever go in trying to be something I'm not. All I can do is be myself, and talk to people, and try to just be as upfront as possible. I think the more upfront I am about what I'm trying to do, the easier the whole thing becomes because people start to get what it's all about.

I think the funniest bit in Greatest Movie *is the scene with the* Mane 'N' Tail *shampoo. And it's funny because you thought it was funny …*

We just stumbled upon it. I had no idea that even existed. And that's one of the things about the way I like to work: we don't shoot things multiple times; we don't do multiple takes. I think that the minute you say, 'Okay, let's do that one more time,' it's gone. The magic of that moment is over. That scene is funny because it's real. What I really want to have happen in my films, especially things that I'm in, is that you're going on this journey with me. It's a vicarious journey. When I learn something, you'll learn something. When I feel something, you'll feel something. When I think something's funny, hopefully you'll think it's funny as well. I love that scene also, because of the ridiculousness of it: there's a shampoo for people *and* horses. Come on, that's amazing! It's phenomenal!

Are there any subjects that you can't apply humour to? Are there any subjects where humour just does not work?

I think that in narrative films it's easier to deal with certain topics with humour. *Life is Beautiful* is a great example. It dealt with World War II, with concentration camps, and it's a fantastically funny, entertaining movie that is really dark in terms of subject matter. I think that, from a documentary standpoint, there are probably things along those lines that it would be hard to make funny because they are so dark. I think there are just things that you can't make funny or you shouldn't try to make funny, just because of the subject matter. I think that in documentaries there are subgenres, just like in movies there are dramas, thrillers, comedies. I think that's the same thing in documentary films, so you have documentary comedies, documentary dramas, documentary thrillers, documentary horror films, and so on. There are things that should be comedies, and there are things that should be dramas and thrillers.

There are a lot of ideas, funny ideas, in Greatest Movie. *Do you have a team of writers?*

It's myself and my writing partner, Jeremy. He and I write almost everything. I wrote the commercials that are in the film and then he and I together wrote everything else. He's a great sounding board. He and I have worked together now for seven years and we share one brain. We know how the other person thinks. He can get completely into my head and understand how I'd tell a story and how I would say something. And I think that makes it work.

In Greatest Movie *there are more gags as such than in your other films, like the running gag with the POM juice.*

Yes. Advertising those products was part of our sponsorship contracts. So when these things come on screen, whether it's me eating an Amy's Pizza, or drinking a POM, or wearing Merrells shoes, or driving a Mini Cooper, or getting gas at a Sheetz, those things suddenly have a humour in them. Knowing that these things have all been paid for by somebody just to make sure they're in a movie makes them really funny from the start, just because that's the world we live in, where people will pay for anything. People will buy anything. Anything's for sale.

There's a real sense of showmanship about your films. Is that just a natural thing? Is that what you're naturally like?

Yes, I'm the carnival barker of documentaries. I'm the guy out front saying, 'Come on in! You're going to love it. It's the greatest thing ever!' I think there's something exciting about trying to make a lot of these topics and issues as broad as we can, to reach the largest possible audience. And I think whatever you can do to achieve that can only help your film, including some of the stunts that we do to promote a film. Like with *The Greatest Movie Ever Sold*, we bought the name to a town in Pennsylvania. We bought that for $25,000. We had this big renaming ceremony where all the media came. And this is just an extension of the movie. It has nothing to do with the filming at this point. It's just *promoting* the film. I gave the cheque to the mayor of the town and they changed the name of their town to 'POM Wonderful Presents: The Greatest Movie Ever Sold, Pennsylvania'. That's amazing, that we were able to make that happen! It is a big kind of P.T. Barnam-esque stunt, a thing that gets everybody talking. And it was picked up around the world. So we're making it into an event and making it something like: 'Wow, I have to see that. It's historical! It's that important!' It's bigger than a documentary. When we started calling it *The Greatest Movie Ever Sold*, the goal for me was to make a documentary blockbuster. So we coined this term of a 'docbuster' – again, to make it seem bigger than a regular documentary.

Do you need to be a naturally funny person to make a funny film?

I've met some really unfunny people who are comedians, especially in Hollywood. I've met a lot of people who will sit at a table and talk to you and they are some really unfunny people. But when they start writing on a page some really funny things come out. But I think, if you're going to be on camera especially, there's got to be a sense of humour. You have to have a sense of humour.

The tone of your films – the sense that they're going to be funny and entertaining – a lot of that comes from the animations, doesn't it?

For me, I want to have things in my films that kind of jump off the screen, and even as you're getting an onslaught of information, it's given to you in a way that is (a) understandable and (b) kind of engaging and palatable. There's something delicious about this spoonful of medicine I'm giving you. And, yes, the animations also set a tone. They let you know that the approach will be irreverent. From the beginning, I want people to come into the film and know it's okay to laugh at this, that this is going to be fun and there are going to be funny parts – really funny parts. And then, as we bring you in, as we pull the rope and get you closer, at some point we cut the rope and it gets serious. Like there are scenes, whether it be in *Super Size Me* or *Where in the World?* or *Greatest Movie*, where the tables do turn and you're not laughing. There get to be some really serious moments. Like in *Super Size Me*, when my health is falling apart and all the doctors are telling me to quit; or in *Where in the World?*, where we're in the middle of a Taliban ambush in Afghanistan. There are moments that are incredibly serious, and what we try to do is we want to get you to those moments, through humour, so once we peel back the layers of onion you don't mind crying for a while.

How did you come to make films the way you do: funny, authored, with your presence on screen?

Well, it started with *Super Size Me*, though it was never the intention that I was going to be on screen. The original idea was I'm going to get somebody else to do this. I'm going to get somebody else to eat all this junk food, because my girlfriend was like: 'You can't do this.' But the more I started talking about it internally with my director of photography and other people in my office, it became clear that there was no way I could know for sure that when that guy went home at the end of the night he wouldn't be, like, sneaking in some broccoli, or munching on some bok choi while no one's looking. And so I was like: 'We can't do that because there's no guarantee that this person will live up to the parameters that we're setting within the film.' So I did it out of necessity with *Super Size Me* more than anything else.

Did you ever do stand-up?

Yes, years ago. When I was in college I did, and improv. And then when I got out I just started focusing on filmmaking.

Have you ever been attracted to making a funny film about a character, like, say, Winnebago Man?

I love *Winnebago Man*. And *King of Kong* is a great movie. *Exit Through the Gift Shop*. You know, these are films that all follow these great, quirky people and tell incredible stories. I'm just finishing a film right now about Comic-Con, the biggest comic book convention in the world that happens every year in San Diego; 150,000 people go there. We've made a movie where we follow seven different people into Comic-Con and we kind of tell their story. I didn't want to make a movie that was kind of like, 'Laugh at all these nerds and geeks'. I wanted it to be much more of a celebration of this thing that we all love, with really interesting characters. I'm not in one frame of that movie which is great. I'm not narrowing that movie which is a good thing.

The thing that those films all have in common – and also I think Anvil *and* Best Worst Movie *– is that you're rooting for someone, and they're redemptive. They're all about characters who have struggled but sort of come out okay. And that's quite like the feel of your films. You're that character in your films.*

Yes. You're championing an underdog in those films. These are people who you want to cheer on, people who, you know, have all bets against them. These are people who you want to win; you want them to win so bad. And within my films there's always something much bigger than me that I'm exploring, something that is infinitely bigger than all of us. In my films generally, it's not just me. It's me kind of representing us, saying, 'This is bigger than us, but let's figure it out together.' And it does tend to be against the odds, you're right, especially with *Greatest Movie*, where we called every ad agency and not one ad agency would help us. We called every product-placement company and none would help us put products in the movie, and only two would even go on camera.

There's something about your films that makes an audience feel they could emulate them. There's something YouTube-ish about them. Like Super Size Me *– the spirit of it is: 'Why not? I'll get a camera. I'll do it and see what happens.'*

Which I think is great. I met some kids just this week, and they were like: '*Super Size Me* was the movie that made me want to become a filmmaker and it made me get off my arse and actually make a film.' You know, 'For years I've been wanting to make a film and after seeing your film I realised that I could.' Because that's how easy it is! That's how bad my movies look! My movies look so bad that everybody's like, 'Shit, I can make a movie that looks that good. Get a camera and strap it to the back of a monkey!' A great thing happened in the early 2000s, which was a real democratisation of filmmaking. You know, when I was in film school, we were still shooting on 16mm and editing on Steenbecks and using a guillotine to actually cut the film. That was like the late '90s. And then suddenly there were great video cameras that were affordable. And now anyone with a camera and a computer and a good idea can make a movie. You didn't need money, you just needed sweat equity; you needed time. I think that really changed filmmaking, and that's how *Super Size Me* got made. You know, we made that movie with a Sony PD150, a little three-chip camera. We edited the whole thing on Final Cut. It was a revolution. It gave people who had never had the ability to make movies, (a) the access and (b), I think, the courage. And long may it continue.

12 Documentaries and music

Julien Temple

Julien Temple is a multi-award-winning director with a particular interest in music. His involvement in punk in the 1970s led to a friendship with The Sex Pistols, which produced a number of remarkable documentaries, including *The Great Rock 'n' Roll Swindle* (1979), the story of the band from the perspective of their manager, Malcolm McLaren; and *The Filth and the Fury* (2000), a counter-piece to the earlier film, told from the perspective of the surviving members of the band.

Other documentary projects include: *The Future Is Unwritten* (2007), a very personal and moving film about the life of The Clash frontman (and Temple's close friend) Joe Strummer; *Glastonbury* (2006), a feature documentary about the British music festival, drawing on both footage filmed by Temple himself and material shot by festival goers over the event's forty-year lifespan; *Oil City Confidential* (2009), a vivid history of the Essex-based pub-rock band Dr Feelgood; *Requiem for Detroit?* (2011), a beautiful and inspiring film about the decline of a once-great metropolis, home to American car production and the Motown music industry; and a pair of biographical documentaries about the brothers who founded the influential British rock band The Kinks – *Ray Davies: Imaginary Man* (2010) and *Dave Davies: Kinkdom Come* (2011).

Temple has also directed a large number of music videos for artists such as The Rolling Stones, Neil Young, Blur and David Bowie, as well as *Absolute Beginners* (1986), a musical adaptation of Colin MacInnes' book, which was one of the most expensive feature films in British cinema history.

Julien Temple, during the making of Requiem for Detroit? *Picture courtesy of Julien Temple.*

What role does music play in documentaries?

I find it quite strange being interviewed as a documentary-maker, because I don't really think of my films as documentaries. I come from a fictional background, and I think any film, whether it's a documentary or a fiction film, is an amazing manipulation of reality. And if you can obtain some kind of personal truth, that's about as good as it gets. So I come from a totally different tradition from a lot of the other people who are in this book. I don't come from any tradition, I hope. Well, I come from the punk tradition where you really mix and match and smash things together and see what happens. It's very manipulative. It's not a kind of objective, observational, fly-on-the-wall sense of making a film. You know, the BBC have all these modules you have to do about telling the truth before they'll let you make a film. And my first instinct is to take the module apart and create provocative lies and make people question and challenge what they're seeing. That's the way I would approach any film, whether it's a fiction film or a documentary.

I've made documentaries about music and musicians, but I don't think you can film music; I think it's invisible. I think you move to it, you don't film it. Certainly, fingers-on-guitar-frets and so on is a waste of film or tape. If you lined those shots up, you could get round the solar system twenty times. To me, music is like a tool you can use. You can strain things through music, and you can *see* through music, and you can tell stories with music. It's a great, propulsive energy to have at your disposal, both in terms of the audio but also the particular cutting style that certain kinds of music seem to demand. I don't make films about music; I make films about the people that make the music, the people who listen to the music, the world that the music came from. And I use the music to kind of power the film, like gasoline.

It seems to me that music has the power to complicate and bring subtlety, which is a great thing for a documentary.

You can't make a film that tells people things they already know. You've got to try to find ways of making them look at something that seems familiar in a different way, I think, and music does that quite well.

You can paint with music. In the Detroit film I was very lucky to be able to use any music I wanted for the first time in my life because of the BBC blanket licence agreement [an arrangement whereby the BBC pays an annual fee to PRS for Music, which allows everyone making films for the BBC to use any PRS-managed track without having to obtain (and pay for) a separate individual licence to cover its use]. And I found myself putting a little brushstroke of Sinatra in there, just five seconds or so. I think it's how you use music. It can be incredibly emotionally revealing. You can tell a story and drive a narrative by music. I think, if you use it in the right way, you can provoke a whole series of responses: not just physical and adrenaline-based, but intellectual, you know? I love that idea of playing music against type, so it becomes a kind of an idea, like an edit or a cut. Something like 'School's Out', which is a Detroit song, when you play that over a school that's being pulled down by climbing vines – because Detroit is this abandoned city that's being reclaimed by nature – and it's 'School's Out Forever!': that's an ironic but also argumentative use of music. And that's really exciting to me. If you want a bit of a car chase and you just pump up the volume, I think that's a very boring use of music.

You know, I've never really recovered from hearing 'You Really Got Me' as a kid under the blankets on a crystal radio set. It just came through from a pirate radio station when I was a little kid. And just the power of that, and the kind of questions that it raised, and the sense that there must be other ways of looking at things or feeling things than you were being taught at school and by your parents ... that still really reverberates with me. And I was lucky enough to grow up in that moment in London where you had The Kinks and The Stones and The Who and The Small Faces. And each week, these songs seemed to be talking directly to us as an audience and opening up new ways of seeing your life, and new ideas about what it was possible to feel and do with your life. That was very, very powerful – an extremely exciting thing. And I was lucky enough to revisit it with the punk thing when I was older, and I felt the same excitement, the same connection.

It's very clear, watching your films, that music can be incredibly evocative of a time and place. A piece of music can take you straight back not just to the time it was created but to the time in your life when you heard it.

Yes, it's a form of time travel, and I like that a lot about it. But I think it takes you on many journeys, not just back into where it came from. It can take you deep inside yourself. You know, it's a powerful thing, music. And it belongs with motion, you know? I think people always moved around fires to music, and in a way film is just capturing people doing what they do. That's what people did when they had nothing else: they'd bang a drum and dance around a fire. That to me was an early movie.

Are there any rules for combining images and music that you've learned? Or is it more a matter of trial and error when you're making a film, and when you're in the edit?

If there are rules, I really try to not learn them, you know? I really believe that, if you feel you've learned some kind of formula, you're fucked. I like the idea of being very terrified when I start a new film, which is partly what made me want to go to Tijuana for the thing I'm doing at the moment [Tijuanalandia, billed as a musical exploration of the past, present and future of the Mexican border town]. I think you've got to be scared of what you're about to do and feel that you don't know anything. You want to do it as though you're doing it for the first time. And you want to mess up, and you want to make mistakes, and learn. And you want to get depressed, so that you can climb out of the pit of depression. I think it's a very emotional thing making a film, and you have to try to become intensely involved in it and live it as much as possible. And put yourself through a kind of emotional narrative arc, you know? I really love the idea of diving in without a plan and feel you're drowning in a film and struggling to find a way out. And, in that kind of desperation, you find things you would never have planned. I don't see the point of doing another film unless you try to do something you haven't done before.

I remember when I was starting off as an exec, an old-hand editor said to me that you can tell that there's good music in a documentary when you don't notice it.

Well, I love jabbing it right in your face at times. I think that's brilliant, you know? And I like silence. Silence is part of music. I really think there are no rules. It would be great if you didn't notice music, if that's what you want to do. But sometimes it's really great if you stuff it down people's throats. You know, he probably wouldn't like the same kind of music that I like, that guy, anyway. But I do think music has different functions. There's a hypnotic kind of music that can lull you into sleep, which could be good at certain times. But I always find a bit of 'Anarchy in the UK' goes down nicely.

So, no rules for things that you should do with music. Conversely, are there any rules for what you shouldn't do? What's the worst thing that you can do with music?

I've mutilated music in many ways and I look to discover new ways of doing that with every film. I love slowing it down. I love playing it out of sync when people are singing. I mean, these are probably seen to be bad things, but I don't think you can do anything terrible with music. You try it and see whether it does what you need it to do at that point in time. You might want to set fire to the tape while it's playing, I don't know – see what that sounds like.

I always cringe when I hear music where the reason it's there is that the title of the track is in some way relevant to a theme that you're seeing. So if someone in a film is having a lazy weekend, then you hear The Kinks – you know, screamingly obvious, literal choices.

Yes, yes. I'm doing a film about Ray Davies at the moment, and I was looking at an earlier one, and they put a load of literal images to 'Waterloo Sunset', which was the worst thing. It destroyed the kind of Blakean mystery of the song stone dead by being so literal and unimaginative. But I like being really dumb at times and making people laugh at you when you make a film. I think it's really important that you have a sense of the ridiculousness of it, in one way. You've got to be able to take the piss out of the process. That seems important to me, as well as making people laugh. I want people to laugh more than anything else, at times. I think, if you create the circumstances for a well-engineered laugh that has a kind of undercurrent of making people think, that is the best thing. And sometimes music can help create that, because when people laugh they understand what you're saying.

When you're making a film like Requiem for Detroit?, *do you have a soundtrack in your head as you're going into it, or is the soundtrack something that is a response to what you found when you were filming?*

Well, you know, one of the reasons I really wanted to make that film about Detroit was that I was aware of it being one of the most amazing continuums of music from one city. Detroit has just endlessly created amazing music, whether it's '40s Be Bop or '20s Swing, or punk in the '70s, or rap in the '90s, and the whole Motown thing, obviously. So I knew there was just an incredible resource there, but I didn't know how I was going to use it at all.

I've always been a fan of those films about cities, like *Berlin: Symphony of a Great City*. But I don't think it's a documentary. I think it's a kind of art piece about Berlin, really. Or the Humphrey Jennings' films about Britain, which are very abstract with very few words, telling the story through images and music. And I tried to make the music in the Detroit film tell the story, like oral storytelling around a campfire. Again, it's that idea that there's a kind of repository of amazing knowledge in that music, caught like a fly in amber. The music of a time is an incredible way into that time.

Requiem for Detroit? is wall-to-wall music, which people say you can't do. I was kind of painting with it, which was amazing for me. I had access to so much music through the BBC, I could choose a really mad mix. I could just use it to accent and amplify a vibe about the time.

So it's really in the edit where you start making your musical choices?

To me, the editing process is about the sound as much as the image. It's about smashing things together that shouldn't really exist together and seeing if that works, whether it has a kind of resonance, an echo to it. I think there's almost a harmonic way of editing that's a bit like playing an instrument, which, of course, is very hard. You have to learn it. But it's like a different instrument every time. For example, on the *Glastonbury* film, I thought I was being very clever. I did an advert in the paper saying, 'Please send in any footage if you filmed anything at Glastonbury ever. Send it here.' And then this VHS arrived in a padded envelope and I'm like, 'Yes, this is working. This is great.' And then, two weeks later, I was up above my neck in padded bags of all sorts of Super-8 and 35-mill. It was incredible what people sent in. I had two thousand hours of this stuff, and once you start looking at one reel you've got to look at them all, quite rightly, because you find something randomly in the middle of a tape that just jumps out at you. But you then have the problem of how you organise this stuff, because we'd also shot with ten crews at Glastonbury, and I had a huge amount that I'd shot separately as well.

So you get to the point where you are literally trying to digest something that is too big, like a boa constrictor that eats an elephant or something. And it gets to the point where you just think, 'Christ, I can't do it ... I said I'd make a film about this but I can't handle it. I can't deal with it. I can't find a way through it.' But then ... I think it's good to get lost and depressed by it because then the little things that start to make sense or work mean so much to you, that it's like you can haul yourself out. And that energy of getting out of a dark place when you come up on to the sunny mountain upland or whatever, it feels amazing. And you can finally start 'playing' the edit, like a saxophone or something.

Do you think it's essential for documentary-makers to have an interest in music?

I just feel music is part of my life and my way of feeling, of being alive and kind of understanding the arc of my life and the times I've lived through. In a sense, I'm more of a social historian than anything else. That's what I studied at college: history. I like examining cultures and the effect they have on people, and place and time is very important to me. And I think, in that context, music is a really useful tool to unlocking certain mysteries and our emotional connections to particular times and particular places, and to each other.

Have you ever worked with a composer?

I don't like scoring; scoring something means that the music has a supporting role, put on afterwards. You get some guy who hasn't been involved in the process to sit and watch the film and go, 'Oh, I'll put some violins in here,' or whatever. I think music should be designed as you edit, and as you shoot, with certain musical ideas in mind.

But I have worked with composers. I worked with Gil Evans on *Absolute Beginners* which was an amazing trip, to work with him. He was Miles Davis' arranger and composer in the '50s. That was fantastic. I've worked with interesting musicians scoring things, but I do find it's slightly odd that often the budget doesn't allow you to pay a composer to be part of the film, so you sort of bring it to them when it's done. So it's a very one-way use of music. When I use 'found' music, like in the documentaries I've been doing recently, you feel it's part of the actual process of making the film rather than an add-on at the end. Also, it's hard to, you know, discuss music because it's not a verbal thing, so it is very weird sitting down with a composer saying what you want, musically.

How do you do that? How do you communicate with a composer?

Well, it's very much like pidgin English, a kind of child-like discourse. You make sounds and try to explain the emotion that you want from an image or against an image. It's an imprecise science. It's much easier to find something that sounds exactly right or something that's exactly wrong.

I find with composers it's much easier to talk in terms of a feel for the way you want things to sound. So to talk about music sounding polished or serrated, or sandpapery or flaky. I always end up using words like that. It's because, as you say, music is a totally different language which I don't really speak.

I've watched musicians make music and, obviously, a lot of it is instinctive – they live through it. But then they can have really heated arguments using very odd words about music. So I think what you describe is a good way forward.

What are the great examples of using music in documentaries? What about Koyaanisqatsi?

Yes. I haven't seen that for a long time but I like that film. Yes, it was a very bold film and it was also, I think, riding the zeitgeist of the time really, in a weird way. And it had a great hypnotic effect, which is unlike a lot of documentaries where you are supposed to be really attentive, and it kind of encouraged you to get lost in the flow of things. I do think the Dylan film is amazing because you just get a sense of how this guy makes music.

You mean Don't Look Back?

Yes, the Pennebaker film. I love that film. Whenever I see it I get really excited by watching it. It was really pushing the boundaries of what was possible at the time. And I like that sense of films that are doing something really new, because that seems to keep them fresh. Generally, though, I don't really watch documentaries. A good documentary is like a good film to me, you know? You want people to enter into it. Certainly, I don't watch many on TV. Television seems to keep distancing you by telling you what to think, but you should be provoked to think for yourself, really. As a filmmaker, that's what you want your audience to do rather than tell them. This thing of putting in narration that tells them what they are about to see and what they have just seen ... that's very confining I think.

I think it's also true of the way music is usually used in TV. It usually has one clear thing to say. It's not complicated.

Yes. I think they use it in a similar way to narration: to bolster exactly the feeling that's supposed to come through, whereas I think it can be much more interesting to say, 'Okay, let's use Mantovani here.' And you use it for quite a long time and people are saying, 'Why are we listening to so much Mantovani? What's this guy doing? He's lost his mind.' I like that kind of sacrilege. I use a lot of archive and I like the idea of, you know, desecrating, tomb-raiding, getting the bones out and sticking them on top of the coffin and playing around with them. And making stuff have different meanings than it was probably intended to have. I think music should be used in a sacrilegious way.

Let's talk about documentaries about music. It seems obvious that music is a great subject for a documentary, but why is that?

Well, music illuminates people's lives. You know, I'm really a filmmaker about my culture as well as music. I have made a lot of films about England, and about London particularly, and I think that music has an incredible light that it can shed on its time, and why people felt the way that they did at that time. So the intensity of what John Lydon lived through to create his music is really the subject of *The Filth and the Fury*, not just John. It's a way of shining a torch inside their brains, you know?

Also, I think great music has an explicit interest in people, which is maybe something else that makes it good for a documentary.

Yes, I think all great music has to come from someone either really observing people, or really opening up who they are in an incredibly human, revealing way: whether it's Ray Davies, who is an observer but creates these kind of imaginary friends that he then invents stories around, or whether it's someone like Dylan, who's more from within. It's got to be an intensely human revelation and feeling that comes from the music to make it great, I think.

It's very interesting watching The Future Is Unwritten *how interested in people Joe Strummer was, hanging out with people, asking them, 'What's your life like?'*

Well, that was what's so great about punk. It turned the whole celebrity fame thing on its head for a while. No worshipping fake idols. And Joe was a really great listener. And, you know, his songs are really about what he learned from other people about himself.

I think that what documentaries are, when they're good, is going and talking to people, being interested in people and then trying to shape it into something which is true. And I realised that that was what Joe Strummer was doing: making songs which are like documentaries.

Yes, I think that's true.

It seems to me also that music, or at least certain types of music, lends itself quite well to ideas, to exploring ideas and philosophies, in a way that all good documentaries do. There are loads of ideas in The Filth and the Fury *and in* The Future Is Unwritten, *because there are loads of ideas in the music that those films are inspired by.*

Yes. There's probably an element of overload in them, but punk was a kind of anger and, you know, is a reaction to boredom. It was reflecting an incredibly intense sense of being alive in response to a very dead period and dead possibilities. People of a certain generation, and a certain class, I guess, were very, very trapped at that point in time and felt betrayed by their education. They'd been brought up at the fag end of the kind of Victorian mindset of British Empire, and the idea that being British was some important chosen thing. And then you left school and you realised that that didn't really apply for a lot of people. And music, that moment in music, was a very acute way of registering a whole range of responses and feelings about the world. I love that – when a culture throws up music that really questions everything about itself.

Do you think that good music is about ideas?

I think good pop music is. I mean, I think rhythm is not necessarily about ideas; it's just about being alive, you know, and moving. But I think lyrics are really important in the films that I've made. The people I've made films about have written brilliant lyrics. Lyrics don't only mean one thing; they can mean a million things. But the lyrics by the people I've made films about have a provocative, thought-provoking aspect.

I'd say that your films are full of ideas. There are lots of ideas in Glastonbury *as well as* The Filth and the Fury. *I wondered if you're almost an ideas-led filmmaker who has come to music because music is a great way of debating and exploring ideas.*

I think that's probably true, yes, although I try to couch the ideas in humour. And I try to give them a narrative trajectory, so that people don't get really bored of just the ideas. There needs to be an emotional investment for people to want to sit in a cinema for two hours. In the '60s, with The Kinks and The Stones and The Who, the music really was a great catalyst for me intellectually, to start thinking independently. And then punk was a great thing for me because I'd studied history at college and studied revolution and different revolutions, and punk seemed to be something that connected to those ideas of cultures in great turmoil and conflict, where lives were being put on the line for what people believed in. That was very exciting for me as a kind of intellectual. I was an odd part of that punk inner circle because I was, you know, a middle-class cunt with an education, although I had grown up on a council estate. So I had a slightly strange upbringing that allowed me not to lose sight of what a lot of people's lives were about. My father would blast out Beethoven on Sunday mornings across this estate and we'd get dog shit through the letterbox and stuff, so I saw both sides.

Pop music is another reason why music is good territory for a documentary, in that pop is full of great stories and big characters.

Yes. Musicians in post-war Britain have been, you know, the heroes. There were legends about great fighters in previous cultures, or saints, or whatever, but the important cultural figures in our time, since the '60s anyway, have largely been people who have worked in music. That's partly because it's a mass form – it does really dig into the culture and come from the culture because it's trying to sell as many records as it can and reach as many people as it can.

They're pretty wild characters, a lot of them, though – larger than life. They're good characters for documentaries because their lives are so eventful.

Yes, they get into all sorts of trouble. It's usually quite a conflicted life. I think people who are totally happy probably won't make the greatest music. I think someone like Joe was all about contradictions and struggling, you know, to make the music. It wasn't necessarily the easiest thing for him to do. With The Sex Pistols, you have a kind of built-in drama which you would have with any four guys if you locked them up in a room for long enough, I would have thought. But a band is such a kind of intense, captive experience, really, that you're going to get all sorts of heightened dramas between people because of the pressure-cooker situation, especially when you add fame and money and sex into that. It's an incredibly volatile mix. The problem is that it's a bit of a cliché, you know – the band fall out ... It's how you try to make the human emotions of that seem fresh enough so that you're living them with the band, rather than just trotting out another rock and roll cliché.

Musicians give you built-in charisma, as well, which is a good start. Quite often when you're making a documentary and you're casting, you're looking for a good character, someone who has a big personality and a bit of charisma.

If you're making a film about a pop star, you've probably already got a good character, otherwise they wouldn't be a star.

Well, some musicians are really boring old cunts, you know, but others are not. Generally, musicians seem to be a mirror for a much wider thing, and people live their lives through these musicians that I've made films about; to a lesser extent, I suppose, with Dr Feelgood, although for a period people really put their lives on the line with Dr Feelgood. There's something about people living their lives through these songs and through these musicians that makes them somehow absorb the wider culture. That's what's interesting to me, because it really gives you all these lines out into the time and the place that this music was created in.

Another thing that seems quite conducive about pop music, as far as making documentaries is concerned, is that it often has a sense of humour.

Yes. Punk, you know, it had a self-piss-take aspect to it. I think there's huge humour, black humour, in The Sex Pistols. I also think it reaches back beyond rock and roll to a kind of earlier, working-class music, you know music hall and a nineteenth-century response to industrialisation that you had to laugh or you'd go crazy.

It gives you a licence to be funny and playful if there are playfulness and humour in the music.

Yes, it does. The best times I have with an audience watching a film I've made is when they're laughing. When they sit there in rapt silence, you're like, 'What are they thinking? Are they getting it?'

And there's something about the anarchy of punk that gives you this incredible freedom as a filmmaker to do what you like.

Yes, and also the fact of not really having any money. I had this camera with a wide shutter that didn't have the rolling bar, which was amazing. So I could just film shows off the TV as they were being broadcast and film The Pistols, and then just mash it up. And, in fact, that gave you more options than if you'd been going around filming and trying to get something good. It was born out of complete lack of money but it created this great kind of irreverent, anarchic freedom. You could take some newscaster and make him into a kind of Grand

Guignol figure, you know, like a clown, by just manipulating the edit. And that's how I first started feeling you can really play around with this medium and surprise yourself by what you can achieve with found material and chopping it up and making some other sense of it. You know, using archive and different formats was sacrilege at the time – putting video with Super-8 with 35mm with 16mm. It was also very sacrilegious to make cartoons of The Sex Pistols, because they were supposed to be these cool rock and roll guys, whereas now, obviously, you have bands made of cartoons and so on. Then, it was like, 'This is not what you do.' But it was the only way to tell the story at that point because we couldn't stage it. We didn't have the money. But I had friends who were studying animation who could draw it and bring it to life that way.

I watched Glastonbury *just recently, and it felt really moving; I think partly because it's a story of my generation.*

You know, high culture has normally been seen as the repository of history. But I think popular culture is for many people a more direct frame of reference about how things have changed and how the world is organised. Popular music reflects that very vividly. Initially, I wanted to make a film about the way the world has changed and people have changed over the last four decades. And I had some thoughts about what material I could use to illustrate those changes. Then it became really obvious that this one event tells you everything. It's like a big mirror floating around the world reflecting the changes both inside people and outside. Just the idea that in 1971 you turned up to Glastonbury in a pair of jeans with no shoes and now you're walking in with washing machines and what have you. People have evolved in weird ways over that time, and that's the subject of the film.

I felt like the story of Glastonbury *is the story of my life.*

Yes, I felt that too. I mean, I think a lot of the films that I've made are in an odd way autobiographical, you know? The Sex Pistols is the moment when I discovered I could maybe do something. And certainly with Joe, he was born in the same year as me, although obviously we had incredibly different lives on many levels. So there is a sense in making these films of trying to make sense of your own life and the time you've lived through, which I somehow feel a need to do. I don't know why that is particularly.

Maybe another reason why music seems to be such a good subject for documentaries is that music is cool. And, as a subject for a documentary, a lot cooler than what a lot of documentaries tend to be about.

Yes. I'm of a generation that grew up being interested in cool. From the mid-'60s, it was cool to be cool. And it can get you places that not being cool won't get you.

There are documentary purists who would say it's all about vérité; it's all about social realism and you've got to go to a council estate and 'engage'. I do understand all that. But those are reasons why documentaries have been marginalised, whereas making documentaries that are about cool stuff is a reason why documentaries are now so popular.

Yes. Well, I think documentaries can be about the imagination, not just reality. To me, The Sex Pistols and Dr Feelgood are people imagining their way out of situations that aren't that good. They emerge from council estates and places where you want to get out of really, but you're trapped, so how do you do the Houdini act? The Sex Pistols was a version of Houdini to me: people from a council estate sort of life who managed to channel all their feelings and anger into something very positive.

For me, music is great because you can't pin it down; it can't have just one meaning. It's an abstract, rather than a verbal and literal way of communicating. It's very good at communicating just feelings that at times you can't put into words.

Music docs, like the ones that you make, have helped to popularise documentaries generally, I think.

Well, I try to make them very accessible. I have a problem that I was over-educated, unlike people I really admire like John Lydon who wasn't educated and created his own path to wisdom like William Blake. So I'm aware of fighting an over-cerebral response to things. I mean, I think it's good to have a lot of thoughts about things and my greatest pleasure in making films is the research and learning about stuff I haven't understood before. In that sense, it's like an ongoing education, which is a very privileged thing: to be paid to go and learn about something that you don't know about. But I try to make it accessible, and laughter and humour are a big part of doing that. You can have quite complicated ideas that are unlocked for people by having a sense of humour built into them. I think it is good to suddenly take the rug away.

Having said that about popularising docs, there are music documentaries that are quite dull, don't you think?

Well, 'rockumentary' is extremely dull. As dull as it gets. You know, the kind of record company-commissioned old farts at mixing desks saying, 'We came in and did this album and then we did that album and then he had an overdose.' I get called a rockumentarian, and I want to gag when I hear that. I hate it. Because rockumentaries seem to be about music – you know, here's the desk we mixed it on, and here's Eric Clapton with his guitar – but they're never about reaching out into the culture, or asking where that music came from, or why it emerged. If I've done anything in the music documentary world, it is to use the music as a way of viewing the world behind the music.

What about concert films? I think it's a doomed form, really, because it's never going to be as good as being there.

I've done them, or at least I've tried. I did a Madness film [*The Liberty of Norton Folgate*, 2009] where I tried to take on the idea. They wanted me to do this film of them in concert. But it was interesting for me because it was very much a music hall series of songs that they were performing for the first time in an old music hall theatre. So we kind of corrupted the idea of just filming an event. We filmed the concert and then projected it on alleyways and parts of London that kind of linked to this nineteenth-century music hall period. We tried to kind of explode the idea of a concert film and I think there is mileage in that, actually. I don't think it's a totally successful film, but I think that as you sit in the audience at a concert your mind floats around these songs anyway, so why not go with the thoughts that the music evokes and create a film that kind of curls around itself and in and out. And then it could be great. I think the problem with a concert film is that you've got five camera angles over an hour and you're just constantly repeating the same angles so it gets very static. I think you should try to design a concert film so that each song has a different approach to it and is filmed in a different way.

I watched Shine a Light *just recently. Very disappointing.*

Oh, God! I walked out after the second song. I don't think it was very successful at all. I've done some live films. It's quite a good way of making some money without having to exercise your brain too much. I did one about The Sex Pistols' recent tour – I don't know if you saw that? – which was an interesting subject because of the purity of The Sex Pistols. And here's this kind of flogging-a-dead-horse situation, but with a sense of humour about it. It was very music hall as well actually, very surreal. You know, grandfather punks with their little grandchildren punks, all singing these songs like they were incantations, like every word was part of some strange spell that they were casting.

It seems to me that documentaries about music are always better when there's another element, like you were talking about with your films reaching out into the culture. I like Gimme Shelter, *where it becomes about the Hell's Angels and a sort of end of innocence at the end of the '60s.*

Yes, yes, it's a fabulous film. It's one of my favourites because it has this extra-ordinary rosebud event at the heart of it and you really get behind the mask of The Stones because they're terrified by what they've unleashed and what's going on in front of their eyes. It's a very powerful moment, that – there was the Woodstock moment, and then six months later this thing flipping over. There's a kind of connection with the moment and the end of something that's really vivid in it. The Stones are not very good in that concert. You wouldn't see it for the music, but rather for what it's bringing to the surface. There's this hippy world that's been looking like it could change things and do good things in the world, then suddenly it all changes, and you kind of feel that happening in the film which is really exciting. I also really like that film *Dig!* [released in 2004, documenting the love–hate relationship between two bands, The Brian Jonestown Massacre and The Dandy Warhols], which is about human jealousy and rivalry and stuff. It's great.

It seems to me that when you go into the cinema in particular, though probably when you're watching documentary in any context, you want a documentary to be uplifting. And music can give you that. There's something inherently uplifting about music as a subject for a documentary.

Yes, it has the potential for huge uplift, music. But also it can be a downer. It can be soporific. It can be many different things. I mean, I did feel the uplift at the end of *Glastonbury* was really a lot to do with the music. Not necessarily music that I listen to or like, you know: 'Heroes' is not my favourite David Bowie song. I like the Pulp moment in that film where you really get this sense of a band having a chrysalis moment, where the butterfly emerges. In front of a crowd, this band becomes something it wasn't before that moment, and that's really uplifting. And then I wanted to top that. I wanted to build this kind of uplift at the end which certainly the music helped me do. The Bowie is a very anthemic song, but also, somehow, you could use it as a kind of time travel, so that effectively Bowie was playing to crowds across thirty-five years, with hippies from '71 dancing to David Bowie as well as people in the present day. He actually did play the first festival, which I saw. It was amazing because no one knew who he was, really, back then, and he'd just had that one 'Space Oddity' hit. But there he was. So they kept putting him off, and he went on, finally, at about four in the morning, so the dawn was coming up and everyone was asleep. And people were waking you up and saying, 'Wake up! You've got to see this guy. This guy's amazing!' And there he was, just with his guitar in a dress singing along with the dawn chorus of birds. So the idea that he was playing to people through all the years of that event was quite powerful to me.

I wonder if part of music's potential to be uplifting comes from the fact that popular music is basically always youthful and romantic – maybe not romantic, but youthful and sort of optimistic.

Music is usually better when it's young, yes. Although I saw Neil Young a couple of years ago at Glastonbury, and that was amazing. There was this audience of young kids who thought he was like some grumpy old paedophile from the potting shed or something when he came on, and didn't know who he was, really. But by the end they were just like blown away and really part of this journey. That power of an older musician can be amazing.

If popular music has this sort of youthfulness and optimism, it also has a hint of loss in it as well, which is even better for a documentary, if it can have both ...

Well, that's another thing about rock and roll bands: they have a series of built-in trap-doors that people fall through. There is a powerful moment for me in *The Filth and the Fury* when I was filming John Lydon, with a little handycam, in silhouette, in Malibu with this local student sound recordist guy, and John –

this incredibly strident, verbally aggressive, punk ogre – suddenly started crying and talking about Sid. And the kid was completely freaked out. He was like, 'Shall I continue recording this?' and I was like, 'Yes, yes, go on.' He wanted to turn it off. I was like, 'What? What are you doing?' It was a very, very, you know, unexpected and awkward moment because John is intensely, fiercely proud of his persona, and here it was completely dissolving. And he said, 'If you fucking put that in the film I'm going to fucking kill you,' and all sorts of stuff like that. And I was like, 'But it's great. I'm going to put it in the film.' What was really key to that film working was that you got behind the mask. With the Scorsese Bob Dylan film [*No Direction Home*, 2005], which I admire on many levels, you never got behind the mask. And I think, in a film about musicians, you've got to get behind there and discover a human being rather than this pop construct, the hero figure, with all his human frailties and failings and regrets.

Do you think that documentaries about musicians are usually too celebratory?

I think you want to celebrate, but you want to choose subjects that have a kind of failure built into the success. If it's just mega-stardom or whatever, it has no traction dramatically. But very few careers are without tragedy, I would have thought.

The Future Is Unwritten – *by contrast with* The Filth and the Fury, *it's quite a sombre film. There's a huge sense of loss.*

Well, that's because Joe Strummer, who the film is about, was my friend, a very close friend in the end. I shot The Clash at the same time I shot The Pistols, and knew them, but then kind of fell out with them because they were saying, 'You either shoot us or them.' And I was already shooting The Pistols from before. So, for whatever reason, I wasn't friends with Joe for a long time and then he bizarrely turned up at my house with my wife's best friend from school that he'd married, and then bought a place just up the road from me. So we spent a lot of time together towards the end of his life. And, like most people who knew him, it was very devastating for me when he died, because he was a unique person to know and he connected a lot of people together in a really original and special kind of way. There was such a life force about Joe that it was very hard, in a sense, to make the film about him. Talking about him was probably a way of dealing with it, not just for me but for a lot of the people I knew who were friends with him. It was like a way of dealing with the loss. I saw it as a wake, really, where the guy who'd died turns up at his own wake and is sitting next to you at the campfire.

It's hard to make a film about a friend. I don't know how many people have done that but I've only done it the once and it comes with a lot more levels of self-questioning, like: how are you going to portray your friend? You do want to celebrate them but you want to show the flaws – and certainly with Joe he would have kicked the shit out of me if I hadn't shown the flaws, because he was very proud of using the contradictions and the flaws that he knew he had as a kind of energy to burn up, to use. So, yes, it probably is quite sombre. I had a bad time making that film; you know, how to find the right pitch for talking about Joe ...

The key thing about The Future Is Unwritten *is that like all good documentaries – and there's no way of saying it without sounding idiotic – it's about being human, or 'the human dimension', or 'the human experience'.*

Yes. Whether it's a fiction film or a documentary, it's got to try to get close to what it is to be that person or those people: the human emotional core of people's lives.

You've made feature films. What is it about documentaries that keeps pulling you back?

It's the freedom, really, to make mistakes and improvise as you go along. You know, feature film is by its nature a thing that is over-planned, because people are paranoid about the amount of money you're spending. It's basically like throwing a fifty-quid note into a fire every two minutes. So there's a lot of pressure and you've got some banker behind you saying, 'I'm going to rip these pages out of the script.' I have problems with it because it reminds me of being at school with all these parameters and rules set up by the pressure of the budget. So, when you're working with three people rather than a hundred people, it's a more personal experience and you do feel it's possible to use the camera in a more fluid way.

Do you need to be a certain sort of person to make films like The Filth and the Fury?

I'm interested in rock and roll filmmaking, a kind of outlaw version of things: the camera like a gun, breaking rules for the fun of it, and living it hard, you know? Shooting hard, pushing endurance to the limits, getting as much as you can in a day and not stopping until you drop – that kind of thing. I think you need to be able to push yourself into unsafe areas, have a sense of enjoying creative danger. I think directing any film you have to have a certain level of confidence. You know, I'm personally quite a shy person, so I can find that hard if I'm not feeling great. I find it hard to feel that I'm running on full power. I think confidence has a lot to do with it, however you get that. But, having said that, I think it's good to be unconfident as well. I think it's really good to doubt yourself a lot. I would say the best thing is to feel you really are starting from scratch each time you do it. Never feel that you've learned how it's done.

13 Character-led filmmaking

Marc Isaacs

Marc Isaacs is a leading British documentary filmmaker, whose work often centres on finding and following extraordinary characters. He is known for his patience, sensitivity and compassion, and his films have won Grierson, RTS and BAFTA awards, as well as a number of international film festival prizes.

His body of work includes: *Lift* (2001), in which Isaacs installs himself inside the lift of a high-rise block of council flats, and patiently observes the residents as they go about their daily lives; *Calais: The Last Border* (2003), a portrait of the various characters, including business owners and asylum seekers, who find themselves resident in the declining French town; *The Curious World of Frinton-on-Sea* (2008), a film about the people who have elected to settle in England's most conservative seaside resort; *All White in Barking* (2008), a vivid sketch of relationships, preconceptions and tensions in a multicultural London borough; and *Men of the City* (2009), which follows the lives of workers in London's financial centre at a time of great uncertainty and upheaval.

Marc Isaacs. Picture courtesy of Marc Isaacs.

Your films are full of great characters. How do you go about making them?

I usually start the project with quite a vague idea, and it only really comes alive when I meet characters. The way that I do that is by just hanging around. If I have an idea about a place, I'll go to that place, and I'll stalk the place, until something or somebody catches my eye. You meet a character first, and then it affects how the whole film is going to unfold. In a way, you want all the other characters to match up to the thing that you're initially drawn in by, and that first person who fires your imagination. You know, you hope that all the characters will be equally as fascinating as each other. Usually, it works out that you do favour one over the others, in terms of the time you spend and their emotional impact on the film. But some of the other characters will have value in different ways.

Do you choose a precinct or place first, and then see who's there?

It's not a rule, but with a lot of the ideas I've had, I usually start with an idea of a place and a theme. I enter into a particular space, which has certain themes at its heart, and then I'm looking for people and characters that will bring those themes alive. It does depend on how interesting the place is, you know, as to how important it becomes in the final film. But, usually, the place is extremely important to the conception at the beginning.

What drew you to Frinton-on-Sea, for example?

I knew that there was a new strand at the BBC about to happen, and Nick Mirsky, the guy who ran it, wrote a brief as to the kind of films he was looking for, and a couple of my films were mentioned in the document. I'd just read an article in the newspaper about Frinton and the local population campaigning to save a manually operated nineteenth-century railway crossing, a sort of wooden gate, which cuts across the only road into the town, and I sent it to Nick, thinking that he might be interested. I like films to be open-ended and to find a story, you know, through the process of making the film, whereas this, in the beginning, was quite prescribed: a film about the local population fighting over this seemingly very petty issue. I wasn't particularly set on fire by that. But Nick Mirsky said, 'Well, actually, this could be quite interesting. Do you just want to go and have a look?' and I agreed to do that. But it was months before I committed to the film because I wasn't sure of the direction and what it was that I wanted to say through this place. Eventually, at some point, I made a commitment to it, and it became the film that it did. I was drawn to the central idea that these people were imprisoning themselves somehow and shutting themselves off from the world. The gates story could just be a tiny thread and an excuse to look at interesting characters who were shutting themselves away.

So that process where you were deciding whether to make the film was the process of looking for characters you liked and felt drawn to?

Yes, exactly, yes. I would go there regularly. For me, it's really interesting to immerse yourself in a place and, over time, to try to understand how you feel about it. Often, it was totally depressing being there, because it felt like such a small world, with small-town values – totally claustrophobic in some ways. Then I started to meet people who I quite liked and had some kind of fascination with, and that's when it starts to become a film. I didn't want to make a film where you just trash the place – go in as an outsider and stitch everybody up. It's really important for me, even if you have mixed emotions towards the characters, that there is a kind of connection as a filmmaker, in order for the audience to feel something too. So, once that starts to happen, then it feels like I'm on safe ground, in a way. It just has to be something that's kind of working inside of me to drive me forward, really.

Do you always spend quite a lot of time looking for characters?

Yes, although it varies from film to film. I never separate out the usual industrial processes of making a film, where you have a pre-production period, a pro-duction period, then a post-production period. Often one thing runs into another. I remember when I was making *Calais* that I'd been shooting for about four or five months, and I felt something was missing in the film. I'd filmed with Ijaz, the Afghani guy; I'd filmed the Jamaican guy, which was actually just over one day, more or less; and the English bar owner was a sort of constant in the town, and I'd been filming him. It seemed to me there was something missing. I started to imagine the kind of character that I would like, and it became Tulia. She was quite a late addition to the whole process. I probably shot a lot of the material with the other characters and started filming her story from scratch. So, even in the editing sometimes, we have a break, and I go out shooting to solidify the story and the narrative. It's an ongoing process.

What was it that you felt was missing from Calais?

You know, a lot of my films are mosaics, and I hope that the individual parts of the film add up to something more than just the character stories. At the time, Calais had been in the newspapers because of the refugee camp. I was, like, well, maybe that could be interesting, and I went over and did some research. There were lots of interesting things, but, early on, I knew that I didn't want to make a film just about refugees. I didn't feel like there was anything new to say about that as an issue. What was interesting was this sort of transient town. It seemed to me that the whole town was a kind of metaphor for the idea of being a refugee. So, I just wanted to find characters that embodied that somehow, and as many different types of people as possible to talk about it in different ways. So, you have the English bar owner who considers himself a refugee from England, and by the end of the film, he's driving off to another place, kind of running away the whole time. So, I had him in place, and I had the traditional refugee story, if you like. That was quite difficult in itself because I met so many refugees in the town, and it was only Ijaz that really sparked something inside of me. He was so emotive and so likeable. The Jamaican character came about through stalking that little area where people get chucked off the bus at the border. But I felt there was something historical missing in the film.

For me, the whole place has a really rich history, and a lot of it is connected to the theme of the refugee, which, you know, you can trace back to the beginning of time. I just started to think about that more and more. I remember, at one point, wanting to invent a character that was going to be a complete fiction to put into the film because I couldn't find anything. In the end, we just phoned around a lot of the English businesses in the town and met Tulia. She was a really fascinating character. But it also turned out that she was actually a refugee from the Second World War. When I went along to meet her, this story came out about her past and it was just, you know, one of those great moments where you think, 'Okay, this is perfect.' In addition, she had this unfolding story going on in her life, to do with struggling financially and facing bankruptcy and eviction and homelessness, that also seemed a very good fit in terms of the themes of the film. So, you know, there is quite a lot of dreaming things into existence that goes on during the process for me, because I'm always searching for new elements and thinking about what the film could be. So, it's never really over. It's never really defined until quite late on.

What is a good character? People talk about it in TV all the time.

Yes, they do. It's an overused term, isn't it? You know, just go out and find some great characters. It's an impossible question to answer, partly because it's a very personal question, isn't it? For me, I like complexity, and I like characters who represent more than just themselves, and that's usually defined by the theme that's in my head, the bigger idea. You often meet filmmakers, especially young filmmakers, saying, 'I've found a great character. I should make a film about them.' I always think, 'Well, maybe they are a great character, but what do they really represent and what's the film really about?' You could follow any number of great characters and themes would emerge, of course. For me, it's a little bit different, because I have an idea of the broader themes that they should relate to in some way. I like to find characters who bring an idea alive.

I think a great character is many things. There's something about great characters that means that they're instantly fascinating, which is not to say you always have to fall in love with them straight away. I mean, there are many characters in my films who initially you may not like, but, by the end of the film, you've revealed another side to them and shown something different. You feel differently about them, which is about complexity and also about playing with people's prejudices, you know? With Tulia, when she comes on the screen initially your reaction is: 'Who is this woman?!' She looks quite grotesque and she's a complete diva. You would never imagine that she has the kind of story going on that she does. That's really interesting for a filmmaker. I find that quite fascinating.

Is it important that they're likeable?

I think, at the end of it all, it's important that there's something in them that the audience is going to connect with and like – yes, definitely. For example, with the character in *All White in Barking*, Dave, when you first meet him you're thinking, 'Well, he's just the average racist on the street.' And he is, in some ways, of course. I only cast him because there was something about his fragility that I found quite interesting. It seemed to me it was that his fragility and his insecurities were really driving all his quite strong views about what was going on in his town. I felt like, if I could get underneath that, then that would be quite interesting because, for me, that's what a lot of racism is about. Clearly, it's people's own fears, and he seemed like a perfect character to really explore that with. There were plenty of people in that town whom I never would have filmed with because my overwhelming emotion was just one of hate, you know? There was a guy reading *Mein Kampf* in the pub in Dagenham. It could have been a great opening scene, but, if there's nowhere to go with it and you just hate them, it's kind of uninteresting.

You know, it's funny, isn't it? If you look at Nick Broomfield's film *The Leader, His Driver and the Driver's Wife*, I'm almost certain you couldn't sustain a film with just Eugène Terre'Blanche as the main character. After a while, you would just disengage. So, it's a very clever idea to follow the driver, whom, by the end of the film, you have a lot of empathy for.

Do you always know when you're on to a winner with a character? Is it an instinctive thing? An instant thing?

Yes, I think so, though it's not always instant. I think, if a character has a really interesting personality, and there's something about them that you know is going to work, just in simple film terms, that's great, and you can usually do quite a lot with that. However, there has to be something more. I mean, when I first met Monty on the street in *All White in Barking*, I didn't know he was a Holocaust survivor or anything about him. I just approached him because he looked interesting; it was as simple as that. I noticed him from across the street, saw that he had quite an interesting face, and liked the way he was standing outside his shop, and thought he looked like an interesting character. So, that was my initial approach to him, but it was finding out his other story that really nailed it for me. The Holocaust discovery was very interesting, but even more important was the fact that he was having this relationship with Betty, the woman from Uganda. If that wasn't there, I don't know whether he would have been in the film because it might have unbalanced it. I had to find something in him that said something about this town and the themes that I was dealing with in the here and now. It seemed to me that, you know, a woman comes over from Africa, needs a job, and he gives her a job. He needs companionship ... It had all the right elements there.

With Norman, the big guy in *Men of the City*, I discovered quite early on just through talking to him that he'd decided never to have kids and had sacrificed so much for this life in the City. That, for me, gave me somewhere to go with his story. I knew I could reveal things about him slowly to the audience. Those kinds of things are very important to have in the back of your mind, but it sort of goes hand in hand with having a gut feeling about 'great characters', because there's usually something more there when you're drawn to somebody. There's usually a lot going on inside them.

It seems to me that you need to catch a great character at an important or interesting time of their lives. That's almost as important as how good the character is.

Yes, I think that's true. Or you work very hard to shoot moments that seem totally in the here and now and very alive. The thing is, your presence as a filmmaker affects things and creates moments that wouldn't have happened otherwise. So the what's-going-on-in-their-lives question is something that you're a participator in, you know. Just by being there, you're kind of asking people to think out loud about things that maybe they're thinking about only privately or subconsciously. It feels very in the moment, then, because you're there asking questions and drawing it out, and it feels quite raw. Maybe it hasn't been spoken about for a long time.

On that level, there's this funny sort of game that goes on where, when you find the right character, they know why you're interested in them. You know, I never spend much time explaining to characters why I want to film with them. There's a dialogue that goes on – 'I'm making a film etc. etc. It's about this and that' – but, really, the important, profound stuff in the relationship is never discussed, apart from on camera. It's sort of, like, they know why you're there, and why you're interested in them. It's a fascinating dynamic that happens.

Is it about them wanting to be heard?

Yes, I think so. They want to be heard, and, you know, it could have been the right time five years earlier but nobody was there. So, you create the right time, in a way, and they pick up on it. The relationship is very important, and it's crucial you have time because it's not something that happens in the first meeting. You can meet somebody, get a good feeling about them and they seem to be quite interested in what you're doing, but it's only slowly over time where you feel you have the right, in a way, to ask them more personal questions.

Do you get to that point through filming or through hanging out with people?

For me, it's through filming. It's through the filming process because I separate clearly in my mind reality and the film reality. They're completely different worlds for me. So, for example, with Norman in *Men of the City*, I did discover quite quickly that he didn't have children. Once I knew that, I didn't want to talk to him on camera about it until I felt that I had a really good bond with him because, otherwise, it would have felt uncomfortable and it would also probably not have worked as a scene. So, it's one of the last things that I filmed with him, but I knew that for about a year, so it's sort of like you file it away and wait for the right time. For me, that method has worked quite well. You wait until there's trust, and that's really important. It's crucial that the audience feel that they trust the filmmaker. I see so many films where I don't trust the filmmaker on many levels, and it feels very uncomfortable. It feels manipulative and just cheap, in a way, you know?

It seems, watching your films, that you quite like characters who are on the margins. Is that true? Do you have a preference for a certain type of character?

Yes, definitely, that's for sure. I think there's more drama in the lives of people who are on the margins. I mean, it was interesting when the whole idea for the City film came about because my initial reaction was one of horror. What have I got to do with this world? How could I go into banking and find characters that I could have some kind of relationship with? It just didn't seem that this was a film for me. In my initial research, I spent a lot of time looking at people on the margins, like that Bangladeshi guy who's in the film. It wasn't until I met David, the hedge fund guy, that I overcame that resistance. I felt that, Okay, there were many things about him that I couldn't relate to, but there was something quite central that I could – his vulnerability and fragility, despite his apparent power and status – and that actually became very interesting. When I talk to people about that film, he's one of the characters they always remember and can really empathise with in some way, even though they might have quite strong views about who he is and how he behaves and lives his life.

What does it mean to say that a film is character-led?

Often, it is a line that comes up in a synopsis, isn't it – a character-led film about this or that? For me, it's probably just about the prominence of the characters in the story, and means that a film is really about human emotions. You might see a Michael Moore film described as 'character-led'; it's a character-led film about the American health system or whatever. But his films aren't about characters; they're about an argument. He sets out to prove a point through quite ruthless exploitations of characters' views and feelings, just to serve his own purpose. I think that what I do is almost the opposite. It is very important for me that a film is saying more than just what the individual characters' stories are saying, but the means by which I prefer to find my way to that is through the characters. There is a tension about who is leading the narrative, in a way. In *Men of the City*, probably more than in any of my other films, it is my idea of the City that is leading the film, rather than the characters. It's a critique of the city. In *Calais*, the place and the meaning of the place, and the exploration of the idea of transience, is very strong. But I think the characters are so strong that they lead you to that.

It is really important to me that I remain quite open in terms of what I discover in the world out there. That determines how the film is, at the end of it all. I try to keep a really open mind and if I have ideas I am always ready to change them. If I get carried away with a particular character's story, and I'm compelled to film something, that seems fine to me. If that then means that the film becomes more character-led than ideas-led, that's fine. If that is what has touched me during the filming, then I just go with that.

So a film being character-led means that the narrative emerges through your characters?

Yes, but I manipulate a lot and I often construct scenes with characters that wouldn't ordinarily happen in their lives. The most extreme example is the dinner party in *All White in Barking* where I got two characters to meet each other in a way that they never would have if I wasn't there. There are some filmmakers that will just cast a character and follow them. I don't ever use the word 'follow' because I don't really feel like I am following people. Well, sometimes I am – there might be a situation that is going to happen and I will try to observe what is unfolding in that situation. But, you know, most of the time I know why I am there and what I am looking for. It may change, and that is great and you hope that it does and that something surprising happens. But there is a clear sense of what a particular scene might deliver, what it might mean, how it might fit into the wider themes that I am interested in, rather than just following somebody and hoping that something interesting will emerge.

If characters are at the centre of the film and they are driving it forward, it seems to me that you are always well placed to get surprises. There's always that potential to be blown away by something happening.

Yes, that is true. Good point. The first couple of scenes are quite easy because you are just exploring somebody. You are setting them up as a character. You think of an opening scene that would work in the film and you try different things out. It is quite simple. Once you have got that far, the question arises, 'What is their story going to be? How am I constructing their story in relation to the film as a whole?' That is really tricky. That is when I start to intervene quite a lot and create situations that have potential for a kind of planned spontaneity, if you like. I come up with some ideas. I throw them into the mix. Then I take a step back. It just depends on what is going on in that person's life as to how much I feel I have to do that.

I think that, morally, those things are fine and also necessary. That is my approach to documentary filming. I don't consider myself an observational filmmaker in that sense. I have this deep frustration when things just feel unsurprising – when you are out there with the camera and nothing is happening and you are feeling totally frustrated about how boring and banal the reality is that you are a part of. I guess everything is filmed these days. We have seen everything before and for me it is only these personal interventions that rescue the film and create something authentic. It is sort of the only thing that I have, because I feel a lot of the time like everything is so well explored. England and London are quite familiar to me in some ways, but I am constantly looking for those surprises. That is why it takes so much time. That is why the time spent with the characters is really crucial.

How long were you with Laura-Anne on Some Day My Prince Will Come?

Well, I made that film over about a year and a half, but we would go five days every month or something, because it was in Cumbria. That film came about through Channel 4 wanting to do something about first love. They wanted to make a series, actually. My film was the only one that ended up getting made and it was never shown anyway. It's still on the shelf somewhere. There was a complicated history to the film and because it went on for so long, you know, commissioners left and came and went, and Channel 4 sort of changed in the meantime.

I thought it was a lovely film.

I took a long time to find a really interesting setting for the film. I looked for one as if I were making a feature film. For me, it seemed like a great place to make a film about first love – these two little streets by the sea. You have to get on with the people there because there is nobody else, and kids were able to run free. They were sort of free-range kids. They had the railway line there and the sea. It had all the elements for me to create scenes, because there was a lot of creation that needed to happen. You certainly couldn't just turn up and point a camera at kids. I mean, it was totally dull most of the time. So there was a lot of intervention that had to happen in that film.

What sort of stuff?

Well, for me, intervention is a kind of dialogue with the reality that you are faced with. There is a scene in *Some Day My Prince Will Come* where little Steven is snogging his girlfriend on the rocks. Now, I used to watch him snogging at bus stops all the time. As a filmmaker, I was thinking, 'Well, it is not actually that filmic to film at the bus stop. It would be very grabbed and messy and, you know, noisy.' So I wanted to capture some of that kind of early teenage sexual stuff that goes on, but in a way that felt comfortable. It is a dodgy subject matter, quite controversial in some ways, but totally a part of their experience as kids. I thought, 'Okay, I am just going to get them to sit on these rocks.' I set the camera up and sort of tortured them, kept them there for about half an hour, and asked them to kiss each other and they did. In the film, you watch it and it is fine. You don't think about the set up. So it is those kinds of things where I am drawing on reality, but trying to find ways to film it that are more intense, and more interesting in film terms. But that always has to be balanced with your own personal morality as to how far you can go with that. You are the only person that can judge that, really.

Do you think it's true to say that in character-led films the narratives are more human-sized? More real? More three-dimensional?

Yes, I think you are right, in a way. If you look at documentary films that have hit the cinemas over recent years, they are not the kind of films that I make. They are films that purport to offer quite a strong view on particular issues. I mean, in a film like *The End of the Line*, there are characters, but I don't remember a single character from that film. I remember the issue, the argument. It remains a slight mystery to me as to why those films are in the cinema and not the kind of human dramas that I make and other people make, which is what we go to see all the time with fiction films. We don't watch a fiction film for its sense of an issue. You go there and engage with characters and the issue comes out through them. It has almost gone back to an older idea of documentary that it should just be about an important issue. Creative documentary seems to be something that stays on the margins and just exists in film festivals and the occasional screening on television. It makes me very angry because I feel that, you know, I see great films all the time that are in festivals, that only a festival audience gets to see. I know that when people discover these films they are amazed that they exist. They just don't get enough exposure.

The other type of film that you get in cinemas quite a lot is a story that just feels gargantuan, like One Day in September. *It is so huge and unique it is sort of unimaginable in lots of ways – or* Deep Water *– very big, epic stories. Whereas in character-led films the stories are more human-sized because they're about relationships.*

Yes, I think my films are sort of both ordinary and extraordinary. They are ordinary in their premise and in being about ordinary people. I am not seduced in the slightest by sensational stories. For me, personally, I am much more interested in ordinary people's struggles and dramas than a big sensational story. Within that, when you start to dive into people's lives and explore their lives with certain themes in mind, there are always surprises that feel extraordinary to me – not only extraordinary in the details of people's lives, but also in how people are on the camera and in the emotions they are expressing to you. Just the basic, universal human stuff is endlessly fascinating, you know? It tells you so much more about how we live and who we are than a big sensational story. That is often a one-off, outside of reality.

Do you find it liberating to be free of the 'overarching narrative'?

Yes, yes, totally. I am just not a narrative filmmaker like that. I don't think, 'That is a great story. I must tell that story.' For me, documentary filmmaking is a process of discovery and very bound up with my relationship to the world and to life. Every film, for me, is a kind of dialogue with reality and a discovery of reality that reflects back on my own life and how I feel about things. It's that personal journey all the time that sets me alight. That is what I am about; that is what I have come to understand about myself.

I was just watching a Joris Ivens film called *The Pharmacy*. It starts with shots of the port in Shanghai, from his hotel window. The first thirty minutes is just observations of street life, you know? It is sort of fascinating but nothing is happening. There are these banal questions from behind the camera. Then they enter a pharmacy and the rest of the film, eighty minutes or so, is all in this pharmacy, watching people coming in, buying medicine and learning about the society through that. It can get a bit boring but there are moments in that film that are so much more alive and authentic. The fluidity of it is really exciting. You never quite know where it is going. There is a freedom to it and a sort of love of life, in a way, which you don't get in a film that just has this grand narrative from the beginning.

It seems to me that in mainstream British TV, which used to be full of these quite life-affirming character studies and portraits of people, documentaries are all very narrative-driven now, even when there isn't really a narrative there ...

Yes, that is the ridiculous thing, isn't it? You have to deploy a narrative voice-over – a narration to make you feel like there is a narrative when there isn't. It is ridiculous. You know, I was thinking about this the other day. I am filming outside a court at the moment, just telling mini-dramas outside a London magistrates' court. It is quite fascinating, and one of the characters that I have been following came out from the court having had his trial. He was quite animated and in the back of your mind you are thinking, 'Well, we should sort of ham this up a bit.' Then I thought, 'No, fuck it. I am just going to shoot it as it is and just film his reaction.' It is a strange sort of desire for sensation all the time, isn't it? It is odd that we can't just look at life and the small details and be moved by that any more.

Why have documentaries that are portraits become so unfashionable? Is it just the pressure of viewing figures?

Yes, I think it is just a question of ratings, basically. It is the feeling that audiences won't stick with it; they will get bored of it. On a deeper level, I think we are probably quite an apathetic, disengaged society these days, where ordinary things maybe don't really matter that much any more. It is a feeling in the atmosphere that ordinary life is somehow not important. It all has to be dressed up as entertainment.

Do you think character-led films will come around again?

You know, I think they are always there, but certainly in much smaller numbers. If you go to film festivals, for example, these films are being made all the time.

It is just the television 'landscape', to use a horrible word that they always use, that has changed.

Do you think it might swing round, given that there are fashions in documentaries?

At the same time as being quite pessimistic, I always have this sense of optimism, because I feel like the more shit that we are fed, the more space there will be for something different. So I am all in favour of more shit, because it gives me a bit more space when I go along to speak to the BBC or whatever. But it is disappointing, because for newer filmmakers it is much harder for them to get the space and time to find their voice. When I made *The Lift*, I was literally given the money and had no pressure whatsoever. I could just go off and do it. I would never have made that film if I hadn't had the support and freedom that Channel 4 gave me at that time. On the other hand, if you are totally frustrated with the industry, you know ... everyone has got their own camera and a laptop. There are a lot of filmmakers going to see commissioners with material they have shot by themselves.

If it's true that character-led films depend on intimacy, how do you go about creating intimacy?

I think when I'm filming, if I'm not really getting close to the person in question, then it feels a little bit dead to me. It feels like you're just skating over the surface of something. So I think, by nature, I kind of look and search for that intimacy with a character, and it really only works if you genuinely feel something for that person. You can't create it; you can't manufacture it. Sometimes, I might start filming with somebody where there's something that's drawing me to that person, but, for whatever reason, it feels like it's not working. And you should just give up then, really, and recast, because it's so important that you've got that intimacy, that relationship going on. Usually, I think, it all springs from that very first moment where you decide to cast the character. You feel something for them – you feel a kind of genuine empathy in some way – and then the intimacy just comes, you know?

Does self-shooting help with intimacy?

Well, I only ever shoot myself, so it's a bit hard for me to know. There have certainly been many times within films when I've said to the assistant producer, 'Can you just wait outside?' because I've felt frustrated that I wasn't getting underneath the skin of the character enough, and I've thought that if only I was there by myself, in a way where we could both be totally relaxed, it would make for a much more revealing moment. I remember when I was filming with Tulia in Calais that her motivation initially for doing the film was to do with her business. She thought it would be good exposure, and it was only through time that we built a relationship and she started to understand me and I understood her a bit more. But every time we would go around to her house she would lay on a huge spread, and we'd never get to do any filming. It was really frustrating. I wanted to just turn up and be in her life for a couple of hours and create something magical, and instead all these barriers would be there. So one time I just turned up unannounced, and it was just after she'd had problems with the bank, and that's when that scene occurred where she talks about wanting to take her own life. I could tell that there was stuff going on. It's just that I wasn't able to access it, and being on my own in that moment helped tremendously, because if I'd been with somebody else she would have been distracted.

Patience is important in creating intimacy.

Yes, you really have to wait for the right moment. There are so many things that need to come together to make a scene work, especially if it's a scene that you've been planning for a little while. You've got ideas that you want to talk to somebody about and you have to wait for the right moment. When I spoke to Norman in the City film about him not having kids, it was after the day that he'd finally resigned from his job, and I went home with him and he was a little bit drunk. There was a lot in the rushes that was total nonsense because he was playing up to the camera and stuff. I decided to get him out into the space of the garden. And smoking is always great, because it helps people to relax. So he was out there smoking. And I often talk to people quite briefly before I start shooting to try to create an atmosphere and a mood. So I'll say things like, 'Can you just smoke in the garden and really try to think about this question and just start talking when you feel like it?' And nothing is happening; they're not saying anything. But there's an atmosphere because they're already thinking something through and then, seemingly miraculously, they'll just start talking. And then, even if they don't say anything very meaningful, it's really interesting. And I say to them, 'Look, if you just want to pause, just pause and stop talking, it's fine, and then start again when you're ready.'

I think one feature of your films is that they quite often contain revelations and confidences, which is obviously a product of intimacy.

Yes, it usually comes about through having filmed with a character for a period of time, and through questions arising in my mind that I want to ask and explore with them.

There's the girl who talked about being abused in Travellers.

Yes, yes. With a lot of these revelations they've often been discussed briefly with myself before you've seen them in the film. So, for example, in *The Lift*, the guy that comes in and talks about his parents dying in the space of a few months together – we'd had almost an identical conversation outside the lift just before shooting that. It's a question that young filmmakers often ask, 'Can you talk to somebody about something or should you just film it straight away?' It's not a science and you never quite know, but often you can have brief explorations with a character about these kinds of intimate things in their life. And they can repeat it in a very emotional and authentic way, and it doesn't seem any less powerful for it. And it helps you, in fact, because you can be armed with the right sort of questions and find the right way to enquire into those things if you know a little bit about what's happened, rather than just literally shooting in the dark all the time.

I think that making films in the way that you're describing – very patiently, basing it on real relationships – gives you not just surprises, but also great moments. Like when Steve's dad comes out of prison in One Day My Prince Will Come, *and he's looking at him, saying, 'Your hands are smaller than I remember.'*

Yes, yes, I love that moment.

He's like a little animal trying to get to know a bigger animal.

Yes, exactly, yes. I remember there was so much planning that had to go into making that scene work. I mean, I had been filming with Steven for a while. I knew that his dad was in prison, and we'd written to tell him about the filming.

He came home when Steven was at school, and so I was able to meet his father briefly, knowing that Steven would be home in an hour or so. There's a lot of drama to making sure that you can get it all: shooting Steven coming back into the house and then being in this chaotic situation – because there were loads of other kids around – and trying to create a sense of clarity to the situation, ignoring all this madness around you and trying to keep the frame and make that work and hoping something interesting is going to happen. But in a situation like that you are *guaranteed* that something interesting is going to happen. He hasn't seen his dad for such a long time … you just want to position yourself to observe what's happening.

There is so much that is under-appreciated when you watch a film, and rightly so, because you shouldn't be thinking about that as a viewer. But for filmmakers or young filmmakers wanting to learn their craft, it's so important to know how to get yourself in the right place, and position yourself in order to observe something. There are so many obstacles to overcome to be able to just be there.

Character-led films are often more reflective. They're almost about thinking. You often ask questions like, 'Are you happy? Have you ever been in love?'

Yes, for me, that works really well. It's like in *Men of the City* when David is there at his screen making money or losing money and, at the same time, I know there's this story with his kids going on. He's sat there working and also printing out photos of his children, whom he's lost. It's all happening in the same moment, and that's a great time just to throw in a very simple but thoughtful question. He cuts me quite short; he's sort of 'I don't really want to think about that'. But still, the great thing about film is that it's just as powerful when someone does that, because you totally read what he's not saying and what he's not prepared to talk about. I always look for those moments of reflection even within a supposedly busy, dynamic scene.

There's lots of reflection in The Lift, *as well, with people just thinking aloud?*

Yes, it's very driven by existential questions, and it's a very pure film because it's a unique space in which to deal with those themes. But those themes are there in every film of mine, even though they might occupy very different spaces with a very different visual feel to them.

It struck me that character-led films can often feel a bit nebulous – like you can get a bit lost in them, as a viewer.

It probably comes down to this question of what is a narrative. I'm quite fascinated by the line that a film takes and it's something that I'm never really aware of as a filmmaker until a decent rough-cut stage in the editing process, or maybe even further. It's very fascinating and freeing to just follow your nose and your instinct when you're out there shooting and documenting. It's a great feeling to just film whatever you're drawn to. There's always something connecting all your ideas and I have faith that what's connecting them, what's making them relate to each other, is always going to be there in the rushes because the questions and choices are coming from me. Then, when I sit down in the edit, it's another process of really clarifying those ideas and making them work on the screen. And sometimes you're probably right: films can seemingly go off on a tangent. But I love that; I love the sense of having the ability to create tangents, as long as you don't feel lost and you sort of understand why you're seeing what you're seeing and what's going on. For example, in *Men of the City*, I filmed quite early on the guy talking about saving the woman from drowning in the Thames. And when I was filming it, it seemed like a really pivotal scene, though I had no idea where it would play in the film. When I sat down with my editor and we discussed the meaning of the film, we knew quite early on that that scene would be almost the centre of the film, an anchor. It's like a moment of humanity in a world that seems quite inhuman. But working it into the narrative was a very tricky and delicate process. You could see it as a distraction in the narrative of the main characters, something that's getting in the way. But, for me, it's not that at all; it's a pivotal moment.

The narratives in character-led films often don't pay off in a conventional way. I was thinking, for example, of the gay guy in Frinton-on-Sea, where the narrative never quite concludes.

Yes, there's a certain mystery surrounding his story, and part of it is that in reality he told us something that I couldn't ever use in the film, so in that situation I was treading quite a fine line. I think you understand his homosexuality quite quickly. But still, there's this other mysterious thing going on that you never really pin down, that's true. For me, I feel really intrigued by the idea of leaving people wanting more – not out of arrogance but because I think there's something that happens in film where you watch and it's really satisfying if it's not wrapped up, and not closed off. I want it to kind of carry through and stay with you, and as a filmmaker you're in control of that. You can keep a certain mystery or magic to the stories that you're telling, and that, for me, is born out of a sort of attitude towards life really; there should be mystery. Mystery but not confusion. Confusion is bad.

So open-endedness is an advantage, rather than a problem?

I think so. I really encourage and embrace the open-endedness of films. You've invested in these characters and the story, and then it almost starts again when it ends. There's that sense of the story continuing on in the viewer's mind, which, for me, seems something to aim for because you're raising questions all the time. There are more questions than answers, and I want to leave the audience with questions, so that they reflect back on their own lives, because that's what I'm doing myself. Every film leaves me with questions and I don't know whether they ever get answered. They're almost unanswerable. It's just an ongoing exploration from one film to the other. At the end of *Calais*, the English guy drives off in his caravan; we've said goodbye to the Afghani refugee in a queue; and the Jamaican guy has gone to a hotel, having not got his bus back to Jamaica; and we've left Tulia having celebrated her husband's birthday. In a way, the next chapter is ready to unfold and that's maybe what you start thinking about when the film has finished. You close a chapter in people's lives, yet you know it's ongoing. You leave the characters in a state of uncertainty, which is much more real.

When you're making a character-led film and you're meeting characters, do you ever worry that a narrative is just not going to emerge?

No, I never worry about that, funnily enough. I think hard about the progression of the film. I'm always agonising over a sense of progression and asking, 'Can this sustain an hour?' 'What is this thing that I'm creating here? How is it going to unfold and what is the development?' But the 'What is it?' process is very different from thinking there won't be anything, or worrying that nothing is going to unfold. I have total confidence that something will emerge. I just don't know what it is exactly. There are always real low points in a filming process where you feel a bit stuck, or you know there is something happening on a certain date that you feel has some kind of potential, but maybe you don't quite know what it's going to deliver, or you worry that it might get cancelled. But, over the years, you learn to both surrender to these doubts and insecurities and think around them. So, no, I never worry about there being a lack of narrative.

Does the fact that character-led narrative is not obvious, necessarily, mean it's more satisfying when it does emerge, because you found it?

Yes. I remember when we were cutting the Barking film together and it just seemed like there was one surprise after another, and it felt really satisfying. And even in the City film, you don't quite know where it's going and who's going to appear next. That comes about through an openness in the shooting, and freeing yourself from being tightly controlled about the narrative. For me, it's really enjoyable. A lot of TV execs would be terrified of that sort of open-endedness and not knowing where the film was going. And it's a real problem if you're being discouraged from that, because I think that's where you really find your own voice as a filmmaker, in those moments where you go off the prescribed path. But that's just my nature. I've never been the kind of person to stick to the rules in that way. You shut so many doors if you're living in a fearful state all the time about trying things out. It's better to fail spectacularly having tried, than make something that just feels okay – it has a clear narrative, but actually it's totally dull and uninteresting.

The overall effect of your films emotionally, I would have said, is they are often quite sad or bittersweet. Why is that?

I don't know really. I think comedy and tragedy are so bound up with each other that it's impossible to separate out. I could never imagine making a pure comedy, because, for me, there's no comedy without sadness and tragedy. It's all bound up in the same idea.

Is that kind of heartache a result of making character-led films, in the sense that that's what the human condition is like?

Yes, I mean, that *is* what the human condition is like. I wouldn't be interested in making a film about somebody who was just seemingly always happy and life was wonderful. It's not how I feel about life. You know, some days I'm totally fucked off and depressed; other days I have these great moments of joy, and that's just how I feel. I think that there's this sense in the society that we live in that we have to be happy all the time. People go around saying, 'I'm fine. No, I'm fine,' and you know underneath that they are on the verge of a nervous breakdown. I just think that without dwelling on people's misery – because I don't want to do that – even in the sadness there's optimism, because all the characters in my films, I think, are fighting and staying alive. There's a sense that, if you relate to these people and you can identify with them, that gives you some kind of hope, through their ability to survive their problems. I don't want to have to make a happy film just because that's what a broadcaster might want, to cheer up an audience after work. No, no – the opposite. I want to reflect what I feel about life and about being alive.

That's a feature of good character-led films, isn't it? That there is layering and complexity.

You do get comedy laid over tragedies. I'm always looking for comedy. I mean, in a character like Monty in *All White in Barking,* there's so much tragedy in his life, yet what makes him a great character is that he is able to laugh. I always remember the moment in *Calais* when, at his lowest point, the Afghani refugee guy is in tears. It's freezing cold; he's got nowhere to go; and I'm saying, 'Well, why don't you just stay in France?' because he's got the opportunity of claiming asylum there. And there's a moment of silence, and he just says, 'I don't like French people.' And when the film is screened and people watch that, they are crying but then they are laughing and that's how life is, I think.

What sort of person do you need to be to make character-led films?

I think you have to care about people, basically. If I think about the reasons why I made films, I think about the craft, I think about the form – all those things – but what really matters is the way that you deal with the characters, and I think you have to be the kind of person that really, genuinely cares about the people in your film and is engaged with their struggles, their dilemmas, their situation. If that isn't genuine, as a viewer you feel very, very awkward. I remember watching *Capturing the Friedmans* and feeling like it was a fascinating story, but totally questioning the motivations of the filmmaker all the way through. I felt like the filmmaker behind the camera was rubbing his hands with glee at this amazing situation. You know, it's a grand story, and it's fascinating, but then the question of 'why' comes up and I'm left with that more than anything else.

Do you need to be quite a genuine sort of person?

I think you do have to be genuine, but I would never sit here in front of you and say that I'm not manipulative or even quite ruthless when it comes to it, because I am. But I try to treat people as fairly as possible.

A rounded sort of person?

I don't know. I don't know if I'm so rounded. I think you have to be quite humble, but you also need a certain kind of arrogance to be able to make a film, because you have to have a confidence and a belief that you've got something to say. And you have to be the kind of person that is sensitive to those big themes that we all seem to be intrigued by.

I wonder if it's harder to make character-led films if you're young? That's what I mean about being rounded, really. Do you need a certain amount of life experience?

Well, you meet some twenty-year-olds that are extremely mature and have a sense of what it is to be alive and you meet some that aren't. For me, that's crucial: you have to know something about life and have some sense of maturity. It's partly about who you are. It makes total sense to me why I've ended up doing what I'm doing. I was a goalkeeper when I was at school; they are always the outsiders, leaning against the post, observing the game and occasionally being called into action.

Is character-led filmmaking teachable?

That's a really interesting question, because I teach and sometimes you want to pull your hair out because you think the way this person is thinking, they are never going to make an interesting film. And it's a terrible thing to say in some ways. Yet you know when you meet somebody if they've just got that human something. You know, even if the film will be structurally a bit of a mess, they will have something going on that could be really good. So I think you can encourage people, but I'm not sure it is teachable.

So it's more a matter of channelling?

Yes, yes, exactly. It's something that you have, and then you can learn to channel it in the right direction.

What would you say to young filmmakers who want to do what you do?

I think that people should just do it, you know? I feel really strongly that it's so easy just to start. Just film! Film away. Film anything, and just find your own way of doing things. It's really important that people find their own voice, because otherwise I think you can get lost quite easily. I do believe that, if people have the desire, they will find a way to make their own films. And I think, over the years, the most interesting films have come about that way. If you actually studied the backgrounds of documentary filmmakers who really make their own quite individual films, there'd be no obvious route as to how people got into it and how they found their way through. Just film and film and film. Take it home and edit it yourself and try to make sense of what you're doing. It's no different these days to just having a notebook if you want to be a writer. Just pick up a camera and start shooting.

Do you think that films that are character-led come closer to art than documentaries often do?

Hmm. I've always felt really uncomfortable about the word 'art' being associated with documentary. But, having said that, what's really interesting, for me, is those moments in a film that work on the level of art. That's what you're searching for all the time, those moments. I'm trying to capture, I suppose, a sort of poetry of everyday life. That's when it really comes alive for me, when there's a kind of surprising poetry to the moment. What's most restrictive is this sense that you're just there recording reality. Or just 'interviewing' people – like it's just a question and answer session. I never use an exchange with a character if it feels like an interview. There has to be something else going on there. It has to have some magic and atmosphere. Interviews don't have atmosphere. They're just interviews. There's such beauty and transcendence in your dealings with characters sometimes that they just blow you away. And that's the high. You're always searching for those moments. In a film, there are probably only a small number of them but, in a way, those moments really are what you build the whole film around.

What's the goal of character-led filmmaking?

I don't know. What is the goal? I think that I want to make a film that touches people – it's as simple as that. If it doesn't do that or it doesn't do that in as powerful a way as I imagined it could, then it's a failure. I mean, films are always a failure on many levels. You never make a perfect film – you can forget about that. I think that the goal is to find characters and tell stories that really tell us something about the way that we are living.

What is it that you want a viewer to come away with? Do you want them to ask questions, or to come away with a better understanding of something?

I want people to reflect on those themes which are both timeless and universal and also very current: to give time to those themes, to reflect on them, and to question themselves. In *Men of the City*, it's definitely a kind of critique of the City; it's a dystopian vision of the City. But the issues of what the City does to people and the human cost, and is it right, is it wrong ... I feel like my job is to raise questions about all that, rather than to provide answers, because I don't have answers. At the time I was making that film, I was privileged to be able to reflect upon these great themes during a moment of complete meltdown. But even if you live outside the Square Mile, the themes in the film are themes that affect us all. You might think you're outside of it, but you're really not.

I think we live in very arrogant times. There's a sense that the way we live is the only way. I want to question all of that and strip all of the nonsense away, and create some space for us to actually take a step back and reflect on how we are living. That's sort of what I'm doing when I'm making the film, and, if other people get that too, then I think it's quite a valuable exercise. I tend to turn to the characters in a film for some kind of comfort. The human aspect is sort of all we have, really. If we forget about that, then we're deeply fucked, you know?

14 Editing
Andrew Jarecki

Andrew Jarecki is best known for his extraordinary feature documentary *Capturing The Friedmans* (2003), which tells the story of the Friedman family as two members of it are accused of child sex abuse. Arnold Friedman and his son Jesse were both convicted, but Jarecki discovers that the case is not as straightforward as it seems.

As well as specially shot interviews and other material, Jarecki and his editor Richard Hankin were able to draw on a huge archive of astonishingly candid home video, shot by the Friedman family themselves over the course of many years – even at the time of their alleged crimes, and the subsequent investigation and trial. In marshalling this material into a 107-minute-long movie, the film is a masterpiece of editing. Not only does it tell a complicated story in a clear and gripping way, it also pulls off the trick of making the audience feel certain where they stand, only to repeatedly force them to change their point of view. The film is almost about the elusiveness of facts, and the impossibility of ever really knowing the truth.

Capturing the Friedmans won eighteen international prizes, including the Grand Jury Prize at the Sundance Film Festival and the New York Film Critics Circle award. It was also nominated for an Academy Award.

Andrew Jarecki (left), during the filming of Capturing the Friedmans. *Picture courtesy of Andrew Jarecki.*

Directors quite often prefer either shooting or editing. Do you have a preference?

I see the whole filmmaking process as a continuum. You absorb everything you can absorb about the subject matter and you think about it all the time. And the process of trying to get to the essence of the story, which I think is certainly at the core of the whole filmmaking event, for me is just a constant. It's about really trying to understand whatever aspect of humanity we're dealing with. You're often going back over and over and over to try to find different approaches and different ideas about your subject, and that means that there's no hard line between shooting and editing. For me, there's no moment when you say, 'Okay, we're done shooting now. Let's turn it into a film.' You're shooting, you're editing, you're recognising that there are missing pieces in the edit because you haven't explored something as deeply as you'd like to, and you go back and get more.

It takes me a long time to make a film, partly because it's very seldom that my partners and I will say, 'Well, what about the lady who answered the phone at the medical school?' and I say, 'Nah, we don't need to talk to that person.' Usually, if there might be value in an interview or in a piece of evidence that will give you an idea of how somebody acted or whatever, we'll always go to the trouble of getting it, even if it's very time consuming.

With Capturing the Friedmans, *were you editing that for a long time?*

Yes, it took more than three years, I guess, to make that film between the shooting and the assembly of the archival material and the edit. And the editor, Richard Hankin, and I worked together consistently for at least two of those years as our full-time occupation, because that was such a perfect example of an evolving story, where every time you think you've got a handle on it, something new happens.

The story had the unique quality that, on the one hand, you had a historical story that was a real page-turner, but also, while we were making the movie, major events were taking place in the Friedman family, like the youngest son, Jesse, was in the process of going to jail early in the film. And then later we meet him during the period of his incarceration, and then later the film follows him as he actually is released from prison. Then it follows him back to meet his mother, after she hadn't seen him in quite a long time. The filming took place over a long period of time, and there were events in the film that were taking place as we were shooting. So, yes, it took a long time to put together.

I think what's really striking about the editing in Capturing the Friedmans *is that you're never sure what you think. Or rather, you are sure what you think and then you keep changing your mind. Was that a hard effect to achieve in the cutting room?*

When we were making that film, we were reeling most of the time from our own discoveries about the story, and we knew that making the film was as engaging an experience as we had ever had, so we felt that the thing to do in making the film was to try to give the audience the same thrill of discovery watching the film that we had when we were researching it.

The thing I always struggle with in the cutting room is structure. I think it's the hardest thing to get right. What do you reckon?

Yes. I think that's true of almost any piece of art because you only get one chance to introduce your story to your audience. And what you begin with makes a huge difference. If you reveal at the beginning of a story, about somebody that we're going to fall in love with, that that person murdered his wife, then that changes everything about your perception of that person. And if you learn it later then it maybe feels like a fascinating revelation. Or it might feel like a manipulation. So the order in which people learn things, the sequence of that communication, is extremely important.

The other crucial aspect of it is that you have to keep the movie interesting. You have to give the audience a chance to suspend their disbelief, and a chance to engage in the story, and a chance to learn new information about the story. And you want to dole it all out in appropriate doses, so that they're never getting too much information. It's no different than telling a story at dinner. I know, if I'm sitting around with a group of people and I'm telling a story about what happened to me that day, by the time it's six o' clock at night I've already told the story three times to check out which ways work best, and I've realised that if I start the story by saying, 'I was driving in my car,' it's less effective than if I say, 'I was driving in my car but I had left my licence at home.' The timing of when you reveal those pieces of information is crucial. It's essential that you think about it in terms of what's going to keep the audience engaged enough to care.

That must have been a challenge on Capturing the Friedmans *– the timing and the spacing of the revelations through the film?*

Well, it *was* challenging. What you include, what you choose to include, what pieces of information end up in the final cut of the film, all of those things are huge decisions that will strongly impact the way the people read the film. But I never thought of it all as a big manipulation, you know? I never thought, 'Oh, well, what we're doing is we're going to trick the audience.' I just thought the audience should have the opportunity to have the same set of discoveries as we did when we were learning about the story, so that, when you first hear from a cop in the movie, she says, 'There were foot-high stacks of child pornography in plain view literally all around the Friedman house.' And she's somebody that we have a lot of respect for when we first meet her because obviously she's very passionate about her job, and she wants to do the right thing. And then moments later we're going to see the Assistant District Attorney who was present at the raid of the Friedman house, and he says, 'Unfortunately, we didn't find any physical evidence in the house.' And now you're looking at two people who work essentially on the same team in the prosecution of the Friedmans, and it turns out that they have completely different perspectives. So you're forced to ask yourself what everybody's motivation is and who is telling the truth.

Is there a magic structure for a documentary, something that works every time when you're structuring a film?

I certainly have never found anything like that. I think whether you're writing a screenplay for a fictional film or you're writing a documentary or constructing a documentary out of footage, there are certain tenets that are useful. You've got to grab their attention in the first few minutes of the movie. You have to let them know they're in good hands. You have to let them know you're not going to let them float around without critical information unless it's a conscious decision to make a story more intriguing. There are tenets and principles that can work, but I wouldn't even know how to think about talking about structure in the absence of material. It's horses for courses. It's about the story you're trying to tell.

I saw a really interesting film a while back called *TV Junkie*. It's a documentary about a guy who is a local TV news man who has a hopeful, positive outlook on life. He starts a career and becomes a journalist – it's what he always wanted. And then he becomes a drug addict. You see this happen before your own eyes because he films his own life, and he is constantly ducking into the garage and speaking to camera, describing what's going on in his life. So, the structure of that film must be somewhat chronological in order for that to make sense. At the same time, they could choose to make the film open with him going to the hospital for a drug overdose. But then it would give away crucial information that is much more delicious to learn about if you enter the story cold. That movie had a natural desire to be chronological. But there are other documentaries where you would want to start with what's happening today and go back fifty years.

I don't know, maybe there are filmmakers that say, 'Well, usually I start with the back story, and then I explain the characters and get into what's going on.' But it's not true for me. I think it's a choice about your sensibilities as a filmmaker more than anything else, and what's appropriate for the subject.

What sort of relationship do you have with your editor? Do you like your editor to be quite harsh with your material?

The truth is that editing in a documentary is the systematic process of giving up hundreds of fascinating details and stories in favour of a handful of even more fascinating details and stories. I always remind myself that art is waste.

For me, one of the frustrations of editing is you're constantly looking at beautiful sequences that tell you something about the human race, and then having to eliminate them because your movie can't be nine hours long. Your editor can help you through that.

I think, with editors, what you need is somebody who has intellectual honesty and is able to communicate an emotional story, and then you say to that person, 'What would you do here?' They say, 'Well, I think it's important to be really close to him when he admits this fact, so that's why I want to use this angle.' The editor needs to have a similar sensibility to you. You can develop a kind of shorthand. I try not to ride an editor too hard; I try not to say, 'We've really got to have something done by Tuesday.' You don't want him to feel that you're trying to force the story out of him. What you want is to have somebody where the relationship is close enough to begin with that you're not constantly thinking, 'If I'm not looking over this guy's shoulder something bad is happening.' But rather, you're thinking, 'I haven't been in there the whole day. I've been setting up an interview. I'll go in and see my editor and see what brilliant gifts he will be giving me today.' Good editors have an incredible ability to make your story come alive.

In terms of a temperament, do you like editors who are calm, or the more excitable type who have lots of ideas?

Certainly you want somebody with an unlimited number of ideas. You absolutely want to have a lot of opinions in front of you so you can figure out which ones to adopt. It's sort of like improvising as a way of writing music. You know very quickly when you're listening to it: 'That improvisation worked, and I want more of that.' You try it, and it turns out it's really effective when we show this person and then we show images of this thing. All those decisions about what kind of movie you're making are made jointly with the editor. I don't tend to be somebody who says, 'I've delivered all the footage to the editor. He can sort it out.' There are a couple of assistant editors who are going to log the material and add a layer of interpretation to it, but I think the important thing is that you and the editor have a real relationship and you have a close, collaborative way of working. There were plenty of times when I was making *Capturing the Friedmans* when I'd be out filming in the van somewhere, and I would come across some incredible thing, and I'd call Richard, the editor, and say, 'Okay, you're not going to believe this. I'm about to deliver some footage to you that's going to blow you away.' And we'd both get excited. That's the kind of relationship you want: a partnership.

Inside the edit, in the cutting room, do you try to cultivate a particular kind of atmosphere?

I think the atmosphere comes from the people that are there. So, if there's a producer or somebody who makes everyone uncomfortable, then you strive to keep that person out of the room. It has to be comfortable. I also think it's a good idea to bring the subject of your film into the cutting room. Not necessarily to show them every minute of footage you've cut, but because it eliminates some of the distance between the shooting and the cutting. It makes the editor, the assistant editors, the composer and everybody else feel that much more personally connected to the material. I'm really into breaking down those walls. I'm not trying to prevent people from meeting each other; I'm trying to encourage it. I'm not trying to limit the options; I'm trying to increase them and get more people talking about the material, more people saying, 'I thought this, but then I met the guy and, boy, that really opened my eyes, and now I'm not sure what I think.'

So you're looking to make the cutting room into a crucible? A place where ideas are exchanged?

Yes, exactly. If you can, I think it's a good idea to have a bunch of stuff on the walls. If you're working on a case that involves a crime or a family, you want to get photographs of the people in their innocence and earlier years. I think it's healthy, for a lot of reasons, just to have a big bulletin board that's got tons of clippings and maps showing where all these events took place because you want everybody working on the film to be working from the same playbook. You want them all to be absorbing these characters and making them real. Even if somebody's dead, you should get to know them pretty well if you are going to put them in your movie.

Cutting rooms can be quite intense places sometimes?

Certainly. In my life, I don't know if I've ever worked harder than being in the editing room at three o'clock in the morning, knowing you've got a test screening coming up and you've got a set of 150 changes you want to make, and you've got to be cajoling your editor into making the decision to stay up from 3am to 6am doing them, so then you can get a couple of hours of sleep and go to the screening at 10am. That can be very intense.

So, yes, it's intense if the two of you have agreed you need to do something herculean in a short period of time, but, in general, I think the best and most effective mode is to allow the editor to take his or her time. It really doesn't help to stand over them in the formative stages of a film and say, 'Oh, I wouldn't have done that.' If you've chosen your editor correctly and carefully, and if you share a sensibility with the editor (and the editor has a good work ethic), you shouldn't need to look over their shoulder all the time. You should always tell the editor when the work is great. Editors are sitting in the dark for long periods of time. So a big part of it is really just keeping the editor motivated, calling him from the road and saying, 'You'll never guess what this guy just said to me! And you're going to be getting it in an hour.' You need to keep everyone up and enthusiastic. It helps of course if you are genuinely enthusiastic yourself. I usually am when I'm working on something I love.

Also, particularly if you're dealing with dark subjects – and I'm very drawn to dark subjects – you want the atmosphere to be light-hearted, and I think you have to really have fun in the edit room, because you've got to be there a long time. So, hopefully, you're working with people that are funny. A lot of the editors who I've worked with are very funny. They see the absurdity in things. The editor gets to see all the ridiculous behaviour of real people, and they can have fun with it. They get a real line into the way human beings think. And of course the movie's got to be funny, as well as complex and serious and everything else. It's got to be fun to watch. So you need to be enjoying the process of making it.

Do you have a daily routine when you're editing, or is it more a matter of dealing with things as they come up?

There's no routine as such, although I do think that it's a good idea to have a conversation with the editor every day, even if I'm out shooting. I always go out shooting with a detailed question list. And usually I'll send that preliminary question list to the editor a couple of days before and I'll say, 'Hey, can you go over these questions and tell me if I'm missing anything.' Editors are looking for bridges to make sense out of the material, and their input into filming is invaluable.

In the edit on Capturing the Friedmans, *what were the really big creative decisions, the ones that you wrestled over?*

Because we were still shooting the movie, there was an ongoing discussion about when we'd be done. And that's a big thing. It's between you and the editor, you're trying to figure out, you know, at what point is the story finished? What's the movie about? What is the movie? And a big part of that was trying to decide whether we wanted to wait until Jesse Friedman had gotten out of prison. Well, that could have been an event that took years to occur. But we were committed to hanging in there, because we thought that that would be an important conclusion to the story. That was a big decision. A big choice.

Another tough decision in *Capturing the Friedmans* was about a witness who had given us really fascinating but conflicting interviews about the guilt or innocence of the Friedmans. And this is somebody who was ostensibly in and out of the Friedman house, and who was involved in these computer classes that were the subject of so much controversy, about whether or not children were being molested. This witness was hugely important to the case, but ultimately he was not a good interviewee. He didn't want to talk about any of the crucial stuff. He wasn't communicative in the ways that we needed him to be. We worried if we put the movie out and we didn't use any of the interview with him, then all the police officers and people that were going to take issue with the movie were going to say, 'Well, obviously you didn't do your homework.' The editor and I spent a lot of time talking about whether it would be strange to exclude that person from the movie. But ultimately we felt that they were an important part of the case, but not an important part of the movie. They provided a little colour, a little atmosphere, but they didn't provide anything that would warrant the audience's attention. Maybe the audience could get angry with you for leaving something out, but that's not fatal. What's fatal, and what they'll hate you for, is boring them.

What were the biggest problems to solve?

Well, the biggest issue was that we had a very long story and an awful lot to incorporate. We wanted to tell the story of the Friedman family going back a couple of generations, particularly Arnold Friedman and some crucial background information about him. Like when his mother was living in a small apartment with Arnold and his brother, she used to go out and bring men back to the apartment and have sex with them in the bed that they all slept in. And, you know, that's a really interesting story and it tells you a lot about maybe how Arnold was hyper-sexualised at an early age, and there's a lot of interpretation the audience will want to do if you give them that information. For me, that was a really important piece of context, but I'm sure in another version of the movie, or with a different filmmaker or a different editor, that material wouldn't have appeared in the movie.

So we knew there was a certain amount of that kind of background information we needed. But we also needed to deal with the current life of these characters, like the fact that the oldest son, who had come out of a family that was accused of these shocking crimes against children, had seen fit to become a children's birthday-party clown. You know, you can't tell *Capturing the Friedmans* without that. And then, in order to understand the legal case, you have to go into the story of Jesse and his father and the computer classes that they gave in their home. And then you have to go into the marriage because you need to understand how this man could have been a paedophile and yet also raised his family in a fairly traditional way. And then you need to meet the police who prosecuted the case and the accusers who said that this family was not what it seemed. That's a whole legal procedural. And then you need to track the history of these men after the guilty pleas that put them in jail, all the way through the father's suicide and the son's incarceration. I mean, there were so many chapters to this film that took place over many, many years. The first cut of the movie was five and a half hours long.

In the end, the movie was less than two hours. Making those decisions to get it down was hard. You know, when you think about it, there are full-length documentary films that describe events that took place over just five minutes. So it wasn't easy.

The challenge was marshalling all those elements into a narrative?

Yes, lots of elements, including arguably the greatest trove of 'found footage' ever used in a documentary; the fact that the Friedmans had been documenting themselves ever since the turn of the twentieth century all the way through to when the police came to their house in Great Neck, Long Island in the 1980s. That resource gave us the remarkable ability to be inside the house with the central characters on these crucial days we're describing in the film, and to watch for ourselves the interactions between the key characters. It meant that the audience didn't have to look at subjects being interviewed and consider whether or not to believe that person's recollection – they could see the actual events and decide for themselves. As a filmmaker you have to immerse yourself in that material, and hone the material, and you have to keep ploughing through it to see what's repetitious and if there are moments that seem interesting but are actually just distracting.

Was there anything you left out that you really wanted to keep in if only it could have been longer?

I would say not really. There were things that we could have and would have wanted to leave in if the movie were an hour longer. But, ultimately, I think we did a good job of sticking to the stuff that was digestible in under a couple of hours. Any more, I think, would have detracted from the artistic undertaking and from the experience of watching it.

Capturing the Friedmans is, I think, beautifully paced. How do you pace a film? What is pacing, even?

Well, again I think it's like telling the story at the dinner table. I like to lay out little landmines at the beginning of the story that we're going to need in order to make the strongest explosion later when we finally get to the resolution. But it's also about what you don't say. My filmmaking mentor is Mike Nichols, who always says to me, 'The audience doesn't mind not knowing everything. It's okay if you're not constantly telling them what's happening. They don't mind being a little out of the loop, so long as they know they're in good hands.' You need an understanding of how people absorb information. You've got to lead people through. It's just storytelling, really.

In terms of getting that elusive thing, the pacing, right on the film, so it speeds up at the right time and it gives you a bit of air at the right time – is that just a matter of watching it through a lot and really knowing it?

Yes, and watching it with other people. When I was making *Capturing the Friedmans* I was living in Rome, and I couldn't screen the movie for totally English-speaking people because there simply weren't enough of them. So I would download the current cut at night, wake up and burn a disc of it, and then show the movie to a group of people who either spoke not very much English or none at all. I concluded that if they understood what was going on in the movie and felt the right things at the right times, and if they could answer my questions, even without hearing the dialogue and understanding all of it, that would be an indication that we were telling a story in a very clear way, and it was unfolding at the right sort of pace.

In terms of clarity, it's standard in television, I think, for documentaries to have narration. Is it much harder to tell a complicated story without narration?

Not always, but I often think of traditional voice-over in a movie as kind of a resignation. I'm not saying you should never use it. I can appreciate narration in a movie, especially if it's expressing the unique perspective of a charismatic protagonist-filmmaker, like Michael Moore, or Nick Broomfield, or Morgan Spurlock. But often it's a sign of having been on a too-tight edit schedule, and not having had the time to come up with a more creative solution. Either you ran out of money, time, or stick-to-it-iveness. In general, I would say if you're on a very short time frame, you might have to speak into a microphone and tell people what they're seeing. But it just seems like now you're making a PowerPoint presentation instead of a film.

Capturing the Friedmans is such a complicated story, but it's told with such clarity. How did you achieve that?

There's a lot of problem-solving. Usually, these complex stories don't tell themselves. You have to keep digging into the information. You have to keep digging to find the people who have the data you need. I'd say, also, that, if you're having trouble expressing something and people are not understanding it, sometimes that doesn't mean that it's too complicated. Sometimes it means that what you're trying to explain is bullshit, and the reason people aren't accepting it is because somebody's lying; it doesn't feel real to the viewer and so they're not absorbing it. You know, people are very quick to tell you things that aren't true. And in that case you have to go and get somebody else to tell the same story and then get somebody else to tell a different version of the same story, and then at a certain point you start to realise that, you know, you're getting closer to the essence of the thing. But you have to take it seriously that they're not understanding. You can't just say, 'Oh, those people are stupid, they're not paying attention.' A lot of the time the audience is paying attention and they still don't understand something, and so it's up to the filmmaker to get it clarified. And a lot of the time that comes from trying to understand the truth of an issue.

I think one thing that really helps you to understand the story is that your interviewees tell the story so well. They hand over to each other in a really neat way. Was that a matter of finding those perfect bites among the interviews, or did you ask them to do that?

The only time I'll ever really adjust someone's answer is if I'm making a film where I know there's not going to be narration and I'm going to need to have their answer in its fullness, so I need them to repeat part of the question. That's fairly typical – where you'll say, 'Can you just start your answer with a piece of the question?' I think that there are always things that you want people to convey, but they're not going to convey them with conviction if you say, 'Well, I'll tell you what I'd like you to say.' They have to get there themselves.

It has to be real.

You have to let people answer the questions in the way they want to and need to, and then you've got to keep asking the questions until you get it clear enough. You know, you're always free to say, 'I'm not sure I've understood what you're saying.' Sometimes what people have to say is really clunky. But sometimes they say things in amazing, poetic ways, like Vince, the husband of our main character in *Catfish*, who gives the movie its name in the most awkwardly eloquent and poignant speech.

With Capturing the Friedmans, *you must have had so much interview footage. How did you get to grips with it? Did you use transcripts or did you watch the interviews and then respond to them as you were watching them?*

When I'm talking to people initially on the phone, I tend to take very detailed notes; because I type very quickly, I can actually type the whole conversation while it's happening. And that's helpful, because then it gives me a kind of a pre-interview and then I understand what I'm likely to get and I can sort of start doing a pre-edit in my mind, because I start to understand what this person's going to be able to talk about. We usually do transcripts of our interviews as well, and those are invaluable in terms of finding a particular bit of dialogue or a scene.

The one thing I always do use in the edit is a chrono, which is basically a timeline of everything that's happened in the story. When I'm doing my research, we work through it and those chronos end up being, I don't know, twenty, thirty, forty pages of bullet points, date by date. So in the end it enables me to lay out the story chronologically from beginning to end. And in the edit, we totally rely on it. We might start the actual film with the middle of the story and then go back to the beginning and then go to the end, so we're maybe not using the chronological order for the structure of the film. But we've got to know it exists. It's got to be the spine of our process, so that whenever I'm on the phone with the editor I can say, 'You remember when that guy got picked up in Galveston for dismembering his neighbour? Well, that happened two days after this other thing happened, you know. Isn't that interesting?' That's the kind of thing you can only do by starting out with a document that everybody can sort of agree on as the basic rendition of the facts. It's the history of the story – very useful indeed.

How do you like to work with music in the cutting room? Do you experiment a lot?

Yes, I think it starts with the earliest cuts of the film, or even scenes. I'll send the editor a song and I'll say, 'What do you think about this as something to put under this or that sequence?'

Is it a matter of getting your iPod out and flicking through, or do you have more of a sense of where you want to go with the music when you're shooting?

Music is really important to me, and it's really important to the final film. But a lot of the time I just won't think much about it in the early stages. I'm making a film right now, but I haven't really been concerning myself with the music for the film, because it's just too early. We're still too unclear about what the story is and therefore how the music needs to underscore what we're doing or trying to build. So, you should just try to keep it nondescript, I think, early on ... you try to keep it fairly simple. And then as you go you start saying, 'Hey, you know what would be really cool, is to have every piece of music in this just be an old blues harmonica with a violin underneath it or something.'

I knew in *Capturing the Friedmans* that we had a kind of a gothic story and that it was certainly a very emotional, almost Shakespearean story and, you know, it had to do with family and fathers and sons, and it really was a very deep story. I had always thought we needed to have a rich orchestral score because this story was, in many ways, a classical tragedy, and, when we saw that dimension to it, it felt very much like we needed music that would support that idea, and would support the audience's emotional reaction to the film. Then someone put me in touch with Andrea Morricone, who is Ennio Morricone's oldest son, and an amazing composer with a real feeling for theme. And so I started working with Andrea and he completely got the film.

It's got quite a difficult job to do, the music in that film – it is a big, gothic story and it's quite epic in some ways, but it's also very intimate. And it's quite playful, in parts. It's a tough challenge for the music to pull all those different parts of the film together.

Yes, I think that's true. And, you know, that's why your relationship with your composer has to be similar to your relationship with your editor; you really have to bond with that person. You need the person to understand the movie in a very visual way.

I'm often amazed the difference that the right music can make in an edit to a sequence that is not really working. Music can solve a lot of problems.

Oh, yes, music can make an enormous difference. You know, when we were trying to finish *Capturing the Friedmans*, Andrea and I were in his apartment in Rome, and had very intense discussions, sometimes altercations, over music because something wasn't right yet, and it really needed to be, and yet it was a creation of his that he loved. Ultimately, we ended up with something that was much, much stronger and really helped pull the film together. And, you know, that's part of the process.

Did you grapple with the issue of characters being likeable in Capturing the Friedmans? *Because it seems to me you like everybody in a way, and you feel for everyone. Was that something that you felt you needed to address: to try to make people likeable in the edit?*

Well, you want people to be real. But at the same time I'm cognisant that there are moments when people are at their best and moments when people are at their worst. And you'd like, in the end, to have a fair portrait of the person. You know, you'd like to not have chosen the person at their best, nor at their worst. I think generally when you're editing you have to bring some basic moral principles into play. You don't want to take advantage of your subject, and if someone's taking the time to tell you about their lives, you really have to give them the benefit of the doubt and be fair to them. You have to think about not taking their comments out of context, no matter how tempting it might be. You want to have as much compassion for your subject and your characters as you possibly can. And you want to earn people's trust and be worthy of their trust. There is a great documentary called *The Lifestyle* about swingers and wife-swappers in America, and, in order to gain the cooperation and trust of the subjects, the filmmakers agreed to be naked whenever they were shooting a scene in which their subjects were naked. I don't think people will *feel* like they can trust you unless they can *actually* trust you.

I completely agree. But I wondered if with Arnold, the father character in particular, you felt like you needed to try to make him more likeable in the edit? Or was he just likeable? Because, as someone who's accused of being a paedophile, he could easily have been someone that you instantly dislike, which would have made it a less enjoyable and interesting film to watch. Part of the complexity and intrigue of the film is that you do sort of like him; he just seems quite ordinary when he's messing about with his kids on videotape ...

Yes, in other words, he's a real person. That's the thing that sometimes I think people find very frustrating, and that I find very interesting – that both things can be true. It can be true that Arnold Friedman is a charming guy, and is also a paedophile. And, you know, the fact that he's a paedophile doesn't mean that he's a person who doesn't have a heart and doesn't have the ability to even be a good father. Yet he has this terrible other side.

A large part of what you're doing in the edit with a doc is characterisation, isn't it? What you choose to put in and what you leave out, and the way that you combine the elements – you're sort of sketching a character like a novelist does.

Yes, no doubt. And that's why if you show somebody at their best or at their worst maybe you can be criticised for that. You try to show them as best you can for who they are, but, of course, it's going to be influenced by who *you* are, and what *you* think.

Let's talk about some of the other people who come into cutting rooms. What is the role of an executive producer? What's the point of an exec?

I would say the purpose of those people – if the relationship is good – is to say to you, 'Look, you might not have noticed it, but this part of your film is slow', or 'This part of your film makes me hate this character', or 'This part of your film seems to go against everything I've been feeling up to this date and not in a good way'. You know, they are good and pragmatic storytellers who support your vision of the film but are willing to say the unpopular thing like, 'I don't think this works', or 'I think this is too long'.

Do they represent the interests of the audience, to some extent? They're watching it as an audience member but someone who understands filmmaking as well?

Yes, you could say that. I mean, it depends. Sometimes you have a director who's extremely good at understanding what the audience wants and then sometimes you have a director who's really flaky and maybe has a real anti-audience mentality. I think the critical thing is you're making a piece of film that's designed to entertain, inform, enthral, and maybe even better. So, you do have to keep it interesting. You have to reveal the information in a way that takes the audience on a kind of a flight. That's all they want. And an executive producer can help you achieve that. They know the pitfalls and the tricks and the difficulties and the solutions.

Nick Fraser, at the BBC, is a great example of that. He's done that a lot for my brother [Eugene Jarecki, director of documentaries including *Reagan, Why We Fight* and *The House I Live In*] who now swears by Nick. Nick is a really good storyteller, and he can also be very inspiring. He's the kind of person you want to impress. You want him to think that you're smart and that the work you did is good. Shelia Nevins at HBO is another person you just don't want to disappoint. You're trying to surround yourself with people that get you excited about doing what you're doing, and I think Nick and Sheila are both good examples of that. There's a lot of value to people like that.

The films you make are quite often about difficult subjects, and sometimes quite explosive subjects. Do you get lawyers involved in your edit?

I have a lawyer or two, whom I make sure are well informed about what I'm doing and have advised me on it before I start making a film. You want to do the right thing. You don't want to do something that is either legally or morally inappropriate. And they suggest things you need to be careful of. That's a very valuable thing to do right at the beginning. And I think you do better to do that and save yourself a lot of heartache, as opposed to doing it a year down the road and having somebody say, 'Oh, you didn't check with me about the law, and in fact you've made a bunch of stupid mistakes.'

Did you have lawyers much involved in Capturing the Friedmans?

Yes. We had everyone's permission in doing it, and yet we had the parents of the victims of alleged child molestation who had a vested interest in not having the film come out. There's always going to be somebody who says, 'What do we need this for in our town? Why do we want to hear any more about it?' There's always somebody who'll get upset at you about whatever it is you are doing.

Where do you do screenings? Do you usually go to a theatre to show your film, or do you get people to come into the edit?

It depends on what kind of input you're looking for to some extent. And it depends on the stage that you're at. I think it's valuable to bring somebody into the edit room at an early stage, because knowing that the film is still in process gives people a certain amount of comfort to be able to just say anything that's on their minds. They don't have to say, 'Oh, I'm sorry, maybe you're done. I don't know if this comment is going to make any sense or I don't know if this is going to be helpful at this stage.' You don't want them thinking that. You want them to say, 'Oh, that whole second half of the movie just sucked. I thought it was going to be really good, but then at a certain point I just fell asleep.' You want to get the straightest response you can personally get. So I think it's good to bring people into the edit room. The only rule is to have the air conditioning on! People fall asleep, and you just can't have them fall asleep in your movie and then make comments about it. You'll hate them, and they'll hate themselves. For the rest of your life that person who fell asleep in your screening is never going to feel comfortable with you. It'll be what Hemingway calls 'A little something shameful between us'.

So I think that there are times to do a little screening like that in an edit suite. And then there are times – maybe most of the time – when you want to screen for, like, five or ten people. You just want people who give you good input. You want to have some people in there who know nothing about the movie and nothing about documentary and nothing about filmmaking. And you really just want to get people's reactions to the material. Usually, I'll start out with a questionnaire, asking: what are the things you remember the most? How would you describe the movie to a friend? That kind of thing. And then, when you can actually sit down with them an hour later, that's when you discover that they watched the whole movie and missed eighty per cent of it.

It's easy to think of the cutting room as a bunker where you feel safe and you're getting a bit of respite after shooting. And it can make you feel quite protective of the film.

Yes. But you can't be defensive. You have to open it up to people, and be open to input from people. Screening stuff is crucially important because you just don't know what you have until you've shown it to some people. It only becomes a film when you show it.

Afterword

Leon Gast

Leon Gast is the director of *When We Were Kings* (1996), the story of the legendary 'Rumble in the Jungle' fight between Muhammad Ali and George Foreman in 1974. The bout was held in Zaire, which at the time was under the dictatorship of President Mobutu, and was accompanied by a soul music festival that became known as 'the Black Woodstock'. Gast faced a twenty-year legal and financial battle to turn the footage he shot into a film; when he finally did so, it won an Oscar for best documentary feature.

His most recent film is *Smash His Camera* (2010), the story of an infamous (but lovable) paparazzi photographer named Ron Galella. The film is full of mini-narratives within the larger narrative of Galella's career and enduring obsession with Jacqueline Kennedy Onassis, in keeping with Gast's great passion for stories and storytelling.

Leon Gast lines up a shot during the making of When We Were Kings. *Picture courtesy of Leon Gast.*

I've been making documentaries for forty years. I've experimented with the way I make films, and entertained all kinds of theories and ideas about what documentaries are, or should or could be. There's only really one notion that's remained constant as a guiding light – which is that documentaries are all about telling stories.

For me, docs are stories first and foremost. They belong to a human tradition of storytelling that's timeless, and they've become a storytelling art form that deserves to be taken as seriously as writing novels or plays. But also they have a wonderful advantage over other ways of telling stories, which gives them a special power; they're *real* and *true*, and they're plucked directly from the world around us.

We're surrounded by stories. They're everywhere – in newspapers, in the park where you go for a stroll, on the subway, on street corners, in bars and coffee shops, in your own home. Almost all of them will be worth telling. And in some measure or other, they'll all reflect the drama and complexity of being human, and the excitement and wonderment of being alive in the world.

There are as many ways to tell a story as there are stories to tell. You should listen to every bit of advice that's available. And then my advice is to ignore it. After forty years of making films, I know this much is true; if telling stories is within you, you'll find a way. Just pick up a camera and start shooting.

Index